Resources for Implementing

Howell and Nolet's

# CURRICULUM-BASED EVALUATION
## Teaching and Decision Making

*Third Edition*

By

## Kenneth Howell
*Western Washington University*

**Wadsworth**
Thomson Learning™

Australia • Canada • Denmark • Japan • Mexico • New Zealand • Philippines
Puerto Rico • Singapore • Spain • United Kingdom • United States

For more information, contact
**Wadsworth/Thomson Learning**
**10 Davis Drive**
**Belmont, CA 94002-3098**
**USA**
**www.wadsworth.com**

**International Headquarters**
Thomson Learning
290 Harbor Drive, 2nd Floor
Stamford, CT 06902-7477
USA

**UK/Europe/Middle East**
Thomson Learning
Berkshire House
168-173 High Holborn
London WC1V 7AA
United Kingdom

**Asia**
Thomson Learning
60 Albert Complex
Singapore 189969

**Canada**
Nelson/Thomson Learning
1120 Birchmount Road
Scarborough, Ontario M1K 5G4
Canada

ISBN 0-534-55722-8

# Resources for Implementing Curriculum-Based Evaluation

## Kenneth W. Howell, Sheila L. Fox,
## Stanley H. Zucker and Mada Kay Morehead

This resource manual was written primarily to provide you with the materials you may need while conducting a Curriculum-Based Evaluation (CBE). The book contains various assessments and summary procedures. However, few directions are provided as it is assumed you have access to *Curriculum-Based Evaluation: Teaching and Decision Making, 3rd edition.* In fact, many of the materials in this guide are found in that text. They are simply reproduced here to make them easier to use.

*Resources for Implementing Curriculum-Based Evaluation* is not a supplement. It contains concrete, serviceable, and handy information to help the reader carry out the actions presented in *Curriculum-Based Evaluation*. The two texts are aligned, with this one containing assessment and interpretation materials, as well as quick and understandable guides to monitoring and instructional content referenced in the chapters.

*Curriculum-Based Evaluation* draws much of its strength from the principle of alignment. This principle states that greater learning will occur when evaluation and instruction complement each other. The essential ingredient for alignment is the curriculum; curriculum is the body of things a student is expected to learn. In other words, students will learn more if teachers use materials and activities that target needed portions of the curriculum and make decisions from measures that concentrate on those portions of this curriculum. This "evaluate what you teach" and "teach what you evaluate" orientation makes common sense. And, it is effective.

## Dedication
This book is dedicated to all of the staff and faculty in Special Education at Western Washington University. We are particularly thankful to Chuck Atkinson and Pam Hamilton.

> *"You know", David whispered to me, "the right to free speech doesn't give people the right to be taken seriously. They're far too earnest. They'd punch someone who said they were mistaken".*
> *"Like fights in your department."*
> *"No, no, you're quite incorrect in your comparison, that's totally different. In my department, we're paid good tax dollars to fight with each other. I would never do it for free."*
>
> Olsen, J (1998). <u>Wild Places</u>. Charnwood, ACT, Australia: Ginninderra Press.

## Acknowledgments
Many people have contributed to this text. A few are the staff at Heartland Area Education Agency 11 in Iowa, Pam Hamilton, Julie Schmitke, Kim Fricke, Dawn Camacho, Jill Hooper, Gina Lockman, Dana Brown, Kevin Candela, Aumony Dahl, Steve Dahl, and Jennifer Woods. Our thanks go out to all for their efforts in preparing and organizing this resource manual.

# Resources For Implementing Curriculum-based Evaluation

# Part C:  CBE Study Exercises
### 1.  Questions & Answers
### 2.  CBE Process Exercises

# Introduction

**Part A** of *Resources for Implementing Curriculum-Based Evaluation* deals with the processes of developing and utilizing measures. Some of this material may be new to the reader, so explanations are often provided. There is also a section on summarizing the findings that result from an evaluation. This is material that is often ignored. However, it is the only way the information we develop can be delivered to others. There is also an extensive presentation on formative evaluation

**Section B** deals with the application of CBE processes across content. The section contains assessment materials for major content areas, including social skills. Much of the material is taken from MASI – Multilevel Academic Skills Inventory – and occasionally, you will notice a reference to that product. As a purchaser of the text, you are granted permission to copy these materials for your own use, but not your whole district.

Finally, **Part C** contains study material for students who are using *Curriculum-Based Evaluation*, 3<sup>rd</sup> edition by Howell and Nolet. Others might find the exercises useful if they are having trouble shifting assessment paradigms.

# Steps In Developing Effective Programs
## (Exhibit 5.1)

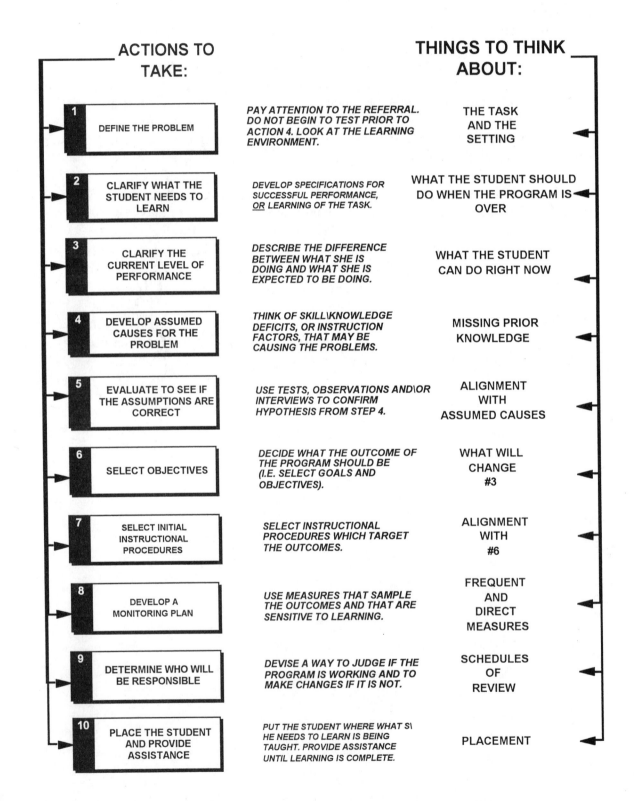

| ACTIONS TO TAKE: | | THINGS TO THINK ABOUT: |
|---|---|---|
| **1** DEFINE THE PROBLEM | *PAY ATTENTION TO THE REFERRAL. DO NOT BEGIN TO TEST PRIOR TO ACTION 4. LOOK AT THE LEARNING ENVIRONMENT.* | THE TASK AND THE SETTING |
| **2** CLARIFY WHAT THE STUDENT NEEDS TO LEARN | *DEVELOP SPECIFICATIONS FOR SUCCESSFUL PERFORMANCE, OR LEARNING OF THE TASK.* | WHAT THE STUDENT SHOULD DO WHEN THE PROGRAM IS OVER |
| **3** CLARIFY THE CURRENT LEVEL OF PERFORMANCE | *DESCRIBE THE DIFFERENCE BETWEEN WHAT SHE IS DOING AND WHAT SHE IS EXPECTED TO BE DOING.* | WHAT THE STUDENT CAN DO RIGHT NOW |
| **4** DEVELOP ASSUMED CAUSES FOR THE PROBLEM | *THINK OF SKILL\KNOWLEDGE DEFICITS, OR INSTRUCTION FACTORS, THAT MAY BE CAUSING THE PROBLEMS.* | MISSING PRIOR KNOWLEDGE |
| **5** EVALUATE TO SEE IF THE ASSUMPTIONS ARE CORRECT | *USE TESTS, OBSERVATIONS AND\OR INTERVIEWS TO CONFIRM HYPOTHESIS FROM STEP 4.* | ALIGNMENT WITH ASSUMED CAUSES |
| **6** SELECT OBJECTIVES | *DECIDE WHAT THE OUTCOME OF THE PROGRAM SHOULD BE (I.E. SELECT GOALS AND OBJECTIVES).* | WHAT WILL CHANGE #3 |
| **7** SELECT INITIAL INSTRUCTIONAL PROCEDURES | *SELECT INSTRUCTIONAL PROCEDURES WHICH TARGET THE OUTCOMES.* | ALIGNMENT WITH #6 |
| **8** DEVELOP A MONITORING PLAN | *USE MEASURES THAT SAMPLE THE OUTCOMES AND THAT ARE SENSITIVE TO LEARNING.* | FREQUENT AND DIRECT MEASURES |
| **9** DETERMINE WHO WILL BE RESPONSIBLE | *DEVISE A WAY TO JUDGE IF THE PROGRAM IS WORKING AND TO MAKE CHANGES IF IT IS NOT.* | SCHEDULES OF REVIEW |
| **10** PLACE THE STUDENT AND PROVIDE ASSISTANCE | *PUT THE STUDENT WHERE WHAT S\ HE NEEDS TO LEARN IS BEING TAUGHT. PROVIDE ASSISTANCE UNTIL LEARNING IS COMPLETE.* | PLACEMENT |

# The CBE Process of Inquiry

| Stage | Purpose | Procedure | Materials | Results |
|-------|---------|-----------|-----------|---------|
| **1: Fact finding** | To find out what the student is doing now. | Assessments are employed and information is summarized. | Wide-band/ survey assessments such as classroom work, general test, and/or status sheets. | The first part of the PLEP is determined and problem areas are identified. |
| **2: Assumed causes for problems are developed** | To think of explanations (missing prior knowledge) for what the student is doing. | Curriculum is analyzed and, if necessary, developed. | Status sheets, tables of specifications, and/or lists of essential prior knowledge. Summaries of student work. | A list of high probability explanations are developed for the problems noted in the results of fact finding. |
| **3: Validating** | To see if the explanations arrived at in the results of step 2 are correct. | Student work is compared with essential prior knowledge noted in the results of step 2. | Narrow band/specific-level assessment materials. | Assumed causes are accepted or rejected based on information collected during this step. |
| **4: Summative decision making** | To select goals and objectives or to recognize the need to repeat steps 2–4. | Assumed causes that have been validated through specific assessment are listed as objectives. New assumed causes are developed as needed. | Status sheets, tables of specifications, and/or lists of essential prior knowledge. Summaries of student work. | The PLEP is completed, and the student's educational program (goals and objectives plus ideas for initial instruction) are produced. A plan for any additional evaluation is also produced. |
| **5: Formative decision making** | To confirm that initial teaching ideas are effective and to monitor progress. | Assessments are repeated, data are visually displayed, and DBPM decision rules are applied. | Direct measures of goals and objectives and DBPM procedures. | Continuous information on the quality of the program and guidelines for making needed changes. |

A-1-b.3      R.I.O.T. Assessment Matrix (Exhibit 5.10)

| DOMAINS | R (Review) | I (Interview) | O (Observe) | T (Test) |
|---|---|---|---|---|
| **I** **Instruction** | Permanent products e.g., written pieces, tests, worksheets, projects | Teachers thoughts about their use of effective teaching and evaluation practices e.g., checklists | Effective teaching practices, teacher expectations, antecedent conditions, consequences | Classroom environment scales, checklists and questionnaires. Student opinions about instruction and teacher. |
| **C** **Curriculum** | Permanent products e.g., books, worksheets, materials, curriculum guides, scope & sequences | Teacher & relevant personnel regarding philosophy (e.g., generative vs. supplantive), district implementation and expectations | Classroom work. Alignment of assignments (curriculum materials) with goals and objectives (curriculum). Alignment of teacher talk with curriculum | Level of assignment and curriculum material difficulty. Opportunity to learn. A student's opinions about what is taught. |
| **E** **Environment** | School rules and policies. | Ask relevant personnel, students & parents about behavior management plans, class rules, class routines | Student, peers and instruction. Interactions and causal relationships. Distractions and health/safety violations | Classroom environment scales, checklists and questionnaires. Student opinions about instruction, peers and teacher |
| **L** **Learner** | District records Health records Error analysis Records for: educational history, onset & duration of the problem, teacher perceptions of the problem, pattern of behavior problems, etc. | Relevant personnel, parents, peers & students (what do they think they are supposed to do; how do they perceive the problem?) | Target behaviors- dimensions and nature of the problem | Student performance. Find the discrepancy between setting demands (instructions, curriculum, and environment) and student performance |

Adopted from Heartland Education Agency (1996) Program Manual For Special Education. Johnston, IA: Heartland Area Education Agency 11.

## Types of Assessments Used for Various Decisions

| Reason For Assessment | Type of Assessment | Typical Materials: | Example: |
|---|---|---|---|
| **To Find Problems** | *Screening* | Must indicate skill in an area. Must be quick and easy to give to large numbers of students. The results need only rank the students so that those who are doing poorly may be identified. | • One minute timed reading from class text.<br>• Teacher ranking of students on peer relations.<br>• Two minute outline for the answer to an essay test item. |
| **To Get Facts About The Student's Current Skills** | *Survey assessment* | Survey, or *broad band,* assessments are similar to screening techniques but they collect a larger sample of behavior in order to allow the evaluator to make judgments about what domains seem to be causing the student problems. | • Multiple reading samples across levels of difficulty.<br>• A review of student records and interviews with teachers and parents.<br>• A review of essay responses the student has written in several classes. |
| **To Get The Information Needed to Solve That Problem** | *Specific assessment* | Must give specific (narrow band) information about the student's knowledge. Must focus on samples of the student's work which are instructionally relevant. They are usually "criterion" or "domain" "referenced." | • Extensive oral reading sample and analysis of specific errors.<br>• Interview with student about the steps she would follow while trying to enter into a game at recess.<br>• Ask student to explain process for answering on essay item. |
| **To See If The Resulting Solution Is Effective** | *Monitoring* | Must be very sensitive to learning (so that they can be used for formative evaluation). They must be quick and easy to use over and over again. They also must accurately and immediately reflect the impact of instructional efforts. | • Charting of one minute timed readings from class text.<br>• Interval observation of student's interactions with students during recess.<br>• Periodic review of student's grades on tests. |

## Constructing Probes

You are about to find out why it is easier, (but not necessarily better) to select a CRT rather than to make one.

Over the next several pages we will focus on: calibrating curriculum, planning a test, selecting writing items, assuring an adequate sample, testing strategies, testing rate, and standardizing criteria. These activities are all necessary in developing curriculum-based measures.

## Calibrating Curriculum

Calibrating a test means adjusting its curriculum coverage to compliment an interval of instructional time. This is a time-consuming task best accomplished during curriculum development. A CTR must measure the same slice (portion) of curriculum being taught by the teacher. This is important for two reasons: (1) It assures adequate sampling and (2) it allows repeated measurement and monitoring. Because special/remedial teachers teach in relation to short-term objectives, which by the convention take approximately 4 to 6 weeks to teach, specific-level tests/observations should be calibrated at 4 to 6 weeks. (If your idea of short term is 10-15 weeks, the principles and procedures we are about to explain also apply, but the time intervals will be longer.)

Step 1. <u>Summarize long-term discrepancy.</u> Find the long-term objectives the student has not met. These are the specified in some form (usually global) in the school district's curriculum guide. Locate where the student (let's call this kid Vicki) is currently working and where she should be working. Subtract this actual performance from the expected performance. For example, suppose the curriculum indicated that Vicki should have mastered 78 separate long-term math objectives. If she has only mastered 50, the summary would look like this:

| | |
|---|---|
| Expected Performance: | 78 |
| Actual Performance: | -50 |
| Discrepancy: | 28 |

Step 2. <u>Establish aim date.</u> Deciding how long it will take to catch a student up is difficult. Usually the duration of service is decided in a child study team meeting with the input of the group. For this example, let's say that the group projects the need for one year of special math instruction.

Step 3. <u>Find the total.</u> Add the discrepancy the number of objectives students in regular programs will be expected to learn during the catch-up period. Remember that to catch up, a remedial student must actually cover more objectives per time unit than a regular student. Vicki has been given one year to catch up. In that year let's assume 20 new long-term objectives will be presented to all students. We now have:

    28 old objectives
   +20 new objectives
    48      Vicki's Progress Goal is 48 objectives in one year.

Step 4. <u>Set a Weekly Goal.</u> This is done by dividing the number of objectives by the number of weeks available for instruction. Throwing out the first and last weeks plus a couple more for state-mandated achievement testing an d parent conferences, let's say that we are going to get 30 weeks of actual instruction during the year. That's 48 objectives divided by 30 weeks or 1.6 long-term objectives per week. (48 / 30 = 1.6).

Step 5. <u>Calibrate the objectives.</u> We think a short-term objective takes from 4 to 6 weeks to teach so our calibration interval is 4 to 6 weeks. To allow time for problems to occur and be corrected we'll take the outside time 6 weeks and multiply it by the weekly factor obtained in step 4 (6 x 1.6 = 9.6) to get a progress expectation of 9.6 math objectives for each 6-week period. The 48 original objectives can now be clumped into five groups of about 10 objectives each. Each group of 10 objectives will be taught together.

Step 6. <u>Consolidate the objectives if possible.</u> This means taking each of the objective chunks produced in step 5 and trying to treat them as one task. It may be that this is not possible and Vicki will end up working on 9 or 10 separate tasks, but if the 10 objectives can be merged into two or three related domains it will limit the number of test Vicki will have to take and the number her teacher will have to write. Consolidation is carried out by examining the content domains in each objective as well as the strategic steps required to carry the objective out. For example, if several objectives cover percents and decimals they can be merged because percents and decimals share the concept of proportion and the application of division.

In the six steps above we used objectives as the basis of calibration. It is also possible to use materials. For example, let's say that Vicki's performance lag has put her one and a half math behind the other students. If the regular students will cover one additional book this year she has a total of 2.5 math books to cover in 30 weeks. If each book has 100 pages, that's a weekly expectation of 8.3 pages (100 pages by 2.5 books / 30 weeks = 8.3 pages a week). 8.3 pages a week is about 50 pages every 6 weeks. To calibrate a probe in this case you go to the text pages and see what they are teaching. This means looking at 50 pages to be covered and devising one or more tests to measure their content. As with the objective method, the aim is to recognize skills that span the entire time period. If four skills are identified you want to produce four 6-week probes, not a series of four covering 1.25 weeks each. (The danger of this system is that assumes the materials are appropriate and that each page is worth doing.)

## Planning a Test

This discussion will describe how to plan a CRT inventory for a 4- to 6-week unit of instruction. A unit of instruction may contain several objectives and each one may require its own probe. Each separate probe in the inventory will measure only one objective. The next few pages will elaborate on the following steps.

1. Recognize content
2. Sequence content
3. Recognize and sequence behavior
4. Recognize and sequence conditions
5. Assemble a table of specifications
6. Discard non-applicable objectives
7. Write items for each square

Step 1. Recognize content. Once the curriculum has been calibrated, take each short-term objective and identify its content element. Content may be factual, strategic, or conceptual.

Recognizing the content elements of tasks is a straightforward, logical, and convergent activity. It begins with a general statement of content from which subtropics are recognized. It is best if several people generate these lists using reference materials, in order to benefit from the thinking of those who know the content area well. Once identified, each item of content should be judged according to the following criteria:

1. Is it relevant? Is the main task of value to the student?
2. Is it complete? Has any of the essential content been omitted?
3. Is it trivial? Is content included which is too easy for the target student?
4. Is it necessary? Is all the content necessary to master the main task?
5. Is it redundant? Do any of the content statements overlap with other content statements? (Thiagarajan, Semmel, & Semmel, 1974)

Step 2. Sequence Content. Even though it seems as if critics of education want teachers to teach everything at the same time, they can't. Therefore, content must be put into a sequence. Sequencing content allows us to recognize a coordinated series of lessons.

If all content topics are of equal difficulty, then the most convenient system for sequencing should be identified and used. Those systems that do not require ordering content according to difficulty are:

Logically--Using this system, content is grouped into units defined by some similarity. Animals, for example, can be grouped according to what they eat. But the study of animals that eat grass isn't necessarily easier than the study of animals who eat cows.

**Chronologically--** Time may be used to present tasks as the content itself evolved or as the content was discovered. Even though it may seem obvious to start at the first, that doesn't make the first step easy. In fact, sometimes it's easier to show people where they are going before you get them started.

**Student interest or teacher priority--** This includes such age-old techniques as teaching what you know while you study up on something to teach next. It also included asking the kids what they would like to know about.

**Utility--** This means arranging the content according to how the student will use it. This involves a little research. One technique is to ask parents if there is a skill they'd like their kids to start using. Utility is one way of ordering content that will vary a lot from location to location.

If the content elements differ in difficulty, they can be ordered by the way they function in the "real" world. For example, a swimming teacher might have objectives specifying "getting into the water" and "kicking in water." Obvious "getting into water" has to come first because it is included in "kicking in water." Similarly teaching a student to "identify faculty arguments" must be preceded by "identify author conclusion" because arguments can only be judged in reference to conclusions.

If content can be sequenced according to difficulty or complexity it should be. The obvious thing to do is to put the easiest material in the first lessons. Prerequisite content relationships (task ladders) are occasionally quite clear and easy to find in the literature. If these relation ships are not clear, then the sequence should be viewed as a hypothesis to be validated through instruction and evaluation. By convention, lists of content start with the easiest (or first taught) at the bottom and the hardest (last taught) at the top.

Step 3. <u>Recognize and sequence behavior.</u> Every objective, must describe what a student will do to show that he or she "knows" the content. Here are some examples:

"On the midterm exam the student will write three definitions of learning with 100% accuracy." What is the "know" word in this objective? Write.

"Given a list of 60 CVC words, the student will pronounce the words within 1 minute with no more than two errors." What will the student do to demonstrate knowledge in this objective? Pronounce the words.

The same behavior occurring under different conditions (e.g., spelling while writing a letter vs. spelling on a spelling test) or at different proficiency level (spelling quickly vs. spelling slowly) may indicate different degrees of knowledge. We can sequence categories of behavior that indicate different degrees of learning. These behavior categories include **response type** (identify/produce) and **proficiency level** (accuracy, mastery, automaticity).

Step 4. <u>Recognize and sequence conditions.</u> The conditions under which a behavior is carried out also indicate different degrees of knowledge. For example, the automatic level involves accurate and quick response under real-world conditions. Conditions can also be arranged into sequences that make the behavior harder to carry out and indicate that a high level of learning has taken place. This is particularly important for special/remedial students, who, as a group, seem to have trouble generalizing what they have learned.

Step 5. <u>Assemble a table of specifications.</u> Assemble content, behavior, and conditions from steps 1-4 into a table of specifications.

Step 6. <u>Discard non-applicable objectives.</u> Look at the table and mark out any squares (objectives) that so not make sense or do not seem to be worth instructional time.

Step 7. <u>Write items for each square.</u> The issue of how many items are needed for an adequate sample is a fairly hot one in test development circles. For the kind of testing we're talking about here (specific-level probes for short-term objectives), 10 items per objective or strategy step is conventional and probably sufficient. For mastery (rate) objectives, the number of items needs to be increased (or the duration of the test modified, as described below) until the student has the opportunity to do 50% more items than called for the objective's CAP. (If the CAP is 60, the total number of items is 90.)

8

## Selecting and Writing Items

The type of item used depends on several factors. Obviously the aim is to select items that are as useful as possible which means they must be both reliable and valid. Items can be categorized into select and supply headings. Supply items are those that require the student to produce an answer and include computation, reading, fill-in-the-blank, cloze, short answer, essay, and project completion. Select items include multiple choice, matching, maze (modified cloze), and true/false.

We would expect to find supply items used for most basic skills (select items are regularly reserved for higher level content or extremely low levels of basic skill knowledge). The best way to choose an item type is to look at the item and ask "Does this item have lifelike stimuli and require lifelike responses, under lifelike conditions?"

Rate Tests. If a test is designed to collect rate data the items should be randomly distributed in terms of difficulty, meaning the sheet will now begin with easy problems and then move to harder ones. The easy and hard problems should be scattered on the page.

When a written test is used, the problems on the sheet should be legible and spaced to facilitate the student's work. To make scoring easier, the number of responses possible in each row can be written down the margin. Note that even when a probe is designed to test regrouping some items may not require regrouping; these non-instances are included to test the strategy for deciding when to regroup.

A student's rate of response depends on skill, the number of opportunities, and the time allowed. If the objective stipulates that 50 digits need to be written in 1 minute, a sufficient number of opportunities must be on the page. Ideally there should 50% more opportunities than the objective calls for. To get the best idea of student rate, students taking rate tests should be encouraged to skip items they do not know.

Including 50% more problems means that few students will never finish a probe. Some kids may become upset when they see all of that work and can't ever seem to get it done. Therefore, you will want to put them at ease by saying, "Work as fast but as carefully as you can. If you come to one you do not know skip it. Don't worry about finishing the page. There are more problems here than anyone needs to do."

The prominent consideration when developing rate tests is to avoid anything that artificially reduces or puts a ceiling on response fluency. It is important to allow many opportunities for the behavior to occur. (We are trying to interpret behavior, so the more have the happier we are.) If you find yourself with low frequencies of behavior, you may solve your problems four ways: (a) extend the time interval for the test, (b) provide more opportunities (items), (c) slice the behavior, (d) move to a response class. We will briefly elaborate on each of these.

**Time.** Time extension is an obvious way to increase the total number of behaviors counted (though not necessarily their rate). Suppose it takes 10 seconds to do a three-place multiplication problem with regrouping. If you allow the students 1 minute, the most she can do is 6. You can raise the ceiling on her behavior by timing for two minutes. In 2 minutes she will have the opportunity to do 12 problems (too much time can cause fatigue. Although successful students can write 100 or more digits per minute, they can't keep up this rate for more than a couple of minutes).

**Opportunities.** Providing more opportunities is also an obvious way to obtain an increase in frequency. If there are only five problems, the ceiling count must be five. Change the number to 20 and you provide the opportunity for more behavior.

**Slice (re-calibrate).** Sometimes you can "slice" a behavior to raise the frequency. When you slice, you segment the behavior and count components. For example, if you want to "stop smoking," you can count (a) packs a day, (b) cigarettes a day, or (c) puffs a day. As a rule, higher frequency behaviors are easier to change than low frequency ones. Therefore, puffs are easier to change than packs, and since decreasing both leads to "stop smoking" it is better to count puffs. Examples of academic slicing include counting digits instead of problems, or syllables spelled instead of words.

**Classes.** The last way to increase frequency is to count an entire class of behavior instead of one member of the class. This is done by first defining a response class. A response class is composed of behaviors that are so closely related that changing one raises the probability of changing them all. To illustrate, imagine that you work in a correctional institution, and Jennifer is sent there for stealing cars. "Steals cars" might be your pinpoint and decreasing "steal cars" your main objective. Unfortunately, there are no cars parked along the hallways of your reformatory, so during Jennifer's whole stay she never does pinpoint and is never punished for it. Similarly you may reward her day and night at 10-minute intervals for "not stealing cars" but the treatment may seem somehow peculiar to her. So what do you do? You make up a response class called "respects property of others" and intervene on and count all instances of "property crimes" including stealing extra desserts and entering rooms without permission. You hope that you will ultimately decrease the stealing of cars. Be redefining the pinpoint to include all samples of the class "property crimes," you have raised the possible frequency.

## Standardizing the Test

CAP is the standard of performance specified in the objective. Usually it is assumed that the performance level is specified in the CAP represents minimal competency at the skill. Our actual ability to establish these minimal competency level (or maximum in-competency levels, if you're a cynic) can be questioned.

Ideally, CAP will have already been established as part of the school program's curriculum development. If now, the burden may fall on the individual evaluator. In this case, you will probably want to follow one of the following procedures. These procedures are not particularly simple, but curriculum-based evaluation is impossible without curriculum expectations.

Academic CAP. In educational literature, criteria will be found which have been established: (a) by guessing (the worst way), (b) by asking experts, (c) by employing standardization techniques, and (d) by using research validating the effect of meeting different criteria or subsequent learning. Each technique has advantages and disadvantages. For the teacher, the best ways to get criteria are to consult experts or standardize the objective.

**Expert Judgement.** One way to determine how well students should do something is to ask someone who already knows. In many cases, particularly in the basic skills, CAPs have already been established. To find them, you should consult educators, texts, or journals that deal with the content in question. Because opinions will almost certainly vary, some test developers use the levels specified by experts as an initial estimate and then administer the test to see if the standard seems to separate instructed and uninstructed students.

**Standardization.** When CRT is standardized, people who are successful at the task are selected. This group is not randomly assembled. Only people who are judged to be experts at the task and who are in the same grade as the target student are selected for the standardization population. Then they all take the test and their median (middle - not average) score is found. This middle score can then be used as the CAP.

The hardest part of this system is deciding which students to sue for the standardization procedure. We recommend grade-level peers rather than age-level peers. This means that if a student has been retained, you should compare him to students at his current grade level. We have found that few academic skills vary simply as a function of age; they are more apt to vary as a function of instruction and practice. A student who should be in the eighth grade but who was retained in the seventh grade has only been taught seventh grade material. Therefore, even though he is older than most seventh graders, he should still be used to establish CAP for him.

As a rule you can accept students selected by the teacher as the ones who have mastered the target skill. Teach judgement is the ultimate standard to which tests are compared in validity studies (though it is safer to use a few students from several teachers than a lot from one). The teacher's judgement can be improved by making the selection question very specific. For example, "Name the 10 best students at addition and the 10 worst students at addition."

If the scores for the successful students are extremely variable, you may wish to collect a larger sample. For example, if the scores you got from an addition probe were 94, 92, 73, 70, 60, 55, 40, 35, 22, you wouldn't think that the median (60) was particularly descriptive of the group because the extreme scores, 94 and 22, vary form the median as much as 273%. The easiest way to tell if a score is descriptive is to rank the scores in a frequency distribution and then to look at it.

The procedure for determining CAP for academic skills is as follows:

1. Devise a test.
2. Select a standardization population of successful grade level peers.
3. If the example is less than 10, locate additional successful students in another class.
4. Administer the test exactly as it will be given to the special/remedial students.
5. Find the median score.
6. Rank order or graph the scores to see if the median score describes the successful group.
7. If most of the scores fall close to the median, accept score as CAP.
8. If the scores don't fall close to the median, double the sample size and repeat the process or review the procedure used to select the sample.

Interestingly, CAPs determined by using this procedure do not vary from class to class as much as class averages do.

Social Behavior CAP. The norm (average) is not particularly relevant to academic skills, but it is to social skills. The average has greater relevance to social behavior because in most situations the behavior of others is a primary cue individuals use to decide how to behave. In our culture, while we don't want to be called average, we don't like being considered abnormal either. The use of using average behavior as the target for special students is discussed in some detail in chapter 13. The best approach for establishing CAP for social behavior is the ecological approach.

# Hospitable Hints
(Prepared by John & Michelle Hosp )

| Prior to Assessment | Getting Started |
|---|---|
| 1. Determine test to be given (published or curriculum-based)<br>2. Practice giving test (review the night before, put hints on index cards or tabs)<br>3. Determine optimal assessment time for student (may be sleepy in the morning, but alert all afternoon)<br>4. Rearrange schedule (student's and yours) if necessary (and notify others affected)<br>5. Choose a setting (with minimal distractions) for assessment<br>6. On morning of assessment, make sure student is present<br>7. Collect/organize necessary materials (stopwatch, pencils, clipboard, scrap paper, test booklets, etc.)<br>8. Make a "Testing—Please Do Not Disturb" sign | 1. Place the "Do Not Disturb" sign on the door, turn off phone/beeper, ask office not to call you over the P. A.<br>2. Establish rapport if necessary (talk about a student interest until he/she is comfortable)<br>3. Explain purpose of assessment (i. e. to help you help them better)<br>4. Explain that some of the items will be easier while others will be harder<br>5. Allow the student a chance to ask questions<br>6. Ask the student which hand they write with and adjust seating/materials accordingly |
| **During Assessment** | **Clean-up** |
| 1. Keep hints (index cards) and manuals with tabs within reach for easy access that won't interrupt the flow of assessment<br>2. Be inconspicuous when recording answers (use a clipboard or book to keep out of student's view)<br>3. Be consistent with feedback (do not give indication if answers are correct or not, respond to effort not accuracy, i. e. "You're working hard on these")<br>4. Allow for short breaks if needed<br>5. Note any accommodations made during assessment<br>6. Note anecdotal information on student (i. e. "student put head on desk and yawned 10 times" or "student asked to have 20 of 30 questions repeated") | 1. Allow student to ask additional questions<br>2. Thank student for their time and effort, make sure to be sincere<br>3. If appropriate, set up a time to discuss results with student<br>4. Make sure all materials are accounted for<br>5. Score materials immediately while responses are fresh in your memory<br>6. Note additional anecdotal information (such as "Where'd my wallet go?")<br>7. Put materials away or prepare for next student |

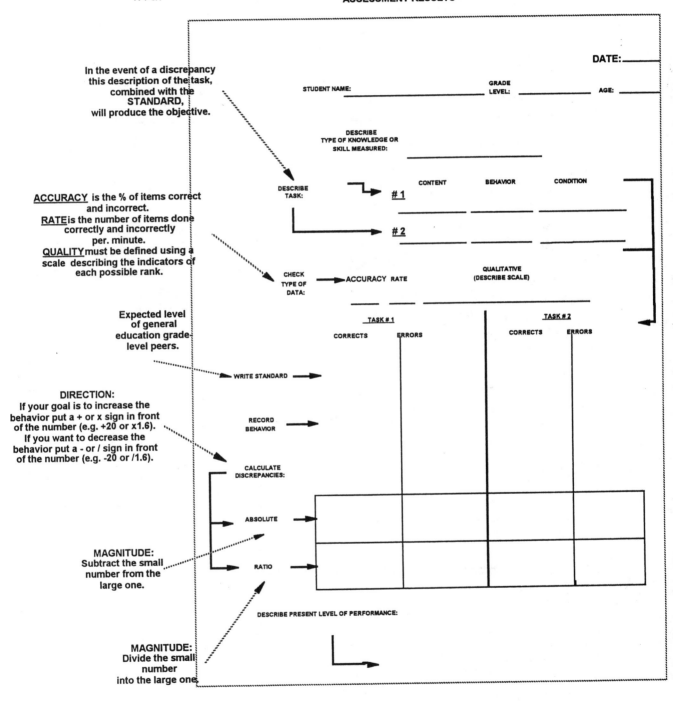

**DIRECTIONS FOR SUMMARIZING ASSESSMENT RESULTS**

A-1-e.1

DATE:_____

STUDENT NAME:_____  GRADE LEVEL: _____  AGE: _____

In the event of a discrepancy this description of the task, combined with the **STANDARD**, will produce the objective.

DESCRIBE TYPE OF KNOWLEDGE OR SKILL MEASURED: _____

**ACCURACY** is the % of items correct and incorrect.
**RATE** is the number of items done correctly and incorrectly per. minute.
**QUALITY** must be defined using a scale describing the indicators of each possible rank.

DESCRIBE TASK:

|  | CONTENT | BEHAVIOR | CONDITION |
|---|---|---|---|
| **# 1** | \_\_\_\_ | \_\_\_\_ | \_\_\_\_ |
| **# 2** | \_\_\_\_ | \_\_\_\_ | \_\_\_\_ |

CHECK TYPE OF DATA:  ACCURACY   RATE    QUALITATIVE (DESCRIBE SCALE)

Expected level of general education grade-level peers.

| TASK # 1 | | TASK # 2 | |
|---|---|---|---|
| CORRECTS | ERRORS | CORRECTS | ERRORS |

WRITE STANDARD

**DIRECTION:**
If your goal is to increase the behavior put a + or x sign in front of the number (e.g. +20 or x1.6).
If you want to decrease the behavior put a - or / sign in front of the number (e.g. -20 or /1.6).

RECORD BEHAVIOR

CALCULATE DISCREPANCIES:

**MAGNITUDE:**
Subtract the small number from the large one.

ABSOLUTE

RATIO

**MAGNITUDE:**
Divide the small number into the large one.

DESCRIBE PRESENT LEVEL OF PERFORMANCE:

13

# WORKSHEET FOR SUMMARIZING
# ASSESSMENT RESULTS

DATE: _____

STUDENT
NAME: _____

GRADE
LEVEL: _____   AGE: _____

DESCRIBE
TYPE OF KNOWLEDGE
OR SKILL MEASURED: _____

DESCRIBE
TASK:

|  | CONTENT | BEHAVIOR | CONDITION |
|---|---|---|---|
| #1 | _____ | _____ | _____ |
| #2 | _____ | _____ | _____ |

CHECK
TYPE OF
DATA:

ACCURACY    RATE         QUALITATIVE
                         (DESCRIBE SCALE)
____    ____    _____

| | TASK # 1 | | TASK # 2 | |
|---|---|---|---|---|
| | CORRECTS | ERRORS | CORRECTS | ERRORS |
| WRITE STANDARD → | | | | |
| RECORD BEHAVIOR → | | | | |

CALCULATE
DISCREPANCIES:

| | | | | |
|---|---|---|---|---|
| ABSOLUTE → | | | | |
| RATIO → | | | | |

DESCRIBE PRESENT LEVEL OF
PERFORMANCE:

14

A-1-E.3
## Using Materials Below Expected Level (student is in the 8th grade)

When the student lacks the skills to work productively in materials at her expected level you may need to *test down* and specify a sequence of assistance (or levels of material) as objectives. For example:

Content area: Oral Reading *

| | *at Expected Level (8th)* | | *at best level for Instruction (4th)* | |
|---|---|---|---|---|
| **Material:** | 8th-grade history text | | 4th-grade history text | |
| **Standard:** | 140 correct <7 errors | | 140 correct <7 errors | |
| **Behavior:** | 15 correct  22 errors | | 63 correct   8 errors | |
| **Discrepancy:** | | | | |
| → Absolute: | +125 | -15 | +87 | -1 |
| →Ratio: | x9.3 | ÷ 3.1 | x2.2 | ÷1.1 |

Oral reading Goal: The Student will read the **6th**-grade history book with expected rate and
  accuracy.

Objectives:

  3. Will read **6th**-grade history text at a rate of 140 mph with 95% accuracy (<7 errors).
  2. Will read **5th**-grade history text at a rate of 140 mph with 95% accuracy (<7 errors).
  3. Will read **4th**-grade history text at a rate of 140 mph with 95% accuracy (<7 errors).

*In this case the annual goal specifies **6th**-grade level text because the team has decided that the discrepancy found in the initial assessment (to move from 4th to 8th grade in content area reading) can't be removed in one year. The goal is acceptable because it is reasonable and specifies a decrease in the student's overall discrepancy.

In the examples above we are only presenting one area of content. There may be other areas related to oral reading (e.g. vocabulary, blending, or use of morphographs) that would also need to be taught.

## Criteria for Judging the Product of an Evaluation

- Is the student briefly described?
- Is the test briefly described?
- Is the test reliable and valid?
- Are dates and scores reported accurately?
- Is the standard (expected score) determined correctly?
- Is the behavior recorded correctly?
- Is the discrepancy calculated correctly?
- Is the goal reasonable for one year, and will meeting it decrease the discrepancy?
- Are the objectives complete in content, behavior, conditions, and CAP?
- Do the objectives lay out a path from the current level of performance to the goal?

Testing Summary

Student Name:

Grade Level:

Date of Test:

Skill Tested:

Test Materials:

Standard:

Behavior:

Discrepancy:

    Absolute:

    Ratio:

    Annual Goal:

    Short-term Objectives:

## Rules for Good Educational Judgement

| Rule | Example/explanation |
|---|---|
| Work with others to define the problem | If possible collaborate. Decide if there even is a problem and if it seems to be related to the curriculum, instruction, environment or student. |
| Focus on solutions not problems | Shift the discussion from what the student is doing wrong to what you want the student to do right. |
| Focus on alterable variables and the curriculum | Think about what the student needs to be taught and what things you can control through instruction |
| Decide what the student will be doing once the problem is fixed. | Operationally define success. Have a clear vision of success and get agreement so that everyone (including the kid) understands what they are working to achieve. |
| Decide if the problem is a priority | Consider the problem in relation to other needs. |
| Isolate the parts | See if there are portions of the problem which can already be solved , or which will be easier to solve than others. Get those out of the way first. |
| Look for simple solutions. | Do not assume that big difficulties always indicate complex problems. There may simply be a missing step or piece of information. |
| Act quickly | The sooner you start working on the problem the sooner you will get feedback on the quality of your solution. You will also get more information on the problem. Besides, the kid is behind already. |
| Reconfigure | If the solution involves several individuals include a mechanism for them to meet and discuss progress. |
| Monitor | Monitoring reduces the need for "front loaded" certainty. If you have good monitoring data and are flexible you can arrive at the best solution by improving the one with which you started |

## Threats to Judgement
### (Exhibit 2.3)

| Threat | Explanation/Example |
| --- | --- |
| Data Characterization (Selective attention) | Seeing what you expect, or want to see. Two people watching the same event don't agree about what they saw. |
| Lack of the knowledge needed to make a judgment | Working on things you don't know about (e.g., trying to teach about the role of minority cultures in U.S. history--when that wasn't taught to you when you were in school). |
| Stereotyping (Over generalization) | Working with someone's label and not their characteristics (e.g., ignoring Ralph and only attending to the fact that he is labeled LD). |
| Failure to define the problem | Not knowing what it is you are trying to do (e.g., deciding to have students work lessons without giving them a pretest). |
| Defining the problem too trivially or narrowly | Concentrating on a trivial aspect of a larger problem (e.g., thinking about the haircut of a student who has no friends). |
| Lack of perspective | Only seeing things one way (e.g., not seeing the problem from the parents' point of view). |
| Fear | Of failure, risk, notoriety, success, responsibility or nearly anything else. |
| Premature resolution | Stopping work too early--failing to be comprehensive (e.g., picking the first solution recommended). |
| Insensitivity to probabilities | Not considering that some things are already more or less likely to work (e.g., adopting specialized reading materials when the general-education class materials haven't been tried). |
| Sample size | Drawing conclusions from too few experiences or examples (e.g., concluding a student can add because he works four problems correctly). |
| Misconceptions of chance | Thinking that unrelated events can affect each other (e.g., believing that flipping three heads in a row somehow alters the 50/50 chance of flipping a head with a fourth coin--it doesn't). |
| Unwarranted confidence | Deciding to do something on the basis of evidence, or advocacy, that doesn't have anything to do with the problem at hand (e.g., deciding a student will have trouble in math because she is bad at reading). |
| Selective or incomplete search | Only considering one category of options (e.g., only considering the use of teaching methods advocated by your friends). |
| Mistaking a corrlational relationship for cause and effect | Just because two things happen at the same time doesn't mean one causes the other (e.g., thinking that a student threw up in class for attention because everyone looked at her when she did). |
| Lack of a supportive environment | Not having a chance to observe others use good judgment or have that use encouraged (e.g., working in a school where everyone routinely makes all of these errors). |

## Questions to Ask before Interpreting an Assessment

Before interpreting the results of any test and/or observation, ask yourself *each* of these questions. If the answer is no (or "unsure") take the specified action(s).

| Question | Explanation/Example | Action |
|---|---|---|
| Are you sure you got an instructionally relevant sample of behavior? | To guide instruction on evaluation must cover the things a student is currently prepared to learn. This means mapping out *both* those things a student can do and those he or she cannot do. An evaluation that yields all "pass" "no-pass" is worthless. | • Continue the evaluation until you find the correct instructional level. |
| Did the student's work represent the student's skills? | Remember that a student may know something but be unable to demonstrate knowledge because of conflicts with the testing situation. Be sure the work represents the student's best efforts. Try giving a pep talk, using preferred tasks, or having a friend present during testing. | • Try to separate knowledge from display. |
| Has the student received instruction on the skills missed? | Don't be concerned when students fail at things they haven't been taught. Ask "Did you ever know how to do that?" or "Has this always been hard?" or "Is it new?" Check with teachers to see if the skill has been taught. | •<br><br>Check to see if a pass is expected. |
| Have you attempted to categorize the errors? | Indicated by incorrect responses whenever particular content is involved (two-place addition, vowel sounds, on biology vocabulary). | • Look for patterns of content errors. |
|  | Indicated by failure to recognize cues (borrows when it isn't necessary) and/or use vocabulary (says "reliable" when talking about "validity"). | • Look for patterns of concept errors. |
|  | Indicated by predictable error patterns and/or incorrect explanation of process. | • Look for patterns of strategy errors. |
|  | Indicated by incorrect statements ("a = eeee" or "2 + 2 = 5"). | • Look for patterns of fact errors. |
| Does the student's skill maintain across different response formats? |  |  |

## SUMMARIZING RESULTS

Evaluation results are summarized by utilizing the basic standard/behavior/ discrepancy model as illustrated throughout the text.

Here are the steps you follow:

-write down the standard
-write down the behavior
-determine the discrepancy
-specify the goal
-specify a series of objectives that map
 intermediate steps between the current level
 of performance (the behavior) and the goal

Here are a couple of examples:

<u>Using materials at expected level</u>
(student in 8th grade)

| | **Oral Reading** | | **Computation** |
|---|---|---|---|
| **Material:** | *8th-grade history text* | | *End-of-text review exercises* |
| **Standard:** | 140 correct | <7 errors p/min | 100% |
| **Behavior:** | 60 | 15 | 65 % |
| **Discrepancy:** | | | |
| Absolute: | +80 | -8 | +35 % |
| Ratio: | x2.3 | 2.1 | x1.9 |

<u>Oral reading goal:</u> *Student will read 8th-grade history book with expected rate and accuracy.*

Objectives:
3. Will read history book aloud at a rate of 140 mph with 95% accuracy (< 5% errors).
2. Will read history book aloud at a rate of 100 mph with 95% accuracy (<5 % errors).
1. Will read history book aloud at a rate of 60 mph with 95% accuracy (<5% errors).

<u>Computation goal:</u> *The Student will accurately work items on end-of-text review tests.*

Objectives:
3. Student will write answers to items with 100% accuracy.
2. Student will explain the process of working [specify content] items with 100% accuracy.
1. Student will identify items requiring knowledge of [specify content] with 100% accuracy.

| Question | Explanation/Example | Action |
|---|---|---|
| Does the student's skill maintain across different levels of proficiency? | If the student cannot do something quickly ask that it be done accurately. If something is done accurately ask that it can be quickly. | • Switch from fluency to accuracy or accuracy to fluency. |
| Does the student's skill maintain across different situations and context? | If a student can't do something in context (add in a story problem) check to see if it can be done in isolation. If a student can do something in isolation (add on a work sheet), check to see if it can be done in context. | • Check the effect of context. |
| Have you missed important skills? | Don't concentrate exclusively on errors. Consider the content the student avoids (if the student never tried to spell words with double consonants, you should check that area). | • Check skills *not* displayed. |
| Does the student know and understand self-skills? | Ask "Will this be easy for you or will it be hard?" or "Which things are you good at and which need improving?" or "Why do other kids get these problems done faster?" | • Ask the student to judge the difficulty of the task or to predict success. |
| | Say "Pretend that you are the teacher. Tell me how to do this." | • Ask the student to explain how to do the task. |
| Do you want to make decisions about how to teach (not just about what to teach)? | Use assisted assessment. Take something the student has failed and try teaching it to him. Observe the student's learning and task-related behaviors. | • Check how the student responds to instruction. |
| | Use instructionally sensitive repeated measures of the skill and monitor progress over time. Compare progress obtained through different instructional approaches. | • Summarize changes in the student's skill. |

# Objective Overlays for Types of Knowledge.

## Factual Knowledge

| Identify Answer (underline, circle, point to, highlight) | Produce Answer (write, say, construct an example) | | |
|---|---|---|---|
| Accuracy | Accuracy | Mastery/Fluency | Automatic |
| <2 + 2 = >.<br><3><br>\|4\|<br>5<br>6 | 2 + 2=<br>(untimed) | 2 + 2 =<br>(at rate) | 2 + 2 =<br>(in check book) |

## Conceptual Knowledge

| Sort Examples from Nonexamples (place, mark, label) | | Specify Attributes (list, mark, name) | | Define Concept (state, write, illustrate) | Contrast/Modify (list similarities, state differences, change attributes) | Explain/Imply (state implications, predict or estimate select strategy) |
|---|---|---|---|---|---|---|
| Far Examples Squares and circles | Near Examples Squares and rectangles | Noncritical Color, size, location | Critical Four sides, straight side | "A Square has four straight sides and 90-degree corners | "Squares have equal sides, rectangles don't." | "To draw square I'll need something to measure the sides." |

## Strategic/Procedural Knowledge

| Identify when to Use Process (sort examples, say label, circle) | Specify Process (say, write, outline, diagram) | | Apply Process (say, write, do (construct product)) |
|---|---|---|---|
| | List Steps | List Rules | |
| "This would be a good time to use self-management." | Set goal; find alternatives; anticipate consequences; make a plan | Problem must be mine; it must be worth the effort; it must be what others want | Use self-management to negotiate getting in the ball game at recess. |

A-1-F.5

**Checklist for Goals and Objectives.**
**(Exhibit 3.5)**

| Status | Question |
|---|---|
| Yes   No | |

1. Do the goals and/or objectives represent an important learning outcome that is a priority for this student?

2. Is there a goal written for each area of need stated in the present levels of performance?

3. Are the goals realistic 1-year accomplishments?

4. Are the goals and objectives easily measured?

5. Are there multiple objectives representing intermediate steps to each goal?

6. Are the goals and instructional objectives appropriately calibrated (sliced neither too broadly nor too narrowly)?

7. Are the goals and instructional objectives useful for planning and evaluating instructional programs

## MONITORING INSTRUCTION:
Formative Evaluation

**INTRODUCTION**  This section provides information about the process of formative evaluation.  The discussion will be housed within a set of procedures referred to as **data based program modification** (DBPM).  Frequent and direct measurement of student growth has be shown, so many times it isn't news to anyone, to be one of the single most effective things a teacher can do. Unfortunately, few of them do it. Our suggestion is the you follow the "minimum/maximum" rule. That rule tells us that students with the minimum skills need the maximum intervention.

There are two critical actions a teacher must take in order to use formative evaluation. First they must define how they will teacher (as it is the outcome of instruction that they will be measuring), next they must measure and summarize the impact of the teaching. So, this section begins with a definition of effective instruction using the Descriptors of TIES Components taken, with permission, from Ysseldyke, J.E., & Christenson, S.L. (1996). TIES II: The Instructional Environment System-II. Longmont, Co: Sopris West. Then there will be an extensive discussion of frequent measurement and the display of results.

**TIES Descriptors for Component 1**
*Instructional Presentation*
Instructional Presentation, a primary component of effective instruction, includes factors related to lesson development, clarity of directions, and checking for student understanding. Lesson Development refers to the presence of an adequate overview; the manner in which the lesson is explained, structured, and sequenced; the variety and richness of teaching examples; the clarity with which the lesson content is presented; the adequacy of guided practice opportunities and degree of teacher-student interaction; the kind of feedback used; and the appropriateness of task directions; kind and amount of examples used; and degree to which task directions are repeated. Checking for Student Understanding refers to the method used to check the student's understanding, the timing of the checking, the degree to which cues and prompts (error correction procedures) are used to promote accurate responses, and the way in which the teacher interprets student inattentiveness.

**TIES Descriptors for Component 2**
*Classroom Environment*
An effective classroom environment is influenced by the extent to which classroom management procedures reduce disciplinary concerns; the extent to which instructional routines maximize productive use of time in the classroom; and the affective tone or climate in the classroom. Classroom Management refers to the kind of rules established to maintain appropriate behavior; how the rules are communicated; the system word to maintain appropriate behavior; and the emphasis placed on student accountability. Productive Time-Use refers to the extent to which non-instructional routines are established and class time is used to increase academic activities. Class Climate refers to

the extent to which the classroom atmosphere is characterized by cooperation, a pleasant atmosphere, and acceptance of individual differences.

## TIES Descriptors for Component 3
*Teacher Expectations*
Establishing high, yet realistic, expectations for student performance, including task completion, quality of work, and use of time in the classroom, is an important characteristic of effective instruction. Teacher Expectations refers to the kind of expectations set for student performance; the communication of the expectations; and the extent to which the student understands the expectations.

## TIES Descriptors for Component 4
*Cognitive Emphasis*
Effective instruction emphasizes the development of thinking skills. Cognitive Emphasis refers to the extent to which varied lessons are planned for the purpose of teaching recall, reasoning, evaluating, and application skills; the extent to which thinking skills necessary to accurately complete a task or master a skill are modeled for the student; and the extent to which learning strategies are directly taught.

## TIES Descriptors for Component 5
*Motivational Strategies*
Encouraging student motivation is an important component of effective instruction. Teachers understand the importance of motivation for learning and consequently use varied techniques to increase student motivation. Motivational Strategies refers to the enthusiasm with which the lesson is presented; the extent to which the lesson is interesting and varied; the kind of motivational strategy (extrinsic vs. intrinsic orientation) used; and the student's sense of self-efficacy

## TIES Descriptors for Component 6
*Relevant Practice*
Students spend approximately 70% of their school day engaged in seatwork practice activities. In order for this time to be effective in promoting positive academic outcomes for a student, the student must engage in relevant practice. Relevant Practice includes the amount of practice opportunity on relevant tasks with appropriate instructional materials. Practice Opportunity refers to the amount and kind of practice. Task Relevance refers to the extent to which the practice activities are related to the lesson presented and are important for attaining the instructional goal in addition to the student's success rate. Instructional Material refers to the academic and affective appropriateness of the assigned materials for the target student to attain the instructional goal

## TIES Descriptors for Component 7
*Academic Engaged Time*
In order to achieve optimally, students must be engaged and actively involved in completing academic tasks and responding to oral and written questions. Both the amount of opportunity to engage in academic work and the rate of student engaged time during completion of the work influence achievement levels. Student Involvement refers to the

opportunities the student has to respond and the extent to which the student actively participates in academic activities. Contextual factors may influence student involvement. Maintenance of Student Engagement refers to the extent to which varied teacher behaviors or systems are used to facilitate time on task.

## TIES Descriptors for Component 8
*Informed Feedback*
Informed Feedback includes feedback and alternative, corrective procedures. The provision of specific, informative feedback and corrective procedures is a necessary step in successfully instructing students. Feedback refers to several characteristics of effective feedback, the type of feedback, and the student's understanding of the feedback. Corrective Procedures refers to the kind of alternative teaching strategies employed, the amount of supervised practice and monitoring provided, and the extent to which student accountability is stressed.

## TIES Descriptors for Component 9
*Adaptive Instruction*
Instruction needs to be modified to accommodate individual needs and differences. Adaptive Instruction refers to the extent to which there is a systematic effort to modify instruction, the options available for modifying instruction, and the degree to which the effectiveness of the modifications is communicated to the student.

## TIES Descriptors for Component 10
*Progress Evaluation*
Effective instruction includes continuous monitoring and systematic follow-up planning for a student. Monitoring Student Progress refers to the kind of student performance data collected, the frequency with which the student's performance is monitored, and the system used for record keeping and communicating to the student. Contextual factors may influence the amount of monitoring for an individual student. Follow-Up Planning refers to the basis for making subsequent instructional decisions for a student and the extent to which reviews are planned systematically.

## TIES Descriptors for Component 11
*Instructional Planning*
Systematic Instructional Planning includes two functions: diagnosis and prescription. Instructional Diagnosis refers to the extent to which student characteristics (e.g., skill level, motivation), task characteristics (e.g., sequence, cognitive demands) and classroom characteristics (e.g., instructional groupings, materials) have been accurately assessed. Instructional Prescription refers to the match between the student's instructional needs and instruction delivered. Student success rate and amount of content covered characterize the degree of task appropriateness for a student. Several factors influence the extent to which instructional planning is optimal for a student's academic progress.

The material in this appendix is taken, with permission, from Ysseldyke, J.E., & Christenson, S.L. (1996). TIES II: The Instructional Environment System-II. Longmont, Co: Sopris West.

## Cross-Reference of TIES-2 Indicators of Effective Instruction to Teacher Actions

**Evaluate**

| TIES-2 Reference | Indicators of Effective Evaluation |
|---|---|
| Component 1, Instructional Diagnosis, Item 1 | 1. The student's level of skill development (e.g., entry-level skills) is assessed accurately. |
| Component 1, Instructional Diagnosis, Item 2 | 2. The student's academic strengths, weaknesses, and interests are identified accurately. |
| Component 1, Instructional Diagnosis, Item 3 | 3. The student's behavioral strengths, weaknesses, and interests are identified accurately. |
| Component 1, Instructional Diagnosis, Item 4 | 4. The student's instructional needs in affective areas (e.g. attitude, self-concept) are identified accurately. |
| Component 1, Instructional Diagnosis, Item 5 | 5. The student's appropriate instructional level is identified. |
| Component 1, Instructional Diagnosis, Item 11 | 6. The gap between the student's actual and desired levels of performance is stated clearly. |
| Component 1, Instructional Match, Item 18 | 7. The student's success rate on assigned tasks is carefully monitored. |
| Component 1, Instructional Match, Item 19 | 8. The success rate is moderately high on new tasks (e.g., 70-85%). |
| Component 1, Instructional Match, Item 19 | 9. The success rate is high on independent practice activities (e.g., 90-100%). |
| Component 1, Instructional Match, Item 21 | 10. The ratio of known to unknown material is appropriate (90-100% for independent work, 70-75% for instruction). |
| Component 1, Instructional Match, Item 23 | 11. Diagnostic teaching is used to ensure a successful instructional match. |
| Component 2, Teacher Expectations, Item 9 | 12. The student understands how to demonstrate mastery of the instructional goals. |
| Component 2, Teacher Expectations, Item 13 | 13. The student knows he/she is held accountable for correcting and completing unfinished work. |
| Component 3, Classroom Management, Item 7 | 14. The student's compliance with the rules is continuously monitored. |
| Component 3, Classroom Management, Item 13 | 15. The student understands the consequences of misbehavior. |
| Component 3, Classroom Management, Item 14 | 16. The student understands the classroom rules and routines. |
| Component 4, Checking for Student Understanding, Item 5 | 17. Initial problems are checked within the first ten minutes of independent seatwork activities. |
| Component 4, Checking for Student Understanding, Item 6 | 18. There is frequent monitoring of the student's success rate on assigned activities. |
| Component 4, Checking for Student Understanding, Item 7 | 19. Error correction procedures, such a cues and prompts, are used to lead the student to the correct answer and to increases the student's accuracy rate. |

| | |
|---|---|
| Component 4, Checking for Student Understanding, Item 8 | 20. The student's errors are used to reteach skills or re-explain procedures. |
| Component 4, Checking for Student Understanding, Item 10 | 21. Student engagement and attention are monitored as indicators of student understanding. |
| Component 4, Checking for Student Understanding, Item 11 | 22. The student's understanding or the appropriateness of the assigned task is checked before the student is assumed to have motivational difficulties. |
| Component 6, Motivational Strategies, Item 11 | 23. Individual instructional conferences are held regularly with the student. |
| Component 6, Motivational Strategies, Item 16 | 24. The student has been asked his/her preferences for how to learn the skills/content. |
| Component 6, Motivational Strategies, Item 17 | 25. The student's success rate is carefully monitored. |
| Component 6, Motivational Strategies, Item 18 | 24. The student is held accountable for completion of quality work. |
| Component 7, Practice Opportunity, Item 3 | 26. Student performance is carefully monitored by the teacher during seatwork (e.g., frequent checking, circulating among students). |
| Component 7, Practice Opportunity, Item 8 | 27. A minimal level of competence is ensured before a homework assignment is given. |
| Component 7, Task Relevance, Item 7 | 26. The student is placed appropriately within the instructional sequence. |
| Component 7, Task Relevance, Item 3 | 27. The student has acquired the necessary prerequisite skills to complete the task successfully. |
| Component 7, Task Relevance, Item 10 | 28. During the beginning stage of practice on a new skill, the student's performance is checked by the teacher. The student's success rate is 70% or better. |
| Component 7, Task Relevance, Item 12 | 29. The teacher's measure of student achievement reflects the material the student has been taught. |
| Component 7, Instructional Material, Item 1 | 30. The student can read the assigned curriculum materials. |
| Component 7, Instructional Material, Item 2 | 31. Assigned materials are at the appropriate skill level for the student. |
| Component 7, Instructional Material, Item 12 | 32. Supplemental materials are provided to help the student attain mastery. |
| Component 8, Feedback, Item 1 | 33. Student performance is monitored continuously. |
| Component 8, Corrective Procedures, Item 8 | 34. Student performance is monitored closely in order to prescribe activities to correct errors. |

| | |
|---|---|
| Component 9, Student Involvement, Item 1 | 35. The student maintains eye contact and follows the lesson presentation and class discussion. |
| Component 9, Student Involvement, Item 2 | 36. The student participates in the lesson presentation (e.g., asks/answers questions, engages in teacher-student discussion). |
| Component 9, Student Involvement, Item 3 | 37. The student is involved in the large group via choral responses, direct questioning, and substantive interaction. |
| Component 9, Student Involvement, Item 4 | 38. The student begins, attends to, and completes assigned work. |
| Component 9, Student Involvement, Item 5 | 39. The student spends little time sitting and waiting. |
| Component 9, Student Involvement, Item 6 | 40. The student returns to work promptly after a break. |
| Component 9, Student Involvement, Item 11 | 41. The student understands the lesson content. |
| Component 9, Maintenance of Student Engagement, Item 3 | 42. Student understanding of the assigned task is checked when the student is unengaged. |
| Component 9, Maintenance of Student Engagement, Item 4 | 43. The teacher scans the class and keeps the student engaged in learning activities. |
| Component 9, Maintenance of Student Engagement, Item 9 | 44. The teacher checks work, discusses, reviews, and provides corrective feedback to the student. |
| Component 9, Maintenance of Student Engagement, Item 10 | 45. Student performance is monitored to ensure an appropriate success rate. |
| Component 10, Adaptive Instruction, Item 8 | 46. During monitoring, the teacher continuously diagnoses errors and prescribes activities to correct incorrect responses. |
| Component 10, Adaptive Instruction, Item 12 | 47. Effectiveness of the alternative interventions is monitored. |
| Component 10, Adaptive Instruction, Item 12 | 48. The student is held accountable for his/her performance and quality of work. |
| Component 10, Adaptive Instruction, Item 14 | 49. The student receives additional review and practice in areas of difficulty. |
| Component 11, Monitoring Student Progress, Item 1 | 50. The teacher circulates among students during seatwork activities to provide assistance and to check work. |
| Component 11, Monitoring Student Progress, Item 2 | 51. The student's success rate is monitored regularly by the teacher. |
| Component 11, Monitoring Student Progress, Item 3 | 52. The student's engaged time is monitored carefully by the teacher. |

| | |
|---|---|
| Component 11, Monitoring Student Progress, Item 4 | 53. Student progress is monitored through both error analysis on daily work and unit tests. |
| Component 11, Monitoring Student Progress, Item 6 | 54. Direct and frequent evaluation (curriculum-based) of student progress toward mastery of objectives is used. |
| Component 11, Monitoring Student Progress, Item 7 | 55. There are enough evaluation items to measure student progress accurately. |
| Component 11, Monitoring Student Progress, Item 8 | 56. Student progress is monitored regularly to make adjustments in teaching strategies that better meet the needs of the student. |
| Component 11, Monitoring Student Progress, Item 9 | 57. Records of student progress are maintained. |
| Component 11, Follow-Up Planning, Item 7 | 58. Student errors trigger the need for corrective or adaptive instructional procedures. |
| Component 12, Student Understanding, Item 1 | 60. The student can explain the purpose of the lesson. |
| Component 12, Student Understanding, Item 2 | 61. The student can explain accurately the task directions (e.g., page numbers. |
| Component 12, Student Understanding, Item 3 | 62. The student can explain accurately how to do problems/assignments (e.g., articulates the steps, processes to follow). |
| Component 12, Student Understanding, Item 4 | 63. The student understands the consequences of inferior quality work. |
| Component 12, Student Understanding, Item 8 | 63. The student's performance is monitored to ensure an appropriate success rate. |

**Prepare for Instruction**

| TIES-II Reference | Indicators of Effective Preparation |
|---|---|
| Component 1, Instructional Diagnosis, Item 6 | 1. There is a logical sequence to instruction. |
| Component 1, Instructional Diagnosis, Item 7 | 2. The steps involved in completing the classroom task are identified accurately through task analysis or similar procedure. |
| Component 1, Instructional Diagnosis, Item | 3. Prerequisite skills needed to perform the task have been considered and accurately identified. |
| Component 1, Instructional Diagnosis, Item 9 | 4. Cognitive demands of the classroom task (e.g., memory, number of steps involved) are identified accurately. |
| Component 1, Instructional Diagnosis, Item 10 | 5. Contextual variables (e.g., instructional groupings, interactions with other students, availability of materials, kinds of tasks) have been considered. |
| Component 1, Instructional Prescription, Item 1 | 6. The student's instructional needs (e.g., strengths, weaknesses, skill level, prior learning) are considered when assigning tasks. |
| Component 1, Instructional Prescription, Item 2 | 7. Appropriate instructional goals/objectives are established on the basis of the student's instructional needs. |

| | |
|---|---|
| Component 1, Instructional Prescription, Item 3 | 8. Instructional goals are matched to the level of skill development of the student. |
| Component 1, Instructional Prescription, Item 4 | 9. The instructional process is guided by the objective or goal to be achieved rather than workbook pages to be completed. |
| Component 1, Instructional Prescription, Item 5 | 10. The priority of each goal/objective is determined. |
| Component 1, Instructional Prescription, Item 6 | 11. The instructional sequence for achieving the goals/objectives is planned. |
| Component 1, Instructional Prescription, Item 7 | 12. Instructional goals/objectives for the student are specific and described in measurable ways. |
| Component 1, Instructional Prescription, Item 8 | 13. Appropriate standards are established for satisfactory performance (or, it is clear how the student is to demonstrate mastery of the goal/objective). |
| Component 1, Instructional Prescription, Item 9 | 14. There is flexibility in choosing instructional materials/methods for the student. |
| Component 1, Instructional Prescription, Item 10 | 15. Instructional planning is not limited by strict adherence to district curriculum objectives or textbooks/materials. |
| Component 1, Instructional Prescription, Item 11 | 16. Teaching strategies, methods, and materials are matched to the student's interests and level of skill development. |
| Component 1, Instructional Prescription, Item 12 | 17. The student's interest or preference for learning materials is considered in planning instruction. |
| Component 1, Instructional Prescription, Item 13 | 18. There is flexible use of grouping structures to accommodate the student's instructional needs. |
| Component 1, Instructional Prescription, Item 14 | 19. Assignments are appropriately paced by the teacher. |
| Component 1, Instructional Prescription, Item 15 | 20. Different lessons are planned to accomplish varied goals (e.g., instruct, practice, generalize, review). |
| Component 1, Instructional Prescription, Item 17 | 21. The student's success rate on assigned tasks is predicted with reasonable accuracy (e.g., 70-85%). |
| Component 1, Instructional Prescription, Item 22 | 22. Potential problems or difficulties for the student on assigned tasks are anticipated by the teacher. |
| Component 2, Teacher Expectations, Item 11 | 23. The student understands the teacher's expectations for neatness. |
| Component 2, Teacher Expectations, Item 12 | 24. The student understands the teacher's expectations for accuracy. |
| Component 3, Classroom Management, Item 1 | 25. A small number of important rules (e.g., talking, out of seat) are selected and reinforced. |
| Component 3, Classroom Management, Item 2 | 26. Expected behavior in the classroom is communicated through discussion of rules and routines. |

| | |
|---|---|
| Component 3, Classroom Management, Item 3 | 27. Behavior that will and will not be tolerated is clearly communicated to the student. |
| Component 3, Classroom Management, Item 4 | 28. Both examples and nonexamples of rules and procedures are used. |
| Component 3, Classroom Management, Item 5 | 29. Classroom rules and routines are introduced at the beginning of the year. |
| Component 3, Classroom Management, Item 15 | 30. There is a system to involve the student in the management of his/her behavior. |
| Component 3, Productive Time Use, Item 1 | 31. The instructional routines for nonacademic class business (e.g., bathroom breaks) are understood and followed. |
| Component 3, Productive Time Use, Item 2 | 32. The physical space of the classroom is well-organized. |
| Component 3, Productive Time Use, Item 3 | 33. The student has easy access to high-use materials and supplies. |
| Component 3, Productive Time Use, Item 4 | 34. The student knows what to do when finished with assigned work. |
| Component 3, Productive Time Use, Item 5 | 35. The student knows how to get help when needed. |
| Component 3, Productive Time Use, Item 6 | 36. There is a sufficient amount of time allocated to instruction in the content area. |
| Component 3, Productive Time Use, Item 7 | 37. There is one academic, task-oriented focus in the classroom. |
| Component 3, Productive Time Use, Item 8 | 38. The lessons, including necessary materials and teaching aids, are prepared in advance. |
| Component 3, Productive Time Use, Item 11 | 39. Lessons begin and end on time. |
| Component 3, Productive Time Use, Item 12 | 40. Transitions are short and brief. |
| Component 3, Productive Time Use, Item 13 | 41. The student is given a warning for transitions between lessons. |
| Component 3, Productive Time Use, Item 14 | 42. Disruptions or interruptions are infrequent and held to a minimum. |
| Component 3, Productive Time Use, Item 15 | 43. Expectations about use of class time are communicated clearly to the student. |
| Component 3, Class Climate, Item 1 | 44. The classroom is a pleasant, friendly, happy environment (one in which the student is not obviously uncomfortable). |

| | |
|---|---|
| Component 3, Class Climate, Item 2 | 45. The classroom is supportive and accepting of individual differences. |
| Component 3, Class Climate, Item 4 | 46. The student's opinions and concerns about the classroom are encouraged and valued. |
| Component 3, Class Climate, Item 5 | 47. The classroom is characterized by a cooperative rather than a competitive atmosphere. |
| Component 3, Class Climate, Item 7 | 48. The student is expected to respond and participate in the classroom. |
| Component 4, Lesson Development, Item 19 | 49. Information is structured for the student in an appropriate fashion (e.g., advance organizers, review, guided practice, independent practice). |
| Component 6, Motivational Strategies, Item 12 | 50. The student believes he/she can do the assignment.. |
| Component 6, Motivational Strategies, Item 13 | 51. Lesson content is relevant to the interests and background of the student (i.e., highlights the student's personal experience). |
| Component 6, Motivational Strategies, Item 14 | 52. Tasks are at the student's appropriate instructional level. |
| Component 6, Motivational Strategies, Item 15 | 53. Teacher-student interactions are positive, encouraging, and emphasize the importance of student effort. |
| Component 7, Practice Opportunity, Item 5 | 54. There is an established system for the student to get help when needed. |
| Component 7, Task Relevance, Item 1 | 55. The instructional scope and sequence are specified clearly. |
| Component 7, Task Relevance, Item 6 | 56. Practice activities are related directly to the student's instructional goal. |
| Component 8, Feedback, Item 11 | 57. An appropriate rationale for the kind of feedback provided the student is present. |
| Component 9, Student Involvement, Item 10 | 58. The student is expected to be an active and involved learner. |
| Component 9, Student Involvement, Item 12 | 59. Class size does not interfere with the amount of oral student responses needed for student progress. |
| Component 9, Student Involvement, Item 13 | 60. Class composition does not interfere with the amount of teacher-student interaction needed for the student. |
| Component 9, Maintenance of Student Engagement, Item 11 | 61. There is a system or procedure for the student to follow if he/she finishes early. |
| Component 9, Maintenance of Student Engagement, Item 12 | 62. Alternative academic options for the unengaged student exist. |

| | |
|---|---|
| Component 10, Adaptive Instruction, Item 1 | 62. There is a systematic effort to adapt instruction so that the student can experience success. |
| Component 10, Adaptive Instruction, Item 2 | 63. The teacher is knowledgeable about the different instructional modifications for teaching the student. |
| Component 10, Adaptive Instruction, Item 3 | 64. The teacher is knowledgeable about many ways for dealing with student behavior or affective concerns. |
| Component 10, Adaptive Instruction, Item 4 | 65. Varied options for modifying the curriculum are available. |
| Component 10, Adaptive Instruction, Item 5 | 66. The teacher is willing to use alternative methods, materials, or goals for the student. |
| Component 10, Adaptive Instruction, Item 13 | 67. The student's needs, in addition to the curriculum to be covered, are used to plan and modify instruction. |
| Component 11, Monitoring Student Progress, Item 15 | 68. Student-teacher ratio does not interfere with frequent monitoring of the student's performance. |
| Component 11, Follow-Up Planning, Item 1 | 69. Predetermined criteria exist for mastery for the student. |
| Component 11, Follow-Up Planning, Item 2 | 70. Student performance data are used regularly to make instructional decisions for the student. |
| Component 11, Follow-Up Planning, Item 3 | 71. Progress through the curriculum depends on mastery of instructional objectives. |
| Component 11, Follow-Up Planning, Item 4 | 72. Review of skills/content is provided. |
| Component 11, Follow-Up Planning, Item 5 | 73. Review and maintenance activities are planned systematically (e.g., daily, weekly, monthly). |
| Component 11, Follow-Up Planning, Item 8 | 74. The student is held accountable for the quality of his/her work and use of class time. |
| Component 11, Follow-Up Planning, Item 9 | 75. Teacher-student ratio does not interfere with the teacher's effort for individualizing subsequent instructional planning. |

**Deliver Information**

| TIES-II Reference | Indicators of Effective Delivery |
|---|---|
| Component 2, Teacher Expectations, Item 5 | 1. The student understands the consequences of not achieving the expected standards of performance. |
| Component 2, Teacher Expectations, Item 6 | 2. Objectives or goals for the instructional less are communicated clearly so that the student knows **what** is to be learned. |
| Component 2, Teacher Expectations, Item 7 | 3. Desired or expected standards of performance are communicated clearly. |

| | |
|---|---|
| Component 2, Teacher Expectations, Item 10 | 4. The student understands the teacher's expectations for task completion. |
| Component 3, Classroom Management, Item 6 | 5. The teacher maintains good eye contact with the student. |
| Component 3, Classroom Management, Item 10 | 6. Reminders about expected behavior are give in advance of an activity (e.g., transition, field trip, assembly). |
| Component 3, Classroom Management, Item 16 | 7. Behavioral disruptions are handled promptly. |
| Component 3, Productive Use of Time, Item 9 | 8. The pace of instructional lessons is brisk, well-organized, and directed by the teacher. |
| Component 3, Productive Use of Time, Item 9 | 9. Directions are clear, simple, sequential, and often written on the board. |
| Component 3, Class Climate, Item 6 | 10. There is some flexibility in changing teaching and behavioral procedures to meet the needs of the student. |
| Component 4, Lesson Development, Item 1 | 11. Prerequisite skills, previous lessons, or prior knowledge are reviewed prior to teaching new content. |
| Component 4, Lesson Development, Item 2 | 12. Background information is provided to assist student understanding and interest and is relevant to the student's experience. |
| Component 4, Lesson Development, Item 3 | 13. An overview of lessons (what is to be learned, how it is to be learned, why it is important) is provided. |
| Component 4, Lesson Development, Item 4 | 14. The student's attention is focused during lesson presentation. |
| Component 4, Lesson Development, Item 5 | 15. the student's attention is maintained during lesson presentation. |
| Component 4, Lesson Development, Item 6 | 16. Modeling and teacher demonstration are used when appropriate to skills/content being taught. |
| Component 4, Lesson Development, Item 7 | 17. Concrete examples are used in instructional lesson. |
| Component 4, Lesson Development, Item 8 | 18. There is a high degree of teacher-directed instruction on skills/content presented. |
| Component 4, Lesson Development, Item 9 | 19. The necessary parts or distinctive features of new skills/concepts are specified clearly by the teacher. |
| Component 4, Lesson Development, Item 10 | 20. A sufficient amount of detail/information is provided in the instructional presentation. |
| Component 4, Lesson Development, Item 11 | 21. The key terms/ideas to be learned are clearly and directly taught. |

| | |
|---|---|
| Component 4, Lesson Development, Item 12 | 22. The lesson explanation is presented in an organized, step-by-step manner. |
| Component 4, Lesson Development, Item 13 | 23. A variety of teaching materials and strategies are used to explain the skills/content being taught. |
| Component 4, Lesson Development, Item 18 | 24. The instructional pace is appropriate for the student's skill level and attention span. |
| Component 4, Clarity of Directions, Item 1 | 25. The student's attention is gained before task directions are given. |
| Component 4, Clarity of Directions, Item 2 | 26. Procedures for completing the task are specified clearly. |
| Component 4, Clarity of Directions, Item 3 | 27. Task directions are logically sequenced. |
| Component 4, Clarity of Directions, Item 4 | 28. The appropriate number of directions are given at one time. |
| Component 4, Clarity of Directions, Item 5 | 29. Directions are of a reasonable and appropriate length. |
| Component 4, Clarity of Directions, Item 6 | 30. Vocabulary in the directions is understood by or clarified for the student. |
| Component 4, Clarity of Directions, Item 7 | 31. Directions are given in both an oral and a written format. |
| Component 4, Clarity of Directions, Item 8 | 32. Examples of the steps the student must follow is provided through modeling. |
| Component 5, Cognitive Emphasis, Item 1 | 33. The lesson purpose is clear and understandable to the student. |
| Component 5, Cognitive Emphasis, Item 2 | 34. Steps for mastering an objective are specified clearly. |
| Component 5, Cognitive Emphasis, Item 3 | 35. The lesson purpose is identified in terms of thinking skills (e.g., memorizing, reasoning, concluding, evaluating) required for completion. |
| Component 5, Cognitive Emphasis, Item 4 | 36. Lesson explanation emphasizes a step-by-step description of the process to follow to solve the problem. |
| Component 5, Cognitive Emphasis, Item 5 | 37. The teacher models how to think through the steps involved in solving the problem (e.g., the mental operations involved). |
| Component 5, Cognitive Emphasis, Item 8 | 38. Appropriate learning strategies (e.g., how to memorize, how to study) are taught. |
| Component 6, Motivational Strategies, Item 1 | 39. The lesson is presented with enthusiasm. |
| Component 6, Motivational Strategies, Item 2 | 40. Teacher interest for the lesson content is communicated clearly. |

| | |
|---|---|
| Component 6, Motivational Strategies, Item 3 | 41. The instructional routine or presentation is varied. |
| Component 6, Motivational Strategies, Item 6 | 42. The rationale for the lesson is communicated and reinforced for the student. |
| Component 6, Motivational Strategies, Item 7 | 43. The value of learning is emphasized in addition to task completion. |
| Component 9, Maintenance of Student Engagement, Item 1 | 44. The student's attention is gained and focused during instruction. |
| Component 9, Maintenance of Student Engagement, Item 2 | 45. The student's attention is maintained during instruction. |
| Component 10, Adaptive Instruction, Item 11 | 47. The student is informed of his/.her instructional needs. |
| Component 11, Progress Evaluation, Item 11 | 48. The student understands both his/her current level of performance and progress. |
| Component 11, Follow-Up Planning, Item 6 | 49. A sufficient amount of review is provided for the student. |

## Ask Questions

| TIES-II Reference | Indicators of Effective Questioning |
|---|---|
| Component 2, Teacher Expectations, Item 1 | 1. The student is called on in the room and expected to answer (i.e., prompts, and cues are provided to assist the student's responses). |
| Component 2, Teacher Expectations, Item 4 | 2. The student has an opportunity to respond actively. |
| Component 3, Class Climate, Item 8 | 3. Cues and prompts are used to assist the accuracy and frequency of the student's responses. |
| Component 4, Lesson Development, Item 15 | 4. Various cueing and prompting techniques are used to elicit accurate responses from the student. |
| Component 4, Checking for Student Understanding, Item 1 | 5. Questions are frequently asked to check or test student understanding. |
| Component 4, Checking for Student Understanding, Item 2 | 6. The student is asked to demonstrate his/her understanding by explaining the process used to solve problems. |
| Component 5, Cognitive Emphasis, Item 6 | 7. The student is asked to explain the process involved in solving problems or completing the work. |
| Component 5, Cognitive Emphasis, Item 7 | 8. The teacher asks the student to "think aloud" while working the problem in order to identify problem areas. |
| Component 9, Maintenance of Student Engagement, Item 9 | 9. Varied questioning techniques to engage the student are used. |
| Component 11, Monitoring Student Progress, Item 5 | 10. The teacher frequently asks the student questions to assess his/her understanding. |

| Component 11, Monitoring Student Progress, Item 14 | 11. Homework is checked, graded, and reviewed with the student. |

### Responds to Efforts

| TIES-II Reference | Indicators of Effective Responding |
|---|---|
| Component 1, Instructional Prescription, Item 24 | 1. Tasks are modified as needed in order to ensure an appropriate success rate for the student. |
| Component 3, Classroom Management, Item 8 | 2. Noncompliance or disruptive behavior is handled immediately. |
| Component 3, Classroom Management, Item 9 | 3. Inappropriate behavior is used as an opportunity to reteach or reinforce behavioral expectations. |
| Component 3, Classroom Management, Item 11 | 4. Nonverbal signals are used to redirect the student while teaching other students. |
| Component 3, Classroom Management, Item 12 | 5. Praise is specific and administered contingently. |
| Component 4, Class Climate, Item 3 | 6. Teacher-student interactions are encouraging, positive, uncritical, and emphasize the importance of student effort. |
| Component 4, Clarity of Directions, Item 9 | 7. Directions are repeated and stressed at difficult points. |
| Component 4, Checking for Student Understanding, Item 3 | 8. The student's understanding of task directions is checked before beginning independent seatwork activities. |
| Component 6, Motivational Strategies, Item 8 | 9. Goal-setting techniques and procedures are used to direct student motivation and to provide feedback. |
| Component 6, Motivational Strategies, Item 9 | 10. Student involvement and choice are used in developing motivation and self-directedness (e.g., contingency contracting opportunities for self-evaluation, self-monitoring, and charting). |
| Component 6, Motivational Strategies, Item 10 | 11. Reward systems and social reinforcers (external orientation) are effective. |
| Component 6, Motivational Strategies, Item 19 | 12. The student understands the consequences of not completing work accurately. |
| Component 6, Motivational Strategies, Item 20 | 13. The student understands the importance of the assigned tasks for real-life performance. |
| Component 6, Motivational Strategies, Item 21 | 14. The student is encouraged to perform (e.g., shown how, told he/she can do the work). |
| Component 7, Practice Opportunity, Item 4 | 15. Prompts, cues, or modeling (i.e., error correction procedures) are used rather than calling on another student to provide the answer. |
| Component 7, Instructional Material, Item 11 | 16. Materials include feedback on student responses during practice. If not, feedback is provided by the teacher. |
| Component 8, Feedback, Item 2 | 17. Feedback about performance is provided within a reasonable period of time (e.g., before beginning a new lesson). |
| Component 8, Feedback, Item 3 | 18. Explicit feedback is provided about the student's behavior. |

| | |
|---|---|
| Component 8, Feedback, Item 4 | 19. Feedback informs the student about which answers are correct or incorrect. |
| Component 8, Feedback, Item 5 | 20. Feedback informs the student why answers are correct or incorrect. |
| Component 8, Feedback, Item 6 | 21. Feedback provides enough information for the student to make the necessary corrections. |
| Component 8, Feedback, Item 7 | 22. Feedback is frequent enough to motivate the student and provide necessary corrections. |
| Component 8, Feedback, Item 8 | 23. feedback is provided in a way that encourages the student to try again. |
| Component 8, Feedback, Item 9 | 24. Process feedback (i.e., prompts and cues to assist student response) rather than terminal feedback (i.e., answer given) is provided. |
| Component 8, Feedback, Item 10 | 25. Task-specific praise about the student's academic work is provided. |
| Component 8, Feedback, Item 12 | 26. The student knows which skills are mastered and which need additional review. |
| Component 8, Corrective Procedures, Item 1 | 27. Re-explanation is provided (not simply providing the student with the correct answer) when the student is confused or makes mistakes. |
| Component 8, Corrective Procedures, Item 2 | 28. Specific suggestions to correct student errors are provided. |
| Component 8, Corrective Procedures, Item 3 | 29. Varied alternative teaching methods to reteach and correct the student's confusion or mistakes are used. |
| Component 8, Corrective Procedures, Item 4 | 30. After correction of errors, the student has an immediate chance to practice the procedure or execute the task correctly. |
| Component 8, Corrective Procedures, Item 6 | 31. The student receives correction or assistance before errors are practiced over and over. |
| Component 8, Corrective Procedures, Item 7 | 32. Prompts and cues to increase the student's accuracy of response are used. |
| Component 8, Corrective Procedures, Item 9 | 33. The student is required to correct his/her mistakes. |
| Component 9, Student Involvement, Item 9 | 34. The teacher probes for correct responses from the student rather than moving on to another student or simply providing answers for the student. |
| Component 9, Maintenance of Student Engagement, Item 5 | 35. The student is directed to another activity when he/she finishes early and is merely waiting. |
| Component 9, Maintenance of Student Engagement, Item 6 | 36. The student is given frequent reminders if he/she dawdles. |
| Component 9, Maintenance of Student Engagement, Item 8 | 37. The teacher circulates among the students during seatwork assignments to check work and assist the target student. |
| Component 10, Adaptive Instruction, Item 6 | 38. Different materials, alternative teaching strategies, increased practice opportunities, or alternative group placements are considered when a student fails to master an objective. |

| | |
|---|---|
| Component 10, Adaptive Instruction, Item 7 | 39. Lesson pace is adjusted to variations in the student's rate of mastery. |
| Component 10, Adaptive Instruction, Item 9 | 40. Tasks are modified until the student is no longer making errors or is making only infrequent careless mistakes. |
| Component 11, Monitoring Student Progress, Item 10 | 41. The student is frequently informed of his/her performance and progress. |
| Component 12, Student Understanding, Item 9 | 42. The student is aware of his/her lack of understanding or confusion with the assigned work. |
| Component 12, Student Understanding, Item 10 | 43. The student knows specific strategies to employ himself/herself in completing the assigned work. |

## Use Activities

| TIES-II Reference | Indicators of Effective Activity Use |
|---|---|
| Component 2, Teacher Expectations, Item 2 | 1. The student is expected to be an active and involved learner. |
| Component 2, Teacher Expectations, Item 8 | 2. The teacher's expectations about the use of time in the classroom are communicated clearly. |
| Component 4, Lesson Development, Item 14 | 3. Substantive teacher-student interaction (e.g., ask/answer questions, repeat directions, provide feedback) occurs. |
| Component 4, Lesson Development, Item 16 | 4. Guided practice opportunities are provided. |
| Component 4, Lesson Development, Item 17 | 5. Opportunities are provided for the student to explain the process or procedures. |
| Component 4, Clarity of Directions, Item 10 | 6. The student begins work after all directions have been provided. |
| Component 4, Checking for Student Understanding, Item 4 | 7. The student has had an opportunity to demonstrate his/her ability to perform the skill before beginning independent seatwork activities. |
| Component 4, Checking for Student Understanding, Item 9 | 8. The student understands how to get assistance when confused. |
| Component 6, Motivational Strategies, Item 4 | 9. Interesting and age-appropriate materials and assignments are used. |
| Component 6, Motivational Strategies, Item 5 | 10. Assignments are varied to heighten student interest. |
| Component 7, Practice Opportunity, Item 1 | 11. Sufficient opportunity for practice of skills/content exists. |
| Component 7, Practice Opportunity, Item 2 | 12. Practice opportunities are provided until the student makes only infrequent careless mistakes. |
| Component 7, Practice Opportunity, Item 6 | 13. The student asks for assistance when needed. |

| | |
|---|---|
| Component 7, Practice Opportunity, Item 7 | 14. Homework is regularly assigned, checked, and reviewed with the student. |
| Component 7, Practice Opportunity, Item 9 | 15. Assigned tasks are designed to included drill work, practice, generalization, and application opportunities. |
| Component 7, Practice Opportunity, Item 10 | 16. Drill work and repeated practice are used to reinforce skills and build student accuracy. |
| Component 7, Practice Opportunity, Item 11 | 17. Speed work is provided to achieve automaticity of basic skills. |
| Component 7, Practice Opportunity, Item 12 | 18. Varied materials and different applications of the skills taught are used to assist with generalization. |
| Component 7, Practice Opportunity, Item 13 | 19. The kind of practice (guided or independent) is appropriate for the student. |
| Component 7, Task Relevance, Item 4 | 20. Practice activities (assigned tasks) are at the appropriate instructional level for the student. |
| Component 7, Task Relevance, Item5 | 21. Task directions contain sufficient detail so that the student understands what to do during practice. |
| Component 7, Task Relevance, Item 7 | 22. Practice activities are related directly to the lesson presentation explained and demonstrated by the teacher. |
| Component 7, Task Relevance, Item 8 | 23. Activities are important for student learning and, consequently, are not simply "busy work." |
| Component 7, Task Relevance, Item 9 | 24. The student's engaged time is high during seatwork practice. |
| Component 7, Task Relevance, Item 11 | 25. The student is able to complete assigned tasks independently during practice. If so, the student's success rate is between 90-100%. |
| Component 7, Instructional Material, Item 3 | 26. Format of assigned materials is easy to understand, clear, and uncluttered. |
| Component 7, Instructional Material, Item 4 | 27. The student can read and understand written directions on the assigned materials. |
| Component 7, Instructional Material, Item 5 | 28. There is ample writing space for the student. |
| Component 7, Instructional Material, Item 6 | 29. The student is assigned the right amount of work. |
| Component 7, Instructional Material, Item 7 | 30. Varied instructional materials are used (e.g., workbook, tapes, films, peer interaction). |
| Component 7, Instructional Material, Item 8 | 31. Necessary modifications for successful completion of assignments are made (e.g., length decreased, concrete aids and cues provided). |
| Component 7, Instructional Material, Item 9 | 32. Materials are age-appropriate, interesting, and visually appealing. |

| | |
|---|---|
| Component 7, Instructional Material, Item 10 | 33. Instructional materials provide ample practice and reinforcement of skills to be mastered. |
| Component 7, Instructional Material, Item 13 | 34. Requirements for successful completion of independent assignments are at the appropriate level for the student (e.g., cognitive processing demands, number of steps/skills involved). |
| Component 8, Corrective Procedures, Item 5 | 35. Practice opportunities are provided until the student makes only infrequent careless mistakes. |
| Component 9, Student Involvement, Item 7 | 36. Many opportunities for the student to respond exist. |
| Component 9, Student Involvement, Item 8 | 37. The student has an equal opportunity to respond when compared with classmates. |
| Component 9, Student Involvement, Item 14 | 38. The kind of task assigned affects the student's engaged time. |
| Component 9, Student Involvement, Item 15 | 39. Seatwork tasks promote active academic student responding (e.g., tutoring, peers, aides, computers). |
| Component 11, Monitoring Student Progress, Item 12 | 40. Opportunities exist for the student to self-evaluate his/her work. |
| Component 11, Monitoring Student Progress, Item 13 | 41. Opportunities to review seatwork assignments are provided. |
| Component 12, Student Understanding, Item 5 | 42. The student demonstrates understanding of the task before beginning or within the first few minutes of independent practice opportunities. |
| Component 12, Student Understanding, Item 6 | 43. The student's success rate is moderately high (e.g., 75%) during initial instruction. |
| Component 12, Student Understanding, Item 7 | 44. The student's success rate is high during independent practice activities (e.g., 90-100%). |

# FORMATIVE EVALUATION
(How to Determine and Analyze Trend)

## Data-Based Program Modification

Here is the main point: *When you are monitoring student performance over time, chart the information in a visual display so that you can <u>see</u> the effect of instruction.  Visual displays will show you when to change teaching actions and will help to keep you from changing when you shouldn't. This will make your teaching more effective.*

There are a number of methods that can be used to chart student performance scores that are derived from curriculum-based measures.  The type of chart used, how frequently the student's performance is measured, and the guidelines used to inform the decision-making process may vary, but there are at least four shared attributes across all Data-Based Program Modification (DBPM) systems.

They are:

1) Assessment items are drawn from the student's curricula;
2) Repeated assessment is conducted across time;
3) The resulting data is visually displayed (usually in a chart); and,
3) The assessment information is used to make instructional decisions.

The first attribute requires that evaluators know the objectives to be taught, and that they then periodically sample student performance using curriculum-based measures to monitor progress toward those objectives. The second characteristic means that student performance must be sampled often enough for learning patterns to emerge. Some teacher judgment is required when deciding how frequently objectives should be measured.  We believe that it is better to err on the side of sampling behavior frequently rather than infrequently. Once data are collected they should be visually displayed for easy access and utility. The final attribute of DBPM is that <u>the assessment information is used to make instructional decisions</u>. Several skills are required to produce these attributes.

### A: Charting

### Step 1. Convert Data

If charting rate of behavior label the vertical axis of the chart "rate (count) per minute." If charting duration, label the axis "minutes." For rate, divide the count obtained for both correct and errors by the number of minutes of the test or observation. This will convert all data into a standard "per-minute" metric. Five days' worth of rate data illustrating common charting problems is shown in Exhibit 1. On Tuesday note that fractions of minutes are treated as decimals and on Wednesday that behaviors occurring less often than once a minute require a chart that goes below 1.

Exhibit 1:

| | Time in Minutes | Count Correct | Count Error | Rate pre Minute (Count/Time) Correct | Rate pre Minute (Count/Time) Error |
|---|---|---|---|---|---|
| Monday | 10 | 40 | 20 | 40/10 = 4 | 20/10 = 2 |
| Tuesday | 1.5 | 8 | 5 | 8/ 1.5 = 5.3 | 5/ 1.5 = 3.3 |
| Wednesday | 20 | 10 | 5 | 10/20 = .5 | 5/20 = .25 |
| Thursday | 1 | 40 | 20 | 40/ 1 = 40 | 20/ 1 = 20 |
| Friday | 7 | 24 | 17 | 24/ 7 = 3.4 | 17/ 7 = 2.4 |

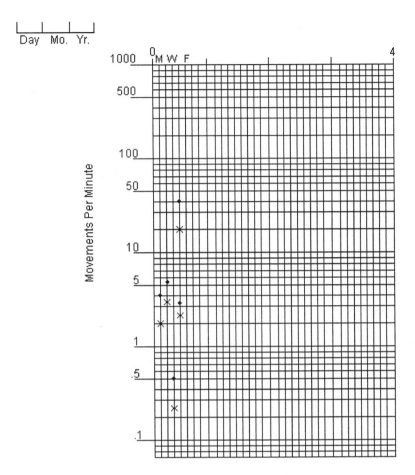

Day  Mo.  Yr.

Figure 15.15

## Step 2. Mark Floors and Ceilings

On the chart note any permanent constraints on the data such as floors (least possible scores) or ceilings (highest possible scores). For accuracy and duration data, the floor is 1. Rate floors are found by dividing the length of the observation (in minutes) into 1. For example, the floor of a 2-minute timing is 1 [yak divide sign] 2 = .5. Floors are marked with dashed lines not crossing the Sunday line, as shown in Exhibit 2.

Ceilings are marked with a dashed line crossing Sunday lines and are either equal to the total available opportunities or the total opportunities allowed by the available time. For example. the ceiling for a behavior that takes 6 seconds to complete would be 10 per minute (6 yak divide /6 = 10). The ceiling for accuracy is 100%.

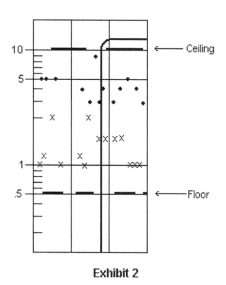

**Exhibit 2**

## Step 3. Mark Aims

Performance aims are the same as CAP for the objective being monitored. Mark performance aims with a wavy line along the line illustrating the performance level . If a performance aim and aim date (date by which the aim is to be met) can both be specified don't bother with a wavy line ; instead mark the intersection of the aim rate and aim date with an **A**. Use an upright **A** for acceleration (correct) behaviors and an upside down for deceleration (error) objectives, as seen in Exhibit 3.

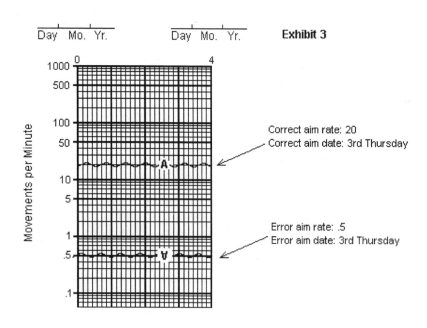

**Exhibit 3**

Correct aim rate: 20
Correct aim date: 3rd Thursday

Error aim rate: .5
Error aim date: 3rd Thursday

Figure 15.17
Marking objectives on the chart

## Step 4. Chart Data

Refer to Exhibit 4 for conventional charting rules.

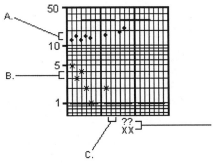

A. Acceleration behaviors (corrects) are charted as dots ( ).
B. Decceleration behaviors (errors) are charted as x's (X).
C. On Days when timings do not occur, don't chart anything.
D. Zero behavior is usually marked below the floor with a
   question mark (?).

Note: Don't connect the dots or x's; it will only confuse the picture

**Exhibit 4**

## Determining Current Performance

When repeated measures of a behavior charted, the median score of the last three recorded days is used to summarize performance. By convention the median is marked on the chart in a teardrop, or bubble, as shown in Exhibit 5. In Exhibit 5 the median rate of **1** was found by simply finding the middle of the last three marks as judged along the vertical axis:

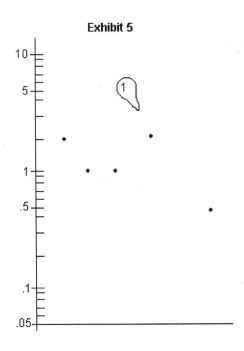

**Exhibit 5**

2
1   -- median
 .7

If the same score is obtained on two days it is counted twice. Therefore, **5** is the median of

**5**
**5** -- median
**10**.

### Determining Current Progress (Trend)

Up until now our focus has been on recording performance (or lack of it) in the form of dots, x's. question marks, ceilings, floors, and teardrops. But formative evaluation is about trends. Here are two ways to note the trend of a set of data:

**Best Fit** This is the least exact way to find a trend; it is also the easiest and most common. The procedure is simple. Take a set of data points, eyeball the data, and draw a line that seems to fit. Obviously this is easier with low variability data, as seen in Exhibit 6.a, than with high variability data like those shown in Exhibit 6.b. It is also easier to do with lots of data points than with only a few. For most students on most behaviors, best fit lines are adequate for decision making.

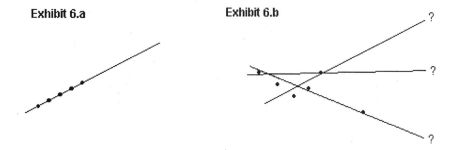

**Exhibit 6.a**     **Exhibit 6.b**

**Median Slopes** The second and more exact way to find a trend is to employ the median slope technique developed by Owen White. This technique is harder to explain than to do and once mastered takes only about 10 seconds to carry out. Each step described below is illustrated in Exhibit 7.

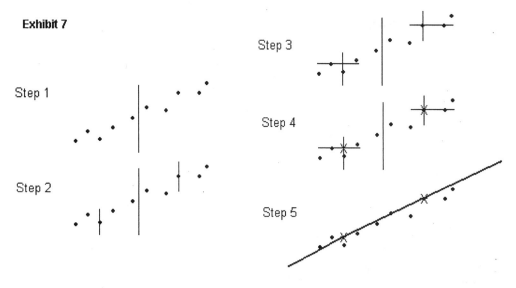

**Exhibit 7**

Step 1

Step 2

Step 3

Step 4

Step 5

Step 1. Divide data in half along time axis.
Step 2. Divide data in quarters along time axis.
Step 3. Switch to the frequency axis. For each half of the data, find the frequency line on which the median score falls.
Step 4. For each half of the data find the intersection of the quarter line and the median frequency line.
Step 5. Connect the two quarter/median intersections to draw the trend.
Here are some hints to follow when finding median slopes.

Medians. As explained above the median of each half of the data is the middle score of each half. Visually it is the dot (or X) that has as many marks below it as above it
When there are an even number of data points, assume the median is halfway between the middle two. For example, the median of

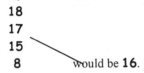

18
17
15
8        would be **16**.

Dividing Data. To divide the data in half or quarters use data, not actual days. This means splitting the data charted, not the calendar days covered.

Half and Quarter Lines. When dividing the data the half line will intersect a dot in cases where there are an odd number of charted points. In these cases the dot is no longer used during calculations. It is not a problem if the quarter lines strike dot, in these cases the dots are used.

A Common Mistake. The most common error people make when calculating a median slope is to draw a line intersecting the median score of each half. The median scores are used only to find the median frequency line. It is the median frequency/quarter intersects that should be connected.

The median slope technique is used to recognize trends in data. These trend lines are summaries of central tendency and, once extended. become our best guess of where a student will be at some future date. Therefore by extending the line to a performance aim we can anticipate when an objective will be met.

## Determining Expected Progress

Formative evaluation is of greatest value when one compares actual progress to expected progress. To make this comparison, find expected progress, in the form of progress aims. The procedure for doing this is simple.

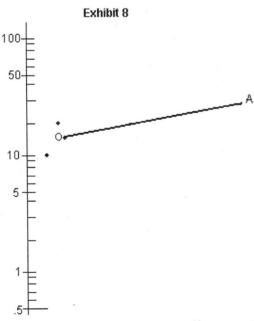

**Exhibit 8**

In Exhibit 8 a student's current performance (as indicated by the median of 3 days of data) is connected to an aim (as indicated by the **A**). The line between the current performance and the aim is called the *minimum 'celeration* line, *objective line*, or *aim line*. The *aim line* is a progress objective and visually represents the path a student must follow to get from where he is now to where you want him to be at the end of instruction. The hardest part of finding the aim line is deciding on the aim date. The aim rate, or performance level, is specified as CAP in the instructional objective and should have been established earlier through a standardization process like the one described in chapter 3. The aim date, however, must be selected by thinking about how long it should take to teach a task (Deno & Mirkin, 1977).

**Curriculum-Determined Aim Dates** Ideally a curriculum will specify when a student is expected to learn each objective. However, few curricula are that specific; even if they are, the date sequence becomes a moot point for special/ remedial students as they are already behind. However, it is possible to recognize how many objectives they must complete in order to catch up and how long that should take.

**Product Completion** The procedure for product completion is outlined in Exhibit 9. In the example the student can catch up in one year by completing one chapter test every six instructional days. This does not mean that his problem will be solved by bombarding him with assignments. It means that he needs sufficient instructional support to complete the assignments at a faster pace than others. This approach should only be used if the assignments involved are meaningful.

| Step | Exhibit 9 | Example |
|---|---|---|
| 1. Identify products to be completed that represent desired learning outcomes. | | End-of-chapter test passed in math. |
| 2. Determine how many of these products the student has already finished. This will be the current level of performance. Mark this on an equal interval graph. | | Performance = 27<br><br>60<br><br>30   •<br><br>0 |
| 3. Decide how many products he would have finished if he were progressing adequately and subtract his current performance from that to find the product discrepancy. | | Ideal products completed   40<br>- Current products completed  -27<br>Product discrepancy   13 |
| 4. Decide how long you have to work with the student to make up the discrepancy and the number of products other students will finish in that time. Add this to number to the product discrepancy. | | If there is one year (40 weeks) to catch the student up and the rest of the class will cover 20 new chapters in that year she must complete 20 + 13 = 33 chapters. |
| 5. Add the products to be completed (33) to those already done. (27). This gives you the performance aim. | | 33  products to be finished<br>+ 27  products already finished<br>60  Total products completed by<br>     the end of instruction<br><br>Performance aim = 60<br>Aim date = 40 weeks<br>from the start of school |

6. Find the minimum 'celeration line by marking the intersection of the performance aim and the aim date. Connect the two points with a line.

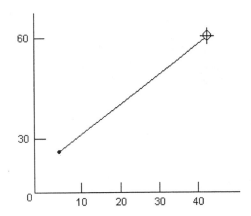

or

| Divide the number of products to be done (obtained in step 4) by the available tiem to find out how many must be completed per week. | 33/40 = .83 chapters a week. With five instructional days a week this figures out to .17 chapters a day (.83/5 = .17), or one chapter every six instructional days. |

**Behavior Change** This procedure is better than product completion because it does not place blind faith in the relevance of every assignment in the text. Instead it uses the assignments as indicators of expected behavior change. It is outlined in Exhibit 10.

| Step | **Exhibit 10** | Example |
|---|---|---|
| 1. Carry out the product completion procedure described above to determinewhat chapter test he needs to be working on now and which one he needs to be working on at the end of instruction. | | Current chapter = 27<br>Target chapter = 60 |
| 2. Determine what objectives/skills will be taught in the intervening chapters. | | |
| 3. divide the objectives into groups that represent reasonably consolidated domains of content and that should be taught during a 4- to 6-week period. (short-term objectives) | | In this case the student is learning fractions. the fraction content is illustrated by the table of specifications. With onw year (40 weeks of instruction) available, a minimum of six 4- to 6-week periods of instruction can be delivered so the table is carved up into six reasonably consolidated domains. |
| 4. Devise a test covering the content of each domain. | | Test titles:<br>1. Converting Fractions<br>2. Adding and Subtracting Fractions With Common Denominators<br>3. Adding and Subtracting Mixed Numbers Without Common Factors Between Uncommon Denominators<br>4. Multiplying and Dividing Fractions With Common Denominators - No Conversion Required<br>5. Multiplying Mixed Numbers With Conversions<br>6. Dividing Mixed Numbers With Conversions |

5. Set performance criteria for each test in the form of an aim rate and intersect it with the aim date of 6 weeks. Mark the intersection with an A. Connect the lower left-hand corner of the chart (0 performance on the first day) to the A to find the minimum 'celeration line. (Few students will actually enter a unit at zero performance so the aim line can be adjusted in most cases.)

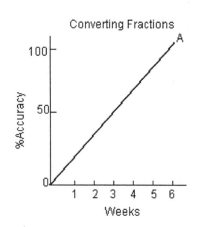

**Student-Determined (Idiosyncratic) Aim Dates** One can use the student's own progress to find the aim date. This procedure has great advantages but also has some risk. Start by collecting several days of data during instruction (this is not a baseline, or no instruction, period) and then finding the median slope for those data. The median slope is then extended to the aim rate. Once the student's current trend is extended to the aim rate, it becomes a *student-determined minimum aim line* and the point where it intersects the rate becomes the *aim date* (Exhibit 11). The risk is obvious: If the student is not learning optimally when the line is drawn it will underestimate potential progress. However, it does have the advantage of indicating a sort of "progress floor." Because the line is based on the student's own progress, it is reasonable to demand this level or more during subsequent learning on the same task.

**Exhibit 11**

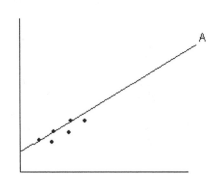

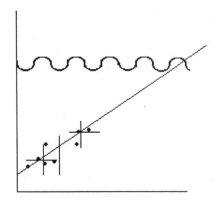

Steps
1. Mark the aim rate and collect several (5 or more) days of dtat as instruction is taking place.
2. Calculate the median slope and extend it to the aim rate.
3. Mark the aim and treat the median slope as a minimum 'celeration rate.

This procedure does have instructional advantages. A teacher can contract with the student to give a reward every day his performance exceeds his own aim line. This procedure puts him in "competition" with himself as opposed to a norm or a behavioral criterion. Because the median slope line typically splits the data in half, so about 50% of the time the student will be rewarded even if his learning doesn't change. This means that a contract based on this line is both individual and highly positive.

## Envelopes

An envelope is simply a pair of dotted lines drawn parallel to the median slope. Envelopes should be drawn so that 80% or more of the data points used to calculate the median slope fall between the dotted lines. Look at the examples in Exhibit 12 and notice how data points that are extremely deviant from the others have simply been ignored when drawing the envelope. Also, notice that the envelope lines are parallel and do not converge as they move up the chart. (This will only be true on a logarithmic graph. On an equal-interval chart the envelope lines should converge as the data converge).

Envelopes are interesting because their width' is determined by variability in both time and behavior. They illustrate clearly the dual nature of learning: that it is indicated by changes in behavior across time.

**Exhibit 12**

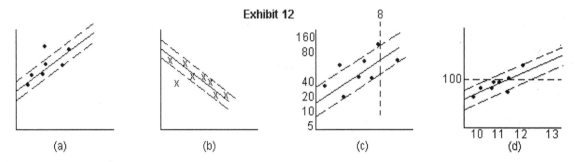

(a)          (b)          (c)          (d)

**Using Envelopes to Make Predictions** Once the envelope has been drawn, it can be extended into the future just like the median slope; like the median slope it can be used to make predictions. Look at the data in Exhibit 13. The median slopes and the envelopes have been extended for the correct and error rates. While the slopes remain the best predictor of the students arrival at the aim, the envelopes indicate the earliest and latest dates that that arrival should be expected. Note that while the correct and error slopes reach their aims on the same day, the variability in errors should cause you to be less certain of the prediction made for the error slope. The prediction for the correct trend could be off by as much as one week without prompting concern about changing the program.

**Exhibit 13**

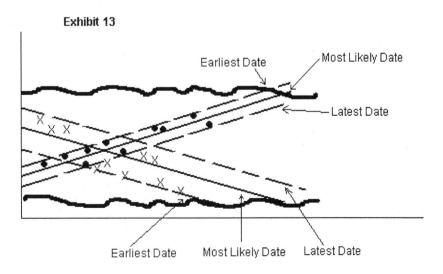

The *bounce*. or variability, in data is due in part to error of measurement. Because the envelope encompasses this error, it describes a students status more accurately than the median slope or an individual data point. For example, look at Exhibit 14, which shows the intersection of the envelope with an aim rate. Notice that on the third Tuesday, the student scores above the aim rate. Does this mean he has met his aim? As an evaluator you can't be sure because the bounce in the data is partially produced by error, which means that the student may have scored above criterion more or less by accident. So you may not want to risk stopping instruction because of this single data point. To guarantee that the student is at aim, you need to monitor him for at least as many days as the width of the envelope indicates. As a rule, a student is not said to have met aim until he is above it on his worst day. However, because aims themselves are seldom absolute, you should introduce a new task after the student's first score exceeds the aim rate, but continue to monitor the original skill for the width of the envelope .

**Exhibit 14**

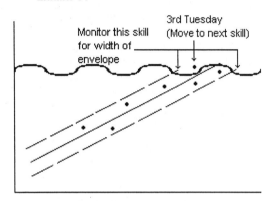

## Using Envelopes to Adjust Aim Dates

Owen White (1983) has suggested using envelopes to adjust aim dates. Because the *minimum 'celeration line* may underestimate what the student can actually do, White has suggested using the top boundary of the envelope as a new *aim line* once the lower boundary reaches the original aim line. This procedure is illustrated in Exhibit 15.

**Exhibit 15**

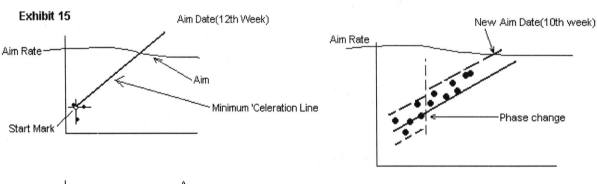

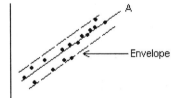

Step 1: Draw original minimum 'celeration line using any of the procedures described in this chapter.

Step 2: Begin teaching and draw the envelope - if the data begin to move above the minimum 'celeration line (as they do at the point indicated by the arrow) carry out step 3.

Step 3: Draw a new envelope and extend the top boundry of the envelope to the aim rate line (keeping it parallel to the minimum 'celeration line) to select the new aim date.

# DECISION MAKING

The remainder of this section will show how formative data can be used to guide decisions about changes in instruction. These changes should be thought of as exercises in fine tuning rather than the major reconstruction of lessons. Obviously no one wants to rip everything apart to start completely over. However. change is necessary and the considerable value of formative evaluation is that it alerts one early so that small adjustments can head off big problems.

## Deciding When to Change

A program should be changed when it isn't working. The more quickly this change takes place the more student time will be saved. If an informal data collection system is being used, teachers/evaluators should set up a routine schedule of program review (every 2 weeks is recommended).

More formal formative systems have the power to alert one immediately if change is indicated. Some authors suggest that changes be made in a program if, for any 3 consecutive days, the data are below (for acceleration) the aim line. For deceleration targets, changes should occur if 3 consecutive days are above the line. If a student is below the acceleration aim line or above the deceleration aim line for 3 days in a row, the chances are less than 6% that he will reach his aim without a change in the instructional program (White & Haring 1982).

## Deciding How to Change

Because there are so many incentive and delivery variables a teacher often must make small changes in programs. Then she can monitor and adjust the treatment until an effective lesson is found. This means comparing the effects of a new treatment to those produced by a previous treatment.

**Comparing** Programs Decisions about instruction can be made by approaching them as if they were research questions to be resolved through single-subject research. In some versions of single subject research each student functions as his own "control" as he is placed in first one treatment and then the other. The ways the student learns in each treatment are then compared to judge their relative effect. The resulting changes can be described in terms of their direction and significance.

Direction Changes in direction are either up (positive) or (down) negative. If progress data are being examined. then a change in direction is called a *slope change*. If performance data are examined, then changes in direction are called *step changes*. The series of illustrations in Exhibit 16 shows various configurations of step and slope changes.

**Exhibit 16**

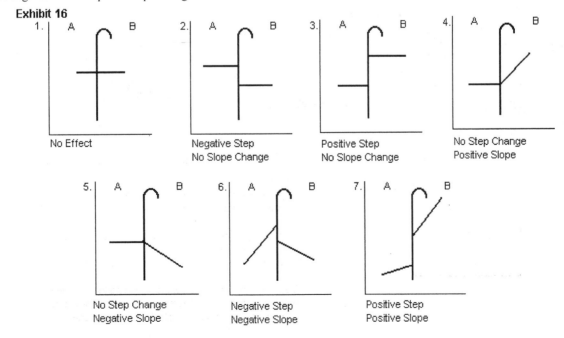

1. No Effect
2. Negative Step / No Slope Change
3. Positive Step / No Slope Change
4. No Step Change / Positive Slope
5. No Step Change / Negative Slope
6. Negative Step / Negative Slope
7. Positive Step / Positive Slope

Note that step and slope changes are independent of each other. Therefore, program changes that have the effect of increasing a student's total performance (positive *step*) may not always increase their progress.

Significance. The whole point of monitoring and comparing treatment is to determine which method is the best for a particular student at a particular time on a particular task. Changes in behavior across time can be summarized numerically but ,these data are often difficult to interpret. The easiest way to summarize and interpret data for individual students is to represent them visually on a chart. On charts that have standard behavior and time axes, the steepest line represents the most behavior change per time unit. Therefore. as a rule, the best program is the one that brings about the steepest slope. To judge significance ask "Did this program change save time?" (by seeing to it that the students arrive at performance aims in the least instructional time). When time is saved teaching one goal another goal can be added. That's how kids who are behind catch up.

Because charts have two dimensions. the effect of a phase change can be noted in two ways. Exhibit 17 shows two treatments (separated by a hooked vertical "phase change" line) and two learning slopes. The dotted lines represent predicted growth in each treatment. Obviously phase **B** is superior; the effect of the change from **A** to **B** can be seen by selecting either a date or behavior frequency for comparison. The net effect of the phase change is that student will be performing 20% ahead in treatment **B** by the 12th Sunday. The student will arrive at the 100% aim two weeks earlier if left in treatment **B**. Therefore, the phase change illustrated in Exhibit 17 is significant if you (as the teacher) believe that saving 2 weeks of instruction is important.

**Exhibit 17**

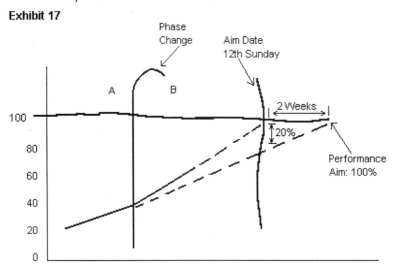

The chart in Exhibit 18 shows the slope effect of a phase change. A step change can also alter the time required to arrive at a behavioral level, as seen in Exhibit 19. In this case, the student was better off in phase A.

**Exhibit 19**

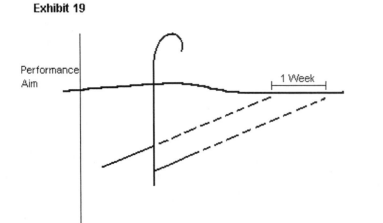

## Summary

Formative evaluation will be most successful when:

- The teacher initially counts only priority behaviors.
- The teacher identifies strategies to make timing and recording behavior easier.
- The teacher evaluates the recorded data frequently (preferably daily).
- Curriculum-based testing or observation is used.
- The system remains a tool for teaching rather than a "cause.' Specific programs of formative evaluation should only be used as long as they help the student.

Strategies to facilitate timing and recording behaviors include:

- Group timings. This works best with written activities. For example: time one-minute handwriting samples, one-minute math fact sheets. one-minute spelling tests.
- Students can record time started and stopped. (This can easily be done with a rubber stamp of a clock on worksheets. Direct them to look at a wall clock and mark the hands on their papers.)
- A kitchen timer or prerecorded tape can be used to time sessions.
- Students can work together to time and record data for each other. This can work well with flashcard drills.
- Students can read into a tape recorder. Teachers can later check correct and error rates.
- Mechanical counters. Single and dual tally counters are available, as well as beads and golf-score counters.
- Teachers should count for a fixed period of time each day. Counting for different intervals confuses the data pattern because such factors as endurance, boredom, and latency of response may enter into the data analysis.
- One-minute timings are easy to chart because the raw score is the same as rate per minute.
- Aides, peers, student teachers, and volunteers can be trained to help develop materials and to count and record behaviors.
- Teachers should count when the behaviors are likely to occur and when other distractions will be minimal.

## THINKING ERRORS

*Directions*

1. During interviews, or specific level testing for Type 2 prerequisites, make a list of things the student says (statements) which seem to reflect errors in thinking.

2. Categorize the errors using one, or both, of the categories: Explanatory Style and Thinking Error.

3. Under the Explanatory style heading review the list of statements and select those which seem to relate to a positive or negative experience. Also list "absolute" statements.

4. You may categorize the same error under more than one heading.

**Explanatory Style**

Mark the appropriate descriptors:

| List statements: | Negative | Performance Oriented | Permanent | Pervasive | Personal |
|---|---|---|---|---|---|
| a. | ❑ | ❑ | ❑ | ❑ | ❑ |
| b. | ❑ | ❑ | ❑ | ❑ | ❑ |
| c. | ❑ | ❑ | ❑ | ❑ | ❑ |
| d. | ❑ | ❑ | ❑ | ❑ | ❑ |

**Other Thinking Errors**

List statements and mark the appropriate descriptors (e.g., 3a, 2d, 1g )

a.

b.

c.

d

e.

## Categories of Commonly Recognized Errors:

**1. Errors in Problem Solving**
- Lack of knowledge
- Stereotyping
- Failure to define problem
- Defining problem to narrowly
- Lack of perspective
- Fear
- Premature resolution
- Insensitivity to probabilities
- Sample size
- Misconceptions of chance
- Unwarranted confidence
- Selective or incomplete search
- Mistaking correlation for cause
- Lack of supportive environment

**2. Irrational Thoughts**
- I must be good at everything I do and it's terrible if I'm not.
- Everybody I meet must like me and it's awful if they don't.
- If people do things to me that I don't like, they must be rotten.
- You can't trust _____ (anyone over thirty).
- When things don't go my way, it's awful.
- Everyone should treat me fairly and it's awful if they don't.
- I have no control over what happens to me in my life.
- I shouldn't have to wait for anything I want.
- When something bad happens to me, I should [think about it all the time].
- Anyone who walks away from a fight is a punk.
- I must be stupid if I make mistakes.
- I always have to win and it's terrible if I don't.
- People should not have to do anything they don't want to do.
- School is dumb. You don't need to go to school.

**3. Helpless Cognitive Set**
- Something must be completed correctly in order for me to be a success
- I should only pick easy things to do.
- If I fail it is because I am dumb.
- If I fail it is because the task is to hard.
- If I fail I should stop working because it means I have encountered a task that is too hard for me.

# Reading Comprehension Status Sheet.

| If the Student Makes This Error: | Then This Is the Problem Area: | And This Is the Objective: | Does the Student Have the Skills? |
|---|---|---|---|
| | 1. Monitors meaning | | Yes No Unsure ☐ ☐ ☐ |
| Student is unaware of and continues reading when she makes errors that violate the meaning of the text. Student employs no strategies for monitoring meaning of reading. | Attends to reading and notes errors that violate meaning. | Upon request, student will explain the following meaning-monitoring tasks: self-correct when making errors that violate meaning rereading confusing portions of texts/passages making predictions regarding upcoming events identifying when additional information is needed to answer questions reading with expression. CAP 100% | |
| Student does not ask questions about material being read. | Self-questions. | When asked to do so the student will generate questions about up-coming events in the passage. These will be based on: q Previous text q Titles and subtitles q Illustrations. CAP 95% | |
| Student reads passages at the same rate and only one time regardless of difficulty or understanding. | Rereads confusing portions of material or adjusts reading rate on difficult sections. | Given passages at [expected or intermediate curriculum levels], the student will, upon encountering difficult or confusing materials, employ one or more of the following tactics: Reread Adjust rate. CAP 90% | |
| Student makes random predictions without reflecting on what has happened and ignoring other cues (pictures, etc.). | Can predict upcoming events in the passage. | Given a series of passages at [the expected or intermediate levels], the student will make pre-dictions about each upcoming passage that reflect a logical extension of the previously read material. CAP 90% | |
| Student makes random guesses to answer questions posed about readings. | Identifies when additional infor-mation is needed, or specifically what kind of information is needed to answer questions. | Given questions related to pass-age read, student will pick out important details necessary to answer questions and report a rule or strategy for locating the information. CAP 100% | |
| | 2. Selective attention to text | | Yes No Unsure ☐ ☐ ☐ |
| Student reading is halted and laborious. | Reads with expression and/or automation. | Given a passage at [expected or intermediate curriculum level], student will read it aloud [at automatic level]. | |
| Student is unaware and continues reading when she makes errors that violate the meaning of the passage. | Student corrects errors that violate meaning. | Given signals, the student will immediately locate and correct errors that violate meaning made in oral reading. The signals may be given after words, phrases, sentence, or paragraphs. CAP 95% | |

| If the Student Makes This Error: | Then This Is the Problem Area: | And This Is the Objective: | Does the Student Have the Skills? |
|---|---|---|---|
| Student reads passage as if it is independent of all previously learned information. | Connects text to prior knowledge. | Upon request, student will supply and/or explain the process of drawing from background knowledge. CAP 100% | |
| | **3. Adjusts for text difficulty** | | Yes No Unsure |
| Student reads texts/ passages as quickly as possible and for completion only. | Allocates study time according to passage difficulty. | Given a passage [at expected or intermediate curriculum level], containing difficult wording or confusing information, student will allocate additional study time necessary to employ clarification strategies. | ☐ ☐ ☐ |
| Student unable to identify purpose(s) for reading(s) (entertainment vs. information). | States purpose for reading. | Prior to beginning passages, student will state their purpose for reading (entertainment or information). | |
| Student does not realize when errors have been made that violate the meaning of passages. | Identifies and self-corrects reading errors that violate the meaning of the passage. | Given signals, the student will immediately locate and correct errors that violate meaning made in oral reading. The signals may be given after words, phrases, sentences, or paragraphs. CAP 95% | |
| Student reads materials at same rate regardless of text difficulty and/or importance (information vs. entertainment). | Adjusts reading rate appropriately. | Student will adjust reading rate according to difficulty and/or importance of materials. | |
| | **4. Connects text with prior knowledge** | | Yes No Unsure |
| After reading a passage/text, student supplies an unrelated or tangentially related "best title" or main idea. Student identifies supporting information as the main idea. | Answers "best title" and main ideas questions accurately. | Student will identify answers to "best title" and main idea questions for [expected or intermediate curriculum level]. CAP 100% | ☐ ☐ ☐ |
| Retells or paraphrases story using supporting or obscure details. Retells story word for word. | Retells story with emphasis on major points. | Given a passage [at expected or intermediate curriculum level], student will retell the content. CAP 3 | |
| Does not say why something was written, or gives an unlikely purpose. | Describes author's purpose for writing. | When presented with a variety of writing selections the student will provide a likely purpose for each. The purpose will be likely if it accurately reflects the known, and/or logically assumed, intent of the author. | |
| Student has to reread entire portions of the text to find answers to questions. | Can locate information in the passage that answers assigned questions. | Given passages [at appropriate level], student will locate, by scanning, answers to assigned questions. CAP 100% | |
| Student does not discriminate between credible and deceptive presentations. | Can accurately apply stated criteria to the story to judge its value as an information source. | When supplied with a variety of written presentations the student will sort them according to legitimacy. The student will then provide an explanation of her sorting, which will include the use of [specified critical reading rules]. CAP [determine within class]. | |

| If the Student Makes This Error: | Then This Is the Problem Area: | And This Is the Objective: | Does the Student Have the Skills? |
|---|---|---|---|
| Student does not recall information immediately after she has read it. Student reads each passage as if it is a brand new idea. | Uses information gained from reading the passage to focus on subsequent topics/information in the passage. | Given a series of passages at [expected or intermediate levels], student will identify key information/ideas to search for supported by previous passage(s). The ideas/information will reflect content that the author/teacher thinks critical. CAP 90% | |
| | 5. Clarifies | | Yes No Unsure |
| Student has no clarification strategies. | Knowledge of clarification strategies. | Upon request, student will supply and explain possible clarification strategies: (CAP 100%) adjusting reading rate identifying important details strategies to determine meaning decoding self-correction asking for help. | ☐ ☐ ☐ |
| Student reads passages at the same rate and only one time regardless of difficulty or understanding. | Adjusts reading rate for material that is not understood. | Student will adjust reading rate according to difficulty and/or understanding of materials. | |
| When asked to paraphrase or retell story, student provides obscure or irrelevant details. | Is more likely to recall important passage details, not trivial ones. | Given passages at [expected or intermediate levels], student will identify [by underlining or reporting], important passage details related to one or more of the following categories: main idea relevant information characters descriptions actions conflicts resolutions. CAP 100% | |
| Student makes references to previously learned information when answering questions, even when irrelevant to the question or passage read. | Answers comprehension questions in terms of stated information in passage, not necessarily prior knowledge. | The student will provide text-dependent answers to questions drawn from reading samples. To establish that the answers are text-dependent, following production of the answer, the student will find and mark those portions of the passage that support her answer. CAP: agreement with instructor or exemplar student. | |
| Student uses a single strategy (reading text one time through) to determine the passage's meaning. | Uses multiple strategies to metacognitive | Upon request, student will determine passage meaning. awareness of strategies for determining the meaning of the passage by supplying and/or explaining the following skills: identifying the main idea looking at the pictures rereading (current and previous passage) | demonstrate |

| If the Student Makes This Error: | Then This Is the Problem Area: | And This Is the Objective: | Does the Student Have the Skills? |
|---|---|---|---|
| | | request assistance creating questions for answering defining unknown vocabulary words. CAP 100% | |
| Student decodes words by individual letter/sound correspondences. | Uses multiple strategies to decode words. | Student will employ meaning-based strategies and decoding to read passages (at expected CAP). | |
| Student is unaware she is making reading errors that violate meaning. | Self-corrects errors that violate meaning. | Given passages at [expected or intermediate curriculum levels], the student will not make, or will spontaneously correct, errors in reading that violate meaning. CAP: no more than 5% uncorrected errors. | |
| After exhausting her strategies for clarification of word meaning, student guesses and moves on or quits. | Asks for assistance. | Whenever student has exhausted her clarification strategies, she will ask for assistance. | |

| | Enabling Skills | | Yes  No  Unsure |
|---|---|---|---|
| | 1. Decoding | | ☐    ☐    ☐ |
| Student decodes words without fluency or accuracy. | Passage reading. | Student will read passages at [specify] level with a rate of [specify] and [specify]% accuracy. | |
| Student inserts words that violate meaning and/or guesses at words. Student rereading improves passage accuracy considerably. | Reads passages with 95% accuracy. | Given passages at [expected or intermediate levels], student will read [at specified rate] with 95% accuracy. | |
| Student commonly inserts words that violate meaning and/or guesses at words. Student frequently must "sound out" words. Student misapplies decoding rules. | Reads passages at 95% accuracy. | Given passages at [expected or intermediate levels], student will read [at specified rate] with 95% accuracy. | |
| Student frequently makes errors that violate the meaning of the passage/text. | Makes few errors that violate meaning. | Given passages at [expected or intermediate curriculum levels], the student will not make, or will spontaneously correct, errors in reading that violate meaning. CAP: no more than 5% uncorrected errors. | |

| | 2. Vocabulary | | Yes  No  Unsure |
|---|---|---|---|
| Student fails to demonstrate comprehension but passes tests of decoding and prior knowledge. | Passage-dependent vocabulary. | Student will identify or produce correct definitions for terms selected from [specified] reading passages. CAP 100% | ☐    ☐    ☐ |
| Student defines words only in isolation or provides their most common definition while passage reading. | Can define words in passage. | Given passages at [expected or intermediate levels], the student will supply the correct definition for vocabulary words that are underlined or pointed to by the teacher. CAP 100% | |

| If the Student Makes This Error: | Then This Is the Problem Area: | And This Is the Objective: | Does the Student Have the Skills? |
|---|---|---|---|
| Student misses context-[expected or dependent vocabulary questions. | Can modify the definition of words in passage according to context. | intermediate levels], the student will supply the correct definition for context-dependent vocabulary words that are underlined or pointed to by the teacher. CAP 100% | Given passages at |
| Errors on maze or cloze exercises excessive (cloze errors . | Balance of errors on maze and/or cloze exercises does not show | Given a 250-word [maze or cloze] passage at [expected or intermediate | |

63

| If the Student Makes This Error: | Then This Is the Problem Area: | And This Is the Objective: | Does the Student Have the Skills? |
|---|---|---|---|
| 60%; maze errors . 40%) and often syntactically correct but semantically incorrect. | excessive semantic errors. | level], student answers will be [80% or 45%] semantically correct. | |
| Comprehension increases and errors decrease dramatically when key words are introduced curriculum level], prior to reading. | Comprehension does not increase dramatically and/or decoding errors are introduced prior to reading. | When provided an unfamiliar passage at [expected or intermediate do not decrease when key words student will read it aloud [at specified rate and with specified accuracy]. | passage at [expected or intermediate |
| Student makes many non-meaningful substitutions of words or words that violate the meaning of the text/ passage. | Makes few nonmeaningful substitutions. | Given passages at [expected or intermediate level], student will not make or will spontaneously correct, word substitution errors in reading that violate the meaning. CAP: not more than 5% uncorrected errors. | |
| Student confuses the meanings of referents contained in sentences. When retelling events in a story, student reports them in the incorrect tense. referents both near and far from the designated wording in the passage.) | Uses pronouns and tenses correctly. | Given passages at [expected or intermediate level], the student will supply the correct definition for referents that are underlined or pointed to by the teacher. CAP 100%. (These will include | |

| | **3. Syntax** | | Yes No Unsure |
|---|---|---|---|
| | | | ☐ ☐ ☐ |
| Student makes excessive syntactic errors when completing comprehension exercises. | Syntax errors during reactions to reading. | When making written or spoken reactions to passages, the student will use correct syntax 100% of the time. | |
| Errors on maze or cloze exercises excessive (cloze errors . 60%; maze errors . 40%) and often semantically correct but syntactically incorrect. | Balance of errors on maze does not show excessive syntactic errors. | Given a 250-word [maze or cloze] passage at [expected or intermediate level], student answers will be [80% or 45%] syntactically correct. | |
| Primary language is other than that of the text. | Primary language is same as texts. | Given a passage in student's primary language, student will complete a [maze or cloze] exercise with [80% or 45%] accuracy. | |
| Oral language contains excessive syntax errors that violate the standard of adult speech. | Oral language adequate, particularly in the use of subject-verb agreement, tense, and pronouns. | Student will produce by [imitation, with prompts, or spontaneously], sentences with subject-verb agreement, correct tense, and pronouns. CAP: adult speech or [an intermediate level]. | |

| If the Student Makes This Error: | Then This Is the Problem Area: | And This Is the Objective: | Does the Student Have the Skills? |
|---|---|---|---|
| | **4. Prior knowledge** | | Yes No Unsure |
| | | | ☐ ☐ ☐ |
| Student's performance on comprehension exercises varies considerably when student already has key prior knowledge or vocabulary before reading a passage. | Comprehension does not vary dramatically according to familiarity with the passage topic. | Given a [maze or cloze] passage at [expected or intermediate level] on an unfamiliar subject, student will [select or supply correct choices] with [80% or 45%] accuracy. | |
| Student provides incorrect definitions for words with context-dependent meanings. | Can correctly define words in passage. | Given passages at [expected or intermediate levels], the student will supply the correct definition for vocabulary words that are underlined or pointed to by the teacher. CAP 100% | |
| Performance on comprehension activities varies considerably when key concepts and ideas are previewed prior to reading. | Comprehension does not improve dramatically when a passage is previewed and unstated ideas are explained prior to reading. | Given passages at [expected or intermediate levels], student will maintain passing scores on maze/ cloze tests with no assistance. CAP 100% | |

64

B-1.2

| | | |
|---|---|---|
| During comprehension exercises, student uses only concrete information provided in the passage. | Can relate information in passage to personal experience or to other sources of information (other passages, books, authors, classes, etc.). | When supplied with questions pertaining to the theme of a passage, the student will answer the questions correctly and support the answers with information not supplied in the passage. CAP: teacher judgment or exemplar comparison. |
| Student omits unstated ideas when completing comprehension activities and/or discussing the passage. | Can discuss unstated ideas accurately. | When supplied with topics pertaining to the theme of a passage, the student will discuss and/or debate the topics while including information supplied, and not supplied, in the passage. CAP: teacher judgment or exemplar comparison. |

Source: Howell, K. W., Zucker, S. H. & Morehead, M. K. (2000b). Multilevel Academic Skills Inventory. Bellingham, WA: Applied Research and Development Center. To order contact the Student Co-op Bookstore, Western Washington University. Fax (360) 650-2888. Phone (360) 650-3656. Reprinted with permission.

# Comprehension Interview.

*Directions:*

1. Ask all questions and then, based on the answers, mark the status of categories 1–6 on the status sheet in Exhibit 8.8.
2. In Exhibit 8.8, mark "Pass" if the student seems to correctly answer the question in a category. Mark "No-Pass" if the answers are wrong. Mark "Unsure" if you can't tell and/or think more assessment is needed.
3. If the student's answer is short prompt her by saying "Can you tell me some more about this?" or "Are there any other things you do?"
4. Example correct answers can be found in parentheses following each item.
5. Remember, you are judging the categories, not the individual items (it is possible to mark a category "No-Pass" even if some items are correct).

## Before Reading

(Ask the questions and mark items as correct if they are answered in response to any question under this category.)

"Why do you read this text?", "What might give you a clue about what is in this story?", "How else could you try to find out about a story before you read?"

1. Purpose (learn the information in it, for enjoyment)
2. Title (mentions the title)
3. Illustrations (mentions looking at the illustrations/figures)
4. Prereading questions (mentions making up and asking questions about passage prior to reading)
5. Predictions (try to guess what will be in the next parts of the passage)

## While Reading

(Ask the questions and mark items as correct if they are answered in response to any question under this category.)

"As you are reading what do you do?", "How can you tell if you are understanding while you read?", "Is there anything you try to get done while you read?"

6. Remembers questions and predictions (answer questions, checks to see if predictions were correct)
7. Checks to see if it makes sense (see if I know what it's saying, make sure I don't get confused or lost)
8. Summarizes (stop and think about parts, try to sum up parts, put it in a nutshell)
9. Keeps questioning (make up new questions, think of new predictions, decide what will happen next)
10. Clarifies (when I get stuck I read ahead/back, I use the sentences to decide what the words mean)

## After Reading

(Ask the questions and mark items as correct if they are answered in response to any question under this category.)

"When you are finished reading what do you do?", "What do you do as soon as you finish reading a passage/story?"

11. Summarize (takes time to think it over, try to sum it all up)
12. Reviews (thinks over the questions and predictions to see if answers were found)
13. Uses prior knowledge (try to make sense of it, checks to see if it is out of line with what is already known)

## Reading Awareness

Ask each question, record what student says, try to rate the answers so you can judge the overall category. Examples of correct answers are in parentheses.

14. What's the hardest part about reading for you? (complex material, paying attention to the right stuff)

B-1.3

15. What would help you become a better reader? (help from the teacher, practice)

16. Is there anything special about the first sentence or two in a story? What do they tell you? (tells you what is important, makes the reading easier)

17. How about the last sentence; what does it tell you? (what I should have attended to, what is important)

18. How can you tell which sentences are the most important ones in a story? (where they are in the story, if they tell about the hardest stuff to understand)

**Planning**

Ask each question, record what student says, try to rate the answers so you can judge the overall category. Examples of correct answers are in parentheses.

19. If you could only read some sentences in the story because you are in a hurry, which ones would you read? (the ones that tell about important stuff, the first or last ones)

20. What do you try to tell someone about a story—all the words, just the ending, what the story was about, or something else? (the important stuff, what/who it was about)

21. The other day I asked a girl to read a story and then tell me what she read. Before she started reading, though, she asked me if I wanted her to remember the story word for word or just the general meaning. Why do you think she asked me that? (because she wanted to know why she was reading the story, so she could decide what to focus on)

22. Before you start to read a story, do you do anything special? What kinds of plans help you read better? (I try to find out why I'm reading it, I look it over before I start)

23. If you had to read very fast and could only read some words, which ones would you try to read? (I'd look for clues, like words that are darker)

**Regulation**

Ask each question, record what student says, try to rate the answers so you can judge the overall category. Examples of correct answers are in parentheses.

24. Do you ever go back and read things over? Why? (yes—because I get confused, because I want to read the stuff the teacher talked about twice, because they are the things I need to attend to)

25. What do you do if you come to a word you don't understand? (I put another word in its place, then see if the sentence makes sense; I look it up, I ask for help)

26. What do you do if you don't understand a whole sentence? (pay attention to it, read it over, skip it and come back later, stop and ask for help)

27. What parts of a story do you skip as you read? (the stuff the teacher won't ask about, the stuff I don't think is important)

28. What things do you read faster than others? (the easy things, the things I know about)

Questions 14–28 are based on Paris and Jacobs (1984, pp. 2085–2086): Used with permission.

Source: Howell, K. W., Zucker, S. H. & Morehead, M. K. (2000b). Multilevel Academic Skills Inventory. Bellingham, WA: Applied Research and Development Center. To order contact the Student Co-op Bookstore, Western Washington University. Fax (360) 650-2888. Phone (360) 650-3656. Reprinted with permission.

Status Sheet for Awareness of the Reading Process.

Directions:

For each item, mark "Pass" if the student seems to correctly answer the question in a category. Mark "No-Pass" if the answers are wrong. Mark "Unsure" if you can't tell and/or think more assessment is needed.

Remember, you are judging the categories, not the individual items (it is possible to mark a category "No-Pass" even if some items are correct).

| Is the category of skills OK? | Pass | No-Pass | Unsure |
|---|---|---|---|
| **Before Reading** | ____ | ____ | ____ |
| 1.  Considers purpose for reading | | | |
| 2.  Considers title | | | |
| 3.  Scans illustrations/figures | | | |
| 4.  Asks questions | | | |
| 5.  Makes predictions | | | |
| **While Reading** | ____ | ____ | ____ |
| 6.  Remembers predictions and questions | | | |
| 7.  Decides if passage makes sense | | | |
| 8.  Summarizes while reading | | | |
| 9.  Keeps questioning and predicting | | | |
| 10.  Seeks clarification | | | |
| **After Reading** | ____ | ____ | ____ |
| 11.  Summarizes | | | |
| 12.  Reviews questions/predictions | | | |
| 13.  Fits the story to what is already known | | | |
| **Reading Awareness** | ____ | ____ | ____ |
| 14.  Explains what is hard | | | |
| 15.  Knows how to get help | | | |
| 16.  Knows importance of the first sentences | | | |
| 17.  Knows importance of the last sentences | | | |
| 18.  Explains how to decide what is important | | | |
| **Planning** | ____ | ____ | ____ |
| 19.  Plans priority on parts of passage | | | |
| 20.  Focuses on important information | | | |
| 21.  Determines purpose before reading | | | |
| 22.  Plans before reading | | | |
| 23.  Looks for emphasis in passage | | | |
| **Regulation** | ____ | ____ | ____ |
| 24.  Rereads | | | |
| 25.  Clarifies vocabulary | | | |
| 26.  Deals with sentences she doesn't understand | | | |
| 27.  Skips trivial information | | | |
| 28.  Adjusts reading rate | | | |

# Oral Reading Criteria
(page 222)

| Reading Fluency | | | |
|---|---|---|---|
| Grade | Pass | Unsure | No-Pass |
| Early 1st | +35 wpm | 25-35 wpm | -25 wpm |
| Late 1st | +50 wpm | 40-50 wpm | -40 wpm |
| Early 2nd | +70 wpm | 50-70 wpm | -50 wpm |
| Late 2nd | +100 wpm | 80-100 wpm | -80 wpm |
| Early 3rd | +120 wpm | 100-120 wpm | -100 wpm |
| Late 3rd or above | +140 wpm | 100-140 wpm | -100 wpm |
| Reading Accuracy | | | |
| Grade | Pass | Unsure | No-Pass |
| | + 95% | 90-95% | - 90% |

## Comprehension

| Criteria | | |
|---|---|---|
| | Maze | Cloze |
| Pass | 80% or better | 45% or better |
| Unsure | 60-80% | 30-45% |
| No-pass | 60% or less | 30% or less |

## Comprehension Maze Tests

This section contains eight maze tests and the answers to the tests. The test passages were written using words identified at each grade level in five best-selling basal-reading series. However, because the concept of "grade level" is so impractical you may want to carefully compare the passages to the text material your student needs to read.

These maze tests were constructed to provide opportunities for either semantic or syntactic errors. On the answer sheets the correct response is given in "**Bold**" print, the semantic foil is given in "CAPITAL" letters, and the syntactic foil is given in "lower case" letters. The authors gave these tests to 237 students from grades 1-8 and obtained the following error proportions. The students were predominantly Anglo and middle class. There were very few (if any) non-English speakers in the sample:

### Comprehension Error Types

|  | Semantic | Syntactic |
|---|---|---|
| Total Sample | 67% | 33% |
| Grade 1 | 51% | 49% |
| Grade 2 | 60% | 40% |
| Grade 3 | 55% | 45% |
| Grade 4 | 53% | 47% |
| Grade 5 | 63% | 37% |
| Grade 6 | 64% | 36% |
| Grade 7 | 72% | 28% |
| Grade 8 | 88% | 12% |

Howell, K. W., Zucker, S. H. & Morehead, M. K. (2000). Multilevel Academic Skills Inventory. Bellingham, WA: Applied Research And Development Center.
To order contact the Student Co-op Bookstore, Western Washington University. FAX (360) 650-2888. Phone (360) 650-3656.

## My New Animal

I'll tell you about my new animal. This animal is blue and black and white. It does not have

_____. It does not have _____. It likes
tells, spots, doors                    bad, fur, tail

to be _____ and free.
     outdoors, this, park

Sometimes this _____ wakes me up.
              likes, house, animal

It _____ be very loud. I _____ outside and
  is, can, to              look, like, along

see it. _____ is outside in the _____. It is
       Let, It, I              a, sun, food

outside in _____ snow.
          the, over, happy

This animal likes _____ talk to other animals.
                 go, to, on

_____ likes trees. It likes _____ and
It, They, With                       a, doors, food

bugs and bread.

_____ you know what it _____ yet? It
Do, Has, Mother                  car, do, is

is a bird. The bird is called a blue-jay.

## The Country and the City

People who live in the country are lucky. The countryside is full of open fields and trees. Lots of animals run _____ there. There are
*wild, left, window*

rabbits _____ raccoons and even snakes.
*but, pink, and*

_____ animals live on farms.
*Nobody, Oh, Many*

_____ can see cows and _____,
*You, The, Always*          *horses, hurt, balloons*

sheep and chickens there.

_____ spring comes, there
*Across, When, Land*

are _____ everywhere. The earth
*flowers, numbers, there*

is _____ with wonderful things. Baby
*above, band, filled*

_____ are born. The farms _____
*animals, necks, lots*          *do, are, both*

really busy. There are _____ jobs to do.
*many, after, table*

People _____ live in the city _____
*they, see, who*          *can, pets, are*

lucky too. The city _____ filled with people.
*is, knew, not*

There _____ open places and parks
*are, almost, wake*

_____ pretty gardens. It's fun _____
*angry, with, on*          *to, with, lots*

explore! The wild animals _____ kept in
*line, are, things*

the zoo. _____ can see elephants and
*You, Color, Act*

_____ and snakes there.
*monkeys, bedrooms, sleeps*

*(Continued)*

People _____ animals at home too.
do, cake, have

_____ cats, birds, and fish _____
Dogs, Bags, Grows                         all, two, breath

make good pets. People _____ some pets
blow, keep, apple

outdoors. Some _____ live indoors with
pets, bands, tonight

people.

_____ spring comes to
Anything, Loud, When

the _____, trees get their leaves.
pretty, city, floor

_____ and flowers in windows
Gardens, Buildings, Stay

_____ to grow. Children go _____
start, run, baby                         asleep, but, outdoors

to play.

There are _____ things in the country
bus, wonderful, cut

_____ in the city. Country _____
and, with, zoo                      trees, some, people

visit the city and _____ fun. City people
does, have, herself

visit the country and have fun. They all feel lucky

to live where they live!

## News

Who writes what you read in the newspaper?

Reporters write stories about things that are happening in your city.

There are other reporters _____ live in other cities.
<u>among, newspapers, who</u>

_____ write about what is _____ in
<u>They, Extra, Squirrels</u>      <u>happening, message, pointing</u>

their cities.

A _____ who is far away _____ write a news
<u>city, reporter, that</u>      <u>did, can, business</u>

story _____ send it "over the _____". When you make a
<u>and, but, reporter</u>      <u>far, books, wire</u>

_____ call, your voice goes "_____ the wire."
<u>write, telephone, cooking</u>      <u>over, until, other</u>

The reporter's _____ is sent about the _____ way. The
<u>news, city, some</u>      <u>new, same, get</u>

telephone line _____ the signals.
<u>special, happens, carries</u>

Large machines _____ the signals. They type _____ the
<u>comic, receive, go</u>      <u>out, but, call</u>

story the reporter _____. You do not have _____ wait very
<u>everyone, lived, wrote</u>      <u>to, in, other</u>

long to _____ out what's happening anywhere _____ your world.
<u>find, write, in</u>      <u>wire, for, in</u>

Of course, _____ newspaper pays to get _____ "over
<u>your, dark, with</u>      <u>machine, news, around</u>

the wire."

Reporters _____ not the only people _____ write what you
<u>are, can, story</u>      <u>can, they, who</u>

read _____ the paper. Your friends _____ neighbors write
<u>in, before, news</u>      <u>some, for, and</u>

letters to _____ newspaper. These letters tell _____ those
<u>the, and, line</u>      <u>cities, what, every</u>

people think about _____ in the news. Some _____
<u>events, wires, pays</u>      <u>also, voices, letters</u>

are printed in the _____ so everyone can read
<u>newspaper, telephone, and</u>

_____. They are usually printed _____ a special page
<u>signals, them, pays</u>      <u>early, about, on</u>

called _____ editorial page.
<u>same, in, the</u>

*(Continued)*

LEVEL 3

74

What about _____ "funny papers"? Special writers _____
the, and, call                                             line, write, paper

and draw the comic _____. Newspapers buy their work
strips, telephones, answer

_____ that people will buy _____ newspaper.
in, wait, so                      also, button, the

There are many _____ writers who work for _____
other, long, carries                            the, on, everyone

newspaper. Some write about _____ or books or shows.
in, afternoons, movies

_____ write about cooking or _____. Some write
Some, Voices, Special              begin, bowls, gardening

about sports. Some even make up the crossword puzzles! Would you like

to write for a newspaper?

## The Kids in Our Neighborhood...

The kids in our neighborhood had never organized a club before. That summer, we decided to have one.

Tom's parents said we _____ use their backyard for _____ meetings.
(could, took, never) (being, animal, our)

As soon as _____ started warming up, we _____ a clubhouse there. We
(it, he, also) (said, built, with)

_____ some old boards from _____ house that was being _____
(found, could, junk) (could, into, a) (walked, torn, ahead)

down. We discovered lots _____ other good junk there.
(of, if, aroma)

_____ we were finished. We _____ every afternoon, but
(Finally, Always, Atlas) (answers, were, met)

we _____ figure out what to _____ next. Then someone said
(couldn't, there, organized) (with, do, go)

_____ it would be nice _____ take a vacation together. _____
(that, clubhouse, every) (to, for, parents) (With, An, Found)

idea was born! Where _____ we go and how _____ we earn the money?
(are, would, club) (by, were, could)

_____ answers weren't easy. First _____ had to decide where
(To, Near, The) (we, meetings, roamed)

_____ vacation and how much _____ would cost. We talked _____ over and
(in, were, to) (it, she, decided) (it, her, easy)

finally decided _____ beach was the answer. _____ parents
(on, neighborhood, the) (Someone's, Vacation, Lots)

would have to _____ us and we would _____ money for gas.
(summer, take, figure) (need, finish, warm)

We _____ need money to stay _____. We asked Pat and
(said, with, might) (apologized, overnight, apparent)

_____ to figure out how _____ money we needed. They're
(Mary, clubhouse, raining) (much, easy, over)

_____ good in math.
(but, everyone, both)

With _____ regular summer jobs already _____ the rest of us
(in, the, horn) (taken, warmed, under)

_____ to figure out how _____ raise that money. Finally, _____
(easy, might, had) (to, on, beach) (clubhouse, someone, figure)

had an idea. What _____ a neighborhood newsletter? We _____ charge for
(about, with, take) (also, did, could)

ads. If _____ charged more to buy _____ newsletter than it cost _____
(we, idea, stay) (onto, the, afternoon) (to, in, will)

make, we'd make money! _____ could write interesting stuff. _____
(Money, Everybody, Decide) (And, The, Our)

everyone could sell the _____ and deliver them.
(together, junk, newsletters)

Was it a success? We all had a great time at the beach.

## Sheepdog

Thousands of sheep are lost to predators every year. Sheep are grazing animals. They often must be _____ to roam quite some _____
<br>sheep, left, poisoned                              long, are, distance

from shelter.

Farmers have _____ to help their sheep _____ several ways.
<br>predators, tried, heard                 in, because, new

Some hunt _____ and other predators. Some _____ used to
<br>shelter, coyotes, well                    sheep, go, farmers

use poisoned _____ to kill predators. Most _____ bait has
<br>hunt, farmers, bait                 poisoned, grazing, around

now been _____. Some farmers put up _____ fences to keep
<br>to, outlawed, walked              electric, roaming, train

predators _____, but this is very _____.
<br>but, often, out            gone, also, expensive

Scientists are trying to _____ of new methods that _____
<br>think, bait, year              coyotes, help, farmers

might use. One of _____ new methods is really _____ very old one.
<br>their, because, used            a, to, new

Guard _____ are now being trained _____ used to help protect
<br>shelters, dogs, expensive           and, but, farm

_____.
<br>move, sheep, ways

Guard dogs usually have _____ be imported from other _____.
<br>not, over, to             countries, dogs, tries

Guard dogs are not _____ same as herding dogs. _____ dogs,
<br>but, now, the            Herding, Predator, About

such as border _____, move sheep from place _____ place. They
<br>outlawed, sheep, collies          guard, to, but

also keep _____ from straying away from _____ flock. Herding
<br>now, sheep, farmers           the, away, and

dogs are _____ with the flock only _____ the farmer wants
<br>expensive, lost, usually        when, but, near

to _____ the sheep.
<br>put, dog, move

LEVEL 5

(Continued)

Guard dogs, _____ the other hand, are _____ the sheep
(but, on, new) (method, because, with)

all the _____. They do not control _____ flock, but they do
(time, about, control) (dog, the, around)

_____ intruders. Most guard dogs _____ European breeds. The
(control, keep, bait) (are, flock, do)

Komondor _____ from Hungary and the _____ Pyrenees Dog from
(farmer, uses, Dog) (Great, control, often)

the _____ between France and Spain _____ two examples.
(also, mountains, electricity) (are, can, sheep)

Most guard _____ are long-tailed and _____. Each
(mountains, over, dogs) (sheltered, scientists, floppy-eared)

will grow to _____ weight of about one _____ pounds.
(around, very, a) (hundred, expensive, but)

Usually, all a _____ dog has to do _____ to scare predators away
(guard, lost, grow) (will, is, never)

_____ its barking. If they have to, guard dogs will fight to protect their
(around, place, with)

sheep. They are strong and sure fighters who do not often lose.

## Soapmaking

Soap was first made from animal fats, oils, and the lye from burnt wood ashes.

The ancient Romans may have been the first people to use what we call soap. There was a place _____ (near, just, growing) outside the city of _____ (France, old, Rome) There animals were killed _____ (but, and, almost) burned as sacrifices to _____ (the, a, tell) gods. When it rained, _____ (in, snow, the) fat from the animals _____ (but, wolves, and) the burnt wood ashes _____ (were, had, never) carried downhill to a _____ (riverbank, mountain, talk). Many people washed their _____ (automobiles, astounded, clothes) at that riverbank. They _____ (claimed, soapmaking, imported) it was easier to _____ (transfer, get, usually) their clothes clean there.

_____ (Several, Business, About) centuries passed before crude _____ (were, downhill, soap) cakes were made and _____ (sold, planted, easier). By that time, someone _____ (could, with, had) thought of adding perfume _____ (under, to, bought) soap. Usually, only the _____ (animals, rich, very) could afford to buy _____ (the, killed, in) soap cakes.

Soap was _____ (used, eaten, clothes) in America too. Settlers _____ (became, and, used) fat and grease from _____ (passing, only, cooking) and boiled them with _____ (wood, river, bake) ashes. Bacon grease, tallow _____ (because, Roman, from) sheep, and lard all _____ (washed, found, with) their way into that _____ (will, homemade, outside) bar of soap.

Later _____ (soapmaking, sold, claiming) became a big business. _____ (Many, With, Washed) different plant oils were _____ (planted, lard, imported) to be used in _____ (soapmaking, purchase, burning). Coconut oil, palm oil, _____ (but, and, both) cottonseed oil were added _____ (to, price, also) improve the soap.

Today _____ (several, made, easier) large companies are our _____ (ashes', tallow, country's) soapmakers. Each company makes _____ (but, cooking, many) different kinds of soap, _____ (such, improve, however) as soap for doing _____ (laundry, sell, oil), soap for dishwashing, soap _____ (beside, grease, for) bathing, and soap for _____ (shampooing, into, carrying). All the companies advertise _____ (but, and, imported) each company says their _____ (riverbanks, soaps, advertised) are the best. Millions of pounds of soap are sold every year. What would great-grandmother think of that?

# Maples

Over one hundred species of maple trees can be found in the northern hemisphere, including several which are native to North America. One of the most widely recognized North American varieties is the sugar maple.

The sugar maple was _____ surprise to colonists who _____ in the
a, sugar, but      boiled, location, settled

New England _____. They learned from native _____ how to obtain
yellow, native, area      Americans, five, Lakes

sap _____ the tree and process _____ to produce sugar.
with, rise, from      it, them, with

When _____ sent news of _____ process to England,
they, prominent, she      eastern, this, learn

scientists _____ that a major discovery _____ been made.
surmised, remained, foliage      did, native, had

The sugar _____ is a prominent part _____ the landscape,
maple, widely, England      with, news, of

particularly in _____. The foliage turns a _____ yellow or
Scientists, for, autumn      brilliant, hemisphere, several

orange flushed _____ red. Sugar maples can _____ found from the
with, are, of      do, be, three

eastern _____ of the United States _____ Canada west through
discovery, in, edge      but, and, prominent

Minnesota, _____ southward through northeastern Texas. _____ most
then, with, when      The, By, Red

common location for _____ of sugar maples is _____ England, the
diameters, found, groves      One, Foliage, New

Appalachian mountains, _____ the Lakes states.
evaporate, and, from

Sugar _____ can range from sixty _____ eighty feet in
maples, woody, States      to, location, for

height, _____ a diameter of two _____ three feet. Most maples _____ popular
but, is with      with, sappy, to      go, are, for

as shade trees, _____ their wood is also _____ used in making
but, in, tree      widely, easterly, keep

fine _____ and hardwood flooring.
trees, recognize, furniture

Modern _____ has taken some of _____ romance out of
colonist, equipment, locate      the, by, evaporated

the _____ process. However, _____ old-timers remain to keep
sending, sugaring, are      enough, foliage, fresn

the _____ rhythmically dripping into old-fashioned _____ buckets.
flooring, used, sap      brilliant, sugaring, above

The sap is then taken by sled to the boiling house where it is evaporated. The fragrance of wood smoke still rises from boiling houses, and some of the hot syrup is still poured onto fresh snow for a delicious instant taffy.

## Indoor Plants

Many plants will grow indoors if the proper conditions exist. Plants must have the right soil, neither too acid nor too alkaline, and pots which permit them to grow. They must also have _____ light.
<u>however, humid, adequate</u>

Plants vary in _____ much light they require _____ what type of
<u>how, children, other</u>     <u>and, but, protect</u>

soil _____ prefer. Most plants thrive _____ located by a
<u>you, they, with</u>     <u>when, as, foliage</u>

window. _____ people use special fluorescent _____ to
<u>Permit, Acid, Some</u>     <u>climates, propagate, lights</u>

encourage their plants _____ grow.
<u>to, inexpensive, for</u>

Most plants that _____ grown indoors were originally _____ of the
<u>is, special, are</u>     <u>soils, natives, healthy</u>

jungle, and _____ are accustomed to warm, _____ climates. Sudden
<u>if, they, we</u>     <u>humid, frigid, breathe</u>

changes in _____ conditions are bad for _____ whether
<u>inserting, jungle, growing</u>     <u>plants, greenhouses, thrive</u>

they're use to _____ jungle or not. If _____ purchase a plant
<u>a, in, common</u>     <u>thrive, you, sails</u>

from _____ greenhouse, where it's been _____ a warm, humid
<u>between, diseased, a</u>     <u>in, redecorated, but</u>

environment, _____ transfer it to a _____ garage, it will
<u>and, therefore, ingest</u>     <u>lighted, provide, frigid</u>

certainly _____.
<u>suffer, prefer, indoors</u>

Plants in windowsills can _____ protected somewhat during
<u>encourage, literally, be</u>

the _____ weather by inserting newspaper _____ the plants and
<u>condition, cold, adequate</u>     <u>between, in, used</u>

the _____. Otherwise, plant leaves may _____ and drop off
<u>garage, special, glass</u>     <u>die, start, however</u>

from _____ cold temperatures.
<u>extremely, cause, provided</u>

There are _____ problems in raising houseplants. _____ are
<u>neither, other, beside</u>     <u>Insects, Easily, Windowsills</u>

attracted to them _____ can cause plant diseases. _____ common
<u>hut, varieties, and</u>     <u>Pat, Right, Some</u>

houseplants (for instance, _____) are poisonous and
<u>diffenbachia, greenhouse, inserted</u>

can _____ dangerous to pets or _____ if certain parts of _____
<u>is, climates, be</u>     <u>children, lights, therefore</u>     <u>very, the, on</u>

plant are ingested.

*(Continued)*

Like _____ plants, houseplants breathe in _____ dioxide and
     human, all, diseases                       extremely, drop, carbon

emit oxygen, _____ healthy houseplants can be _____ for people by
           if, purchase, so                    healthy, with, sudden

literally _____ good air to breathe. Houseplants are also a relatively
        providing, whoever, cutting

inexpensive way to redecorate a room. Once started, many common varieties, such as

philodendron, can easily be propagated from cuttings.

# MAZE ANSWERS

## Level 1
### My New Animal

1. tells, **spots**, DOORS
2. bad, **fur**, TAIL
3. **outdoors**, this, PARK
4. likes, HOUSE, **animal**
5. IS, **can**, to
6. **look**, LIKE, along
7. Let, **it**, I
8. a, **sun**, FOOD
9. **the**, OVER, happy
10. go, **to**, ON
11. **It**, THEY, With
12. a, DOORS, **food**
13. **Do**, HAS, Mother
14. car, DO, **is**

## Level 2
### The Country and the City

1. **wild**, LEFT, window
2. BUT, pink, **and**
3. NOBODY, Oh, **Many**
4. You, The, ALWAYS
5. **horses**, hurt, BALLOONS
6. ACROSS, **When**, Land
7. **flowers**, NUMBERS, there
8. ABOVE, band, **filled**
9. **animals**, NECKS, lots
10. DO, **are**, both
11. **many**, AFTER, table
12. THEY, see, **who**
13. CAN, pets, **are**
14. **is**, KNEW, hot
15. **are**, almost, WAKE
16. angry, **with**, ON
17. **to**, WITH, lots
18. LINE, **are**, things
19. You, COLOR, Act
20. **monkeys**, bedrooms, SLEEPS
21. DO, cake, **have**
22. **Dogs**, BAGS, Grows
23. **all**, TWO, breath
24. BLOW, **keep**, apple
25. **pets**, BANDS, tonight
26. Anything, LOUD, **When**
27. pretty, **city**, FLOOR
28. **gardens**, BUILDINGS, stay
29. **start**, RUN, baby
30. ASLEEP, but, **outdoors**
31. BUS, **wonderful**, cut
32. **and**, WITH, zoo
33. TREES, some, **people**
34. DOES, **have**, herself

## Level 3
### News

1. among, NEWSPAPERS, **who**
2. **They**, Extra, SQUIRRELS
3. **happening**, message, POINTING
4. **CITY**, reporter, that
5. DID, **can**, business
6. and, BUT, **reporter**
7. far, BOOKS, **wire**
8. write, **telephone**, COOKING
9. **over**, UNTIL, other
10. **news**, CITY, some
11. NEW, **same**, get
12. special, HAPPENS, **carries**
13. comic, **receive**, GO
14. **out**, BUT, call
15. everyone, LIVED, **wrote**
16. **to**, IN, other
17. **find**, WRITE, in
18. wire, FOR, **in**
19. **your**, DARK, with
20. MACHINE, **news**, around
21. **are**, CAN, story
22. can, **THEY**, who
23. **in**, BEFORE, news
24. some, FOR, **and**
25. **the**, AND, line
26. cities, what, **EVERY**
27. **events**, WIRES, pays
28. also, VOICES, **letters**
29. **newspaper**, TELEPHONE, and
30. SIGNALS, **them**, pays
31. early, ABOUT, **on**
32. same, IN, **the**
33. **the**, AND, call
34. LINE, **write**, paper
35. **strips**, TELEPHONES, answer
36. IN, wait, **so**
37. ALSO, button, **the**
38. **other**, LONG, carries
39. **the**, ON, everyone
40. in, AFTERNOONS, **movies**
41. **Some**, VOICES, Special
42. **begin**, bowls, GARDENING

# MAZE ANSWERS

### Level 4
*The Kids in our Neighborhood*

1. **could**, TOOK, never
2. being, ANIMAL, **our**
3. **It**, HE, also
4. SAID, **built**, with
5. **found**, COULD, junk
6. could, INTO, **a**
7. WALKED, **torn**, ahead
8. **of**, IF, aroma
9. **Finally**, ALWAYS, Atlas
10. answers, WERE, **met**
11. **couldn't**, there, ORGANIZED
12. with, **do**, GO
13. **that**, CLUBHOUSE, every
14. **to**, FOR, parents
15. WITH, **An**, Found
16. ARE, **would**, club
17. by, WERE, **could**
18. TO, Near, **The**
19. **we**, MEETINGS, roamed
20. IN, were, **to**
21. **It**, SHE, decided
22. **It**, HER, easy
23. ON, neighborhood, **the**
24. **Someone's**, VACATION, Lots
25. Summer, **take**, FIGURE
26. **need**, FINISH, warm
27. SAID, with, **might**
28. apologized, **overnight**, APPARENT
29. **Mary**, CLUBHOUSE, raining
30. **much**, EASY, over
31. BUT, everyone, **both**
32. IN, **the**, horn
33. **taken**, WARMED, under
34. easy, MIGHT, **had**
35. **to**, ON, beach
36. CLUBHOUSE, **someone**, figure
37. **about**, WITH, take
38. also, DID, **could**
39. **we**, IDEA, stay
40. ONTO, **the**, afternoon
41. **to**, IN, will
42. MONEY, **Everybody**, Decide
43. **And**, THE, Our
44. together, JUNK, **newsletters**

### Level 5
*Sheepdog*

1. sheep, **left**, POISONED
2. LONG, are, **distance**
3. predators, **tried**, HEARD
4. **in**, BECAUSE, new
5. SHELTER, **coyotes**, well
6. SHEEP, go, **farmers**
7. hunt, FARMERS, **bait**
8. **poisoned**, GRAZING, around
9. to, **outlawed**, WALKED
10. **electric**, ROAMING, train
11. but, OFTEN, **out**
12. gone, ALSO, **expensive**
13. **think**, BAIT, year
14. COYOTES, help, **farmers**
15. **their**, because, USED
16. **a**, TO, new
17. SHELTERS, **dogs**, expensive
18. **and**, BUT, farm
19. move, **sheep**, WAYS
20. not, OVER, **to**
21. **countries**, DOGS, tries
22. BUT, now, **the**
23. **Herding**, PREDATOR, About
24. outlawed, SHEEP, **collies**
25. guard, **to**, BUT
26. now, **sheep**, FARMERS
27. **the**, away, AND
28. EXPENSIVE, lost, **usually**
29. **when**, but, NEAR
30. PUT, dog, **move**
31. BUT, **on**, new
32. method, BECAUSE, **with**
33. **time**, about, CONTROL
34. dog, the, AROUND
35. **control**, KEEP, bait
36. **are**, flock, DO
37. FARMER, uses, **Dog**
38. **Great**, control, OFTEN
39. also, **mountains**, ELECTRICITY
40. **are**, CAN, sheep
41. MOUNTAINS, over, **dogs**
42. SHELTERED, scientists, **floppy-eared**
43. AROUND, very, **a**
44. **hundred**, EXPENSIVE, but
45. **guard**, LOST, grow
46. WILL, **is**, never
47. AROUND, place, **with**

# MAZE ANSWERS

## Level 6
### Soapmaking

1. NEAR, **just**, growing
2. FRANCE, old, **Rome**
3. BUT, **and**, almost
4. **the**, A, tell
5. IN, snow, **the**
6. BUT, wolves, **and**
7. **were**, HAD, never
8. **riverbank**, MOUNTAIN, talk
9. AUTOMOBILES, astounded, **clothes**
10. **claimed**, soapmaking, IMPORTED
11. TRANSFER, **get**, usually
12. **Several**, BUSINESS, About
13. were, DOWNHILL, **soap**
14. **sold**, PLANTED, easier
15. COULD, with, **had**
16. UNDER, **to**, bought
17. ANIMALS, **rich**, very
18. **the**, killed, IN
19. **used**, EATEN, clothes
20. BECAME, and, **used**
21. PASSING, only, **cooking**
22. **wood**, RIVER, bake
23. BECAUSE, Roman, **from**
24. WASHED, **found**, with
25. will, **homemade**, OUTSIDE
26. **soapmaking**, sold, CLAIMING
27. **Many**, With, WASHED
28. PLANTED, lard, **Imported**
29. **soapmaking**, sold, CLAIMING
30. BUT, **and**, both
31. **to**, price, ALSO
32. **several**, made, EASIER
33. ASHES', tallow, **country's**
34. but, COOKING, **many**
35. **such**, improve, HOWEVER
36. **laundry**, sell, OIL
37. BESIDE, grease, **for**
38. **shampooing**, into, CARRYING
39. BUT, **and**, imported
40. RIVERBANKS, **soaps**, advertised

## Level 7
### Maples

1. **a**, sugar, BUT
2. BOILED, location, **settled**
3. YELLOW, native, **area**
4. **Americans**, five, LAKES
5. WITH, rise, **from**
6. **It**, THEM, with
7. **they**, prominent, SHE
9. EASTERN, **this**, learn
9. **surmised**, REMAINED, foliage
10. DID, native, **had**
11. **Maple**, widely, ENGLAND
12. WITH, news, **of**
13. SCIENTISTS, for, **Autumn**
14. **brilliant**, HEMISPHERE, several
15. **with**, are, OF
16. DO, **be**, three
17. DISCOVERY, in, **edge**
18. BUT, **and**, prominent
19. **then**, WITH, when
20. **The**, BY, Red
21. DIAMETERS, found, **groves**
22. ONE, Foliage, **New**
23. evaporate, **and**, FROM
24. **Maples**, woody, STATES
25. **to**, location, FOR
26. BUT, is, **with**
27. WITH, sappy, **to**
28. GO, **are**, for
29. **but**, IN, tree
30. **widely**, EASTERLY, keep
31. TREES, recognize, **furniture**
32. COLONIST, **equipment**, locate
33. the, BY, evaporated
34. SENDING, **sugaring**, are
35. **timers**, to, SYRUPS
36. FLOORING, used, **sap**
37. **fashioned**, houses, HUNDRED

## Level 8
### Indoor Plants

1. however, HUMID, **adequate**
2. **how**, children, OTHER
3. **and**, BUT, protect
4. YOU, **they**, with
5. **when**, AS, foliage
6. Permit, ACID, **Some**
7. CLIMATES, propagate, **lights**
8. **to**, inexpensive, FOR
9. IS, special, **are**
10. SOILS, **natives**, healthy
11. if, **they**, WE
12. humid, FRIGID, breathe
13. INSERTING, jungle, **growing**
14. **plants**, GREENHOUSES, thrive
15. **a**, IN, common
16. thrive, **you**, SAILS
17. BETWEEN, diseased, **a**
18. **In**, redecorated, BUT
19. **and**, THEREFORE, ingest
20. LIGHTED, provide, **frigid**
21. **suffer**, PREFER, indoors
22. ENCOURAGE, literally, **be**
23. condition, **cold**, ADEQUATE
24. **between**, IN, used
25. GARAGE, special, **glass**
26. **die**, START, however
27. **extremely**, cause, PROVIDED
28. NEITHER, **other**, beside
29. **Insects**, Easily, WINDOWSILLS
30. HUT, varieties, **and**
31. Pat, RIGHT, **Some**
32. **diffenbachla**, GREENHOUSE, inserted
33. IS, climates, **be**
34. **children**, LIGHTS, therefore
35. very, **the**, ON
36. HUMAN, **all**, diseases
37. EXTREMELY, drop, **carbon**
38. IF, purchase, **so**
39. **healthy**, with, SUDDEN
40. **providing**, whoever, CUTTING

B-2.1

# STATUS SHEET FOR TASK-RELATED KNOWLEDGE

*Directions:*
1.  Use this status sheet with a group of people who work with the student.
2.  Carefully describe the settings and tasks on which the status designations are based.
3.  Give an overall designation for each of the principal skill areas by marking the appropriate box.
4.  Check or circle all those descriptors which seem to apply to the student or setting.
5.  Employ the indicated actions.

## Part A: Class Support

|  | Yes | No | Unsure | Additional Testing Action 4 |
|---|---|---|---|---|
| The Student Has the Skill and Knowledge Needed to Learn in this Setting: | ☐ | ☐ | ☐ | |

Descriptors:
Instructional presentation
Classroom environment
Teaching expectations
Cognitive emphasis
Motivational strategies
Relevant practice
Academic engaged time
Informal feedback
Adaptive instruction
Progress evaluation
Instructional planning
Checks for student understanding

## Part B: Prior Knowledge of Topic

|  | Yes | No | Unsure | Additional Testing Action 5 |
|---|---|---|---|---|
| The Student Has Required Prior Knowledge: | ☐ | ☐ | ☐ | |

Descriptors:
Has taken prerequisite classes
Received acceptable grades in prerequisite classes
Understands text and presentations
Knows topical vocabulary
Is familiar with related topics

## Part C: Study and Test-Taking Skills

|  | Yes | No | Unsure | Additional Testing Action 6 |
|---|---|---|---|---|
| Study and Test-Taking Skills Are Adequate: Before Class: | ☐ | ☐ | ☐ | |

Descriptors:
Arrives on time
Enters in a pleasant manner
Brings materials to class
Gets ready for learning

| During Class: | ☐ | ☐ | ☐ | |
|---|---|---|---|---|

Descriptors:

86

Follows classroom rules
Listens carefully
Works during class
Asks for assistance
Moves quickly to new activity

| After Class: | ☐ | ☐ | ☐ |
|---|---|---|---|

Descriptors:
Takes materials home
Completes homework
Brings homework back

| Organization: | ☐ | ☐ | ☐ |
|---|---|---|---|

Descriptors:
Organization of materials (use of notebook or folders)
Organization of time (use of calendar, scheduling work)
Organization of content on paper (heading, margins)

| Gaining Information: | ☐ | ☐ | ☐ |
|---|---|---|---|

Descriptors:
Reading expository material
Reading narrative material
Gaining information from verbal presentations (lectures, demonstrations)

| Demonstrating Knowledge or Skills: | ☐ | ☐ | ☐ |
|---|---|---|---|

Descriptors:
Completing daily assignments
Answering written questions
Writing narrative and expository products
Preparing for and taking tests

## Part D: Self-Monitoring and Evaluation

|  | Yes | No | Unsure | Additional Testing Action 7 |
|---|---|---|---|---|
| The Student Monitors and Evaluates Work: | ☐ | ☐ | ☐ | |

Descriptors:
Self-monitors
Recognizes errors
Judges quality of work given criteria
Judges quality of work on own

## Part E: Problem Solving

|  | Yes | No | Unsure | Additional Testing Action 7 |
|---|---|---|---|---|
| The Student's Problem Solving/Self-Monitoring Is Adequate: The student recognizes problems: | ☐ | ☐ | ☐ | |

Descriptors:
Defines problems
Identifies goals
Identifies obstacles
Recognizes types of problems
Anticipates problems

| The student recognizes types of problems: | ☐ | ☐ | ☐ |
|---|---|---|---|

Descriptors:
Identifies open system
Identifies closed system

| The student recognizes solution: | ☐ | ☐ | ☐ |
|---|---|---|---|

Descriptors:
Generates options
Considers resources
Anticipates outcomes
Selects solutions

The student plans:    ☐    ☐    ☐

Descriptors:
Thinks before acting
Explains what will happen
Has immediate goals
Allocates time

The student works:    ☐    ☐    ☐

Descriptors:
Follows plan
Follows schedule

## Part F: Academic Motivation

|  | Yes | No | Unsure | Additional Testing Action 8 |
|---|---|---|---|---|
| Descriptors (The Student Holds and Expresses These Beliefs):<br>My goals are important<br>My learning depends on what I do<br>I'm a success as long as I improve<br>My goals are interesting<br>If I make a mistake I need to work hard to fix it<br>I am an important member of my class and my school | ☐ | ☐ | ☐ | |

## Part G: Basic Learning Skills

|  | Yes | No | Unsure | Additional Testing Action 9 |
|---|---|---|---|---|
| The Student Uses Selective Attention: | ☐ | ☐ | ☐ | |
| Descriptors:<br>Focuses on relevant cues<br>Ignores irrelevant cues<br>Uses effective techniques to focus and maintain attention | | | | |
| The Student Uses Recall/Memory: | ☐ | ☐ | ☐ | |
| Descriptors:<br>Recalls information<br>Uses effective techniques to store and recall material | | | | |
| The Student Uses Motivation: | ☐ | ☐ | ☐ | |
| Descriptors:<br>Perseveres in the face of difficulty<br>Perceives value of task<br>Maintains an adaptive explanatory style (is not "learned helplessness")<br>Indicates feelings of control<br>Uses effective techniques to maintain motivation | | | | |

## Early Reading Skills

*Directions:*

1. Follow directions for each skill.
2. Whenever an error occurs, write down the exact content and conditions of the test.
3. Start with production. If the student does not produce answers, move to identification.
4. Record accuracy and summarize with "pass," "no-pass," or "unsure."

### Record Accuracy

| | Identification | Production | Note Conditions/ Content of test |
|---|---|---|---|
| **1. Page conventions** | ____ | ____ | ____ |
| 1.1 Left to right | ____ | ____ | ____ |
| 1.2 Top to bottom | ____ | ____ | ____ |
| 1.3 Book conventions | ____ | ____ | ____ |
| 1.4 Page by page | ____ | ____ | ____ |
| 1.5 Front to back | ____ | ____ | ____ |
| 1.6 Right side up | ____ | ____ | ____ |
| **2. Book length** | ____ | ____ | ____ |
| **3. Word length** | ____ | ____ | ____ |
| **4. Word boundaries** | ____ | ____ | ____ |
| **5. Sentence boundaries** | ____ | ____ | ____ |
| **6. Letter names** | ____ | ____ | ____ |
| 6.1 Lower-case letter names | ____ | ____ | ____ |
| 6.2 Upper-case letter names | ____ | ____ | ____ |
| **7. Environmental print and logos** | ____ | ____ | ____ |
| **8. Phonology with spoken language** | ____ | ____ | ____ |
| 8.1 Distinguish word in speech streams | ____ | ____ | ____ |
| 8.2 Delete words | ____ | ____ | ____ |
| 8.3 Blend word parts | ____ | ____ | ____ |
| 8.4 Segment words | ____ | ____ | ____ |
| 8.5 Rhyme | ____ | ____ | ____ |
| 8.6 Blend syllables | ____ | ____ | ____ |
| 8.7 Segment syllables | ____ | ____ | ____ |
| 8.8 Delete onset/rime or phoneme | ____ | ____ | ____ |
| 8.9 Discriminate same/different phonemes | ____ | ____ | ____ |
| 8.10 Segment and blend phonemes | ____ | ____ | ____ |

## Passage Summary Sheet with Criteria for Acceptable Performance.

*Directions:* For each passage used, record the number of corrects and errors per minute. Also record the accuracy. For each passage, check the rate and accuracy status (pass, unsure, or no-pass) for each curriculum level.

Rate discrepancy at instructional level:

Obtained rate_____ Expected rate_____

Divide the largest number by the smallest 5 rate discrepancy_____

Accuracy discrepancy at instructional level

Obtained accuracy_____% Expected accuracy_____

Divide largest number into the smallest 5 accuracy discrepancy _____

Label discrepancies 3 if they should increase or 4 if they should increase.

| | Expected Rate | | Obtained Rate | | | Expected | Obtained | |
|---|---|---|---|---|---|---|---|---|
| | Correct | Error | Correct | Error | Status | Accuracy | Accuracy | Status |
| 8 | 140 | 0–7 | _____ | _____ | _____ | 100–95% | _____ | _____ |
| 7 | 140 | 0–7 | _____ | _____ | _____ | 100–95% | _____ | _____ |
| 6 | 140 | 0–7 | _____ | _____ | _____ | 100–95% | _____ | _____ |
| 5 | 140 | 0–7 | _____ | _____ | _____ | 100–95% | _____ | _____ |
| 4 | 140 | 0–7 | _____ | _____ | _____ | 100–95% | _____ | _____ |
| 3 | Early 110 Late 140 | 0–7 | _____ | _____ | _____ | 100–95% | _____ | _____ |
| 2 | Early 70 Late 100 | 0–5 | _____ | _____ | _____ | 100–95% | _____ | _____ |
| 1 | Early 30 Late 50 | 0–3 | _____ | _____ | _____ | 100–95% | _____ | _____ |

Expected level (current grade placement)

Curriculum level (highest level at which mastery criterion is met)

Source: Howell K. W., Zucker S. H. & Morehead M. K. (2000). MASI-R: Remedial Screening Test. Applied Research and Development Center, College of Education, Western Washington University, Bellingham, WA 98225-9090: Reprinted with permission.

## Categorizing Decoding Errors.

### _Error Category Checklist for Meaning Violations_

_Directions:_
- Take a 250-word sample of student reading. The student must be very close to 80-85% accurate.
- Say "read this passage carefully. Ready? Begin."
- Tally each error under the appropriate category.
- Circle the error if it is self-corrected.
- An error violates meaning if it has the potential to impair the student's understanding of the author's message.
- Do not tally mispronunciations of proper nouns.
- Determine the % of total errors for each category.

Total errors: _____

|  | Category 1<br>Violates Meaning | Category 2<br>Does Not Violate Meaning | Category 3<br>Cannot Classify |
|---|---|---|---|
| % of total errors this category | _____ | _____ | _____ |
| % of errors this category self-corrected | _____ | _____ | _____ |

### _Error Pattern Checklist_

**Directions:**
- Take a 250-word passage.
- Compare each error in the passage with the following checklist (ignore errors on proper names).
- Make a mark next to the category in which the error seems to fit.
- Come up with a total of all errors.
- Identify the categories in which most errors occur.
- List objectives, teach, and continue to monitor changes in error patterns.

| Error Categories | Tally Errors | Examples Using "We want to have ..." |
|---|---|---|
| **Mispronunciations** | | |
| Errors are substitutions of real words | _____ | (We want to have ...) |
| Errors are not real words | _____ | (We hant to have ...) |
| Errors are phonetically similar to stimulus word | _____ | (We went to haven't ...) |
| **Insertions** | | |
| Insertions are contextually appropriate | _____ | (We still went to have ...) |
| Insertions are contextually inappropriate | _____ | (We and went to have ...) |
| **Omissions** | | |
| Omission affects passage meaning | _____ | (We went to ...) |
| Omission does not affect meaning | _____ | (We went have ...) |
| **Hesitation** | _____ | (We went to ... have) |
| **Repetition** | | |
| Repeats a portion of target word | _____ | (We went to have ...) [3 repetitions of /w/] |
| Repeats preceding word | _____ | (We went to have ...) [3 repetitions of "to" probably while trying to figure out "have"] |
| Repeats preceding words or phrases | _____ | (We went to have ...) [3 repetitions of "we went to"] |
| **Punctuation** | | |
| Does not pause at punctuation | _____ | (...the store. But it ...) |
| Pauses at end of lines without periods or commas. | | |
| **Intonation** | | |
| Does not use appropriate intonation. | | |
| **Self-corrects** | | |
| Other comments/observations should be written below | _____ | (we went to haven't) |

*Question*
1. Are there clear patterns of errors?

*Recommendation*
If yes, correct the erroneous pattern by targeting it as an instructional objective

B-2.4

### _Decoding Content Checklist_

**Directions:**
- Take a 250-word sample.
- Decide what category each error is from and tally it in the "error" column.
- Count the number of opportunities for *each* type of error that occurred.
- Do not record more than two errors per word. If more than two errors were made on word, categorize only the first two.
- Calculate the % of error per opportunity.
- List objectives, teach, and continue to monitor changes in error patterns.
-

|  | Opportunity | Error | % of Errors in Opportunities |
|---|---|---|---|
| **Words: errors involving whole words** | | | |
| Polysyllabic words | ___ | ___ | ___ |
| • (polysyllabic) | | | |
| Contractions | ___ | ___ | ___ |
| • (haven't, can't) | | | |
| Compound words | ___ | ___ | ___ |
| • (into, football) | | | |
| High-frequency words | ___ | ___ | ___ |
| • (do, make, yes) | | | |
| Silent letters | ___ | ___ | ___ |
| • (hate, light, knit) | | | |
| **Units: errors involving combined letter units** | | | |
| Morphographs | ___ | ___ | ___ |
| • (pre, ing, im, less) | | | |
| Beginnings (prefixes) | ___ | ___ | ___ |
| • (be, post, sub) | | | |
| Endings (suffixes) | ___ | ___ | ___ |
| • (able, ing, ment) | | | |
| R-controlled vowels | ___ | ___ | ___ |
| • (er, ir) | | | |
| Vowel combinations (digraphs) | ___ | ___ | ___ |
| • (ai, ay, ee) | | | |
| Consonant combinations (digraphs) | ___ | ___ | ___ |
| • (sh, kn, ph) | | | |
| CVC words | ___ | ___ | ___ |
| • (bag, pot, fed) | | | |
| **Conversions: errors involving sound modification** | | | |
| Double consonant words | ___ | ___ | ___ |
| • (written, butter) | | | |

| | Opportunity | Error | % of Errors in Opportunities |
|---|---|---|---|
| Vowel + *e* conversions (bite = bit, mope = mop) | _____ | _____ | _____ |
| Individual letters: errors involving individual letters and sounds | | | |
| Vowels | _____ | _____ | _____ |
| Consonants | _____ | _____ | _____ |
| Capitals | _____ | _____ | _____ |
| Lower case | _____ | _____ | _____ |
| Manuscript | _____ | _____ | _____ |
| Cursive | _____ | _____ | _____ |

*Question*
Are there identifiable problems of content?

*Recommendation*
Is yes, target it as an instructional objective.

Source: Howell K. W., Zucker S. H. & Morehead M. K. (2000). MASI-R: Remedial Screening Test. Applied Research and Development Center, College of Education, Western Washington University, Bellingham, WA 98225-9090: Reprinted with permission.

## Decoding Tests

This section contains eight reading passages. These are the ones students will read. You will need to make examiner copies for scoring. Do this by counting the words in the passage and writing the cumulative total at the end of each line. Next place a black triangle on each examiner passage to mark the 100th word in the passage. The triangle will make it easy to determine accuracy because, when the student reaches this mark, you only need to count the number of mistakes prior to it to obtain the proportion of errors. When you make scoring copies of the passages be sure to enlarge them so you will have room to write in the student's errors.

The passages were written using words identified at each grade level in five best selling basal reading series. However, because the concept of "grade level" is so impractical you may want to compare these passages to the text material your student needs to read. Another option is to select pages from classroom materials.

Howell, K.W., Zucker, S.H. & Morehead, M.K. (2000). Multilevel Academic Skills Inventory. Bellingham, WA: Applied Research And Development Center. To order contact the Student Co-op Bookstore, Western Washington University. FAX (360) 650-2888. Phone (360) 650-3656.

## One Day a Mouse....

One day a mouse came to our house. She was in a box. That box was her home. She ate there and went to sleep there. She was a little mouse with a little house.

A cat lives at our house too. The cat saw the mouse. He sat still. He did not move. The mouse did not run. The cat looked hard at the mouse. "I will eat you mouse," the cat was thinking.

The mouse was thinking too. "I see you, cat, and you are bad news!"

I took the mouse to my room. No more cats for this mouse!

## Party for Ben

Last Sunday afternoon, there was a party for Ben. First, Mom baked a big cake. She fixed something for us to drink and we put the food in a pretty basket. We put in some balloons too. Ben likes balloons. Then I got Ben and we were ready to go!

We walked to a place with big trees all around. It was a forest, I think. We looked and looked. At last, we found a nice spot with green grass. Ben rested and we fixed a place for the party.

Mom poured some milk for me. I blew up a big red balloon for Ben. We sang "Happy Birthday" with loud, funny voices. We ate white cake with dark icing and it was good! Then Mom asked some crazy riddles. I told her some riddles from school. We laughed and played some more games.

Then it was time for Ben's presents. Mom gave him a new blanket with soft insides. I gave him a new blue hat and lots of balloons. We both gave him birthday hugs.

We walked home happy. Ben was happy too, but he was tired. I put him on the bed upstairs. That bear had some birthday!

## Cookies

Yesterday, we had just settled down to a good game of checkers. Then Pete said he was hungry for cookies. "Not just any cookies, good cookies," he said.

So there we were. I was just getting ready to do my famous triple jump and this guy gets hungry for cookies. "Okay," I said, "let's go look."

Looking for something to eat with Pete is an experience. You would normally look in a cookie jar or in a cupboard for cookies, right? Pete looks in the freezer first. I guess it makes sense. I mean, people usually freeze things in quantity. And Pete is a quantity eater.

Next, we looked in the oven. Pete always hopes that something will be left in the oven.

I suggested that we might take a look in the cupboard. If there's a pack of Fig Newtons or a box of graham crackers to be had, it's usually in the cupboard. A careful search revealed no cookies.

My family does not own a cookie jar, so that left us with no place to search next. Pete had that look in his eye. He was getting ready to say, "I'm going home to get something to eat." I could see my chance at a triple jump was ready to walk out the door.

"Wait," I yelled. Pete froze in his tracks. "Have you ever heard of applesauce wonders?" I asked. "They're just delicious!"

I ignored his funny look and grabbed the jar of applesauce.

"Makes my mouth water just to think about them," I said. I spread the applesauce on a handy soda cracker. I pushed a marshmallow on top of the whole thing and shoved. it into Pete's mouth. Now Pete asks for "applesauce wonders" everytime he comes to my house.

# Chess

Chess was first played in China, India, and Persia. When armies invaded these countries, they learned the game of chess. They brought the game with them wherever their battles took them.

When the game finally reached Europe, the pieces were given the names they have today. The knight, the bishop, the king, the queen, and the rook (or castle) were all part of European life at that time. That's probably how the pieces got their names.

The object of the game is to win. All pieces are used to protect the king. If a player loses his king, he has lost the game.

Chess is played on a chess board which is set up in squares of two colors. Each piece is allowed to move a certain way. Some pieces can only move forward. Some pieces can only move diagonally. Pieces are moved in order to capture the other player's pieces. Or they can be used to protect a more valuable piece, like the king.

Each player has a full set of pieces. One player has the white pieces. One player has the black pieces. It doesn't matter how many pieces are captured. What matters is whether the king is lost.

Thinking ahead is the key to playing good chess. A player must know each piece and how it can move on the board.

Each player must study the way the other player moves. Then, if that player makes a mistake, the first player is ready to capture his king!

LEVEL 4

## Olympic Games

In ancient times, the Greeks held a series of games every four years. These games tested athletic skill. They came to be known as the Olympic games. They were held at a place called Olympia.

The Olympic games were an important part of life in Greece. The Greeks said they wanted "a healthy mind in a healthy body."

Today these games attract athletes from all over the world. Having a modern version of the games was the idea of one man. His name was Baron Pierre de Coubertin and he was a French nobleman.

The site of the ancient games was discovered when he was a young man. It must have given him an idea that stayed with him a long time. He traveled all over the world. He noticed that young athletes were alike no matter what country they were from. So, in 1892, he presented a plan for the modern Olympic games to the Athletic Sports Union of France.

The idea was not accepted at first. But he did not give up. He wrote letters. He began to prepare for the International Athletic Congress meeting in 1894. He got countries like the United States and England and Sweden to back his plan. When it came time to hold the meeting, he was ready.

His plan was accepted. The first modern Olympic games were planned for 1896 in Athens, Greece. "A healthy mind in a healthy body" could be a goal for athletes all over the world.

# Praying Mantis

The praying mantis is a strange insect. Some people say it looks funny or weird. Others say it's a terrifying monster. The mantis is different. A full-grown mantis looks like a pale green stick almost as big as your hand. It has goggle eyes and can swivel its head to watch something.

That something is usually the insect it's about to eat. The praying mantis eats other insects. Mantises even eat each other. If they're very hungry, they will even eat themselves. This habit of eating everything in sight has led some people to call them monsters.

Like all insects, the praying mantis has three pairs of legs. The two rear pairs are used only for walking. The front legs are also used as arms. They have sharp spines and hooks on them.

This insect is a great hunter. It attaches itself to a blade of grass or a twig. Then it waits patiently for some other insect to come into view. The mantis cannot hear and has no voice, but its eyesight is excellent. Once it sees its pray, it inches slowly toward its victim. Then it rears up on its hind legs and grabs the victim with its front legs.

After eating, the mantis wipes its claws and uses them to clean its face.

Adult mantises die each autumn. But hundreds of mantis eggs are left in special egg cases attached to rocks and twigs. In spring, the baby mantises start the cycle again.

Mantises can be helpful. Insect pests are always a problem for gardeners. Some gardeners do not like to use sprays to kill bugs, so they buy baby mantises to eat the bugs.

LEVEL 6

## Bottle

Imagine there's a message for you in a bottle, bobbing about in the ocean. It's hard to figure the odds against that message ever reaching you. Scientists work with such odds every day. They dispatch many messages in special bottles as part of their study of ocean currents.

The water in the ocean follows certain pathways called currents. Generally, a ship following the currents will arrive at its destination much faster than a ship traveling in a straight line. In fact, that's how ocean currents were discovered.

More than two thousand years ago, the Greeks studied currents. They released bottles from their shoreline and tried to study where they went.

Centuries later, American Benjamin Franklin became interested in currents. After hearing sea captains tell of great ''Rivers'' within the ocean, Franklin began throwing bottles into the sea. He put messages inside with instructions for the finders to write and tell him where and when the bottles were found. Using this method, Franklin charted the Gulf Stream, one of the most powerful currents in the Atlantic Ocean.

Why do scientists still study currents? Changes in currents affect fishing activities and climate as well as shipping. Scientists prevent problems by tracking and predicting changes in currents. Many methods are used to study currents. Specially weighted and sealed bottles, like the mysterious message bottles of old, are just one method scientists use.

**May**

It is alleged that the merry month of May was named after Maia, the ancient Roman goddess of spring. The traditional celebration of May Day might well have originated in the Roman civilization.

During the Middle Ages, English villagers and townspeople celebrated May Day by erecting a Maypole. They attached gaily colored streamers to the Maypole, then proceeded to feast and dance around it. The English may also have established the tradition of crowning a pretty girl Queen of the May.

When colonists immigrated to America, they brought May Day customs with them. Some religious groups considered the May festival to be pagan and sinful, but the traditions survived; and today schoolchildren often create May baskets full of candy and seasonal flowers to leave at the doorsteps of their friends. In many contemporary towns and cities, attractive young women and men are still elected May royalty.

All this celebration of May occurs because the sun ascends higher and higher during May. Daytime temperatures will go up about ten degrees Fahrenheit in temperate latitudes. Even at high elevations, where snow can still be several feet deep, warmer temperatures cause melting and a few hardy plants poke through the snow and slush.

May is a period of changes, and the first day of May is a signal that those changes are about to commence. How will you choose a way to commemorate May?

You could consider talking with your parents, grandparents, and older friends to discuss how May was celebrated when they were younger. You can even investigate May customs in other cultures and foreign countries. Then create your own individual way to celebrate May!

103

# Nonsense Word Fluency[1]
## Dynamic Indicators of Basic Early Literacy Skills
### University of Oregon

<u>Directions for Administration and Scoring</u>

<u>Target Age Range</u>

| Preschool | | | Kindergarten | | | First Grade | | | Second Grade | | |
|---|---|---|---|---|---|---|---|---|---|---|---|
| | | | | Phoneme Seg. Fluency | | | | | CBM Reading G2 | | |
| | | | Letter Naming Fluency | | | | | CBM Reading G1 | | | |
| | Onset RF | | | | | Nonsense-word Fluency | | | | | |
| F | W | Sp | F | W | Sp | F | W | Sp | F | W | Sp |

Nonsense Word Fluency is intended for most children from fall of first grade through summer of first grade. It may be appropriate for monitoring the progress of older children with low skills in letter-sound correspondence.

<u>Materials</u>

1. Student copy of probe – Select font to match early literacy materials in the curriculum.
2. Practice items – Select font to match early literacy materials in the curriculum.
3. Examiner copy of probe
4. Stopwatch
5. Red or Blue Pencil or Pen

<u>Directions for Administration</u>

1.    Place the practice items in front of the child.

2.    Explain the task using these specific directions:

***Look at this word*** (point to the first word on the practice probe). ***It is not a real word. It's a make-believe word. All the letters have sounds*** (point to letters). ***Watch me say the sounds:*** (point to the letter "s") ***/s/,*** (point to the letter "i") ***/i/,*** (point to the letter "m") ***/m/. Altogether the sounds are /s/ /i/ /m/*** (point to each letter) ***or "sim"*** (run your finger fast through the whole word). ***Remember, it is a made up word. You can say the sounds of the letters, /s/ /i/ /m/*** (point to each letter), ***or you can say the whole***

[1] This research was supported, in part, by the Early Childhood Research Institute on Measuring Growth and Development (H180M10006) funded by the U. S. Department of Education, Special Education Programs. Address all correspondence concerning this measure to Roland H. Good III, School Psychology Program, College of Education, 5208 University of Oregon, Eugene, OR 97403-5208, rhgood@darkwing.uoregon.edu.

Revised: 1/16/98

word "sim" (run your finger fast through the whole word). *Make sure you say any sounds you know.*

*Ready? Lets try one. Read this word the best you can (point to the word "lut"). Point to each letter and tell me the sound or tell me the whole word.*

| CORRECT RESPONSE: If the child responds "lut" or with some or all of the sounds, say | INCORRECT OR NO RESPONSE: If the child does not respond within 3 seconds or responds incorrectly, say |
|---|---|
| *That's right. The sounds are /l/ /u/ /t/ or "lut"* | *Watch me:* (point to the letter "l") */l/,* (point to the letter "u") */u/,* (point to the letter "t") */t/.* *Altogether the sounds are /l/ /u/ /t/* (point to each letter) *or "lut"* (run your finger fast through the whole word). *Remember, you can say the sounds or you can say the whole word. Lets try again. Read this word the best you can* (point to the word "lut"). |

Place the student copy of the probe in front of the child.

*Here are some more make-believe words* (point to the student probe). *Start here* (point to the first word) *and go across the page* (point across the page). *When I say "begin", read the words the best you can. Point to each letter and tell me the sound or tell me the whole word. Put your finger on the first word. Ready, begin.*

3.  Start your stopwatch. If the student does not respond with a sound within 3 seconds, tell the student the sound and ask them to try the next sound in the word. If they don't respond, or if they respond incorrectly, point to the next word. If the student does not get any sounds correct in words 1-5, discontinue the task and record a score of 0.

4.  Follow along on the examiner copy of the probe and underline each phoneme the student provides correctly, either in isolation or in the context of the nonsense word. Put a slash (/) over each phoneme read incorrectly or omitted.

5.  If the student struggles with a sound for 3 seconds, say the sound, mark it as incorrect, and point to the next sound.

6. At the end of <u>1 minute</u>, place a bracket (]) after the last phoneme provided by the student and say, ***"Stop."***

7. For repeated measurement when the student <u>clearly</u> understands the directions and procedure, these directions can be shortened by beginning with Number 5.

<u>Directions for Scoring</u>

1. Underline the corresponding letters for phonemes produced correctly in isolation and give credit for each letter sound correspondence produced correctly. For example, if the stimulus word is "sim" and the student says /s/ /i/ /m/, the individual letters would be underlined, <u>s</u> <u>i</u> <u>m</u>, with a score of 3.

2. Use 1 underline for correct letter sounds blended together and give credit for each letter sound correspondence produced correctly. For example, if the stimulus word is "sim" and the student says "sim", one underline would be used, <u>s  i  m</u>, with a score of 3.

3. Underline the corresponding letters for phonemes produced correctly in context. For example, if the stimulus word is "sim" and the student says "sam", the letters "s" and "m" would be underlined because those letter sounds were produced correctly, with a score of 2.

4. Put a slash (/) through the letter if the corresponding phoneme is omitted or pronounced incorrectly. For example, if the stimulus word is "sim" and the student says "sam", the letter "i" would be slashed because the letter sound was incorrect.

5. Letter sounds pronounced twice while sounding out the word are given credit only once. For example, if stimulus word is "sim" and the student says, /s/ /i/ /im/, the letter "i" is underlined once and the student receives 1 point for the phoneme "i" even though the letter "i" was pronounced correctly twice (a total of 3 for the entire word).

6. Letter sounds produced in isolation but out of order are scored as correct. For example, if stimulus word is "sim" and the student says, /m/ /i/ /s/, all letters would be underlined, <u>s</u> <u>i</u> <u>m</u>, with a score of 3.

7. Blended letter sounds must be correct and in the correct place (beginning, middle, end) to receive credit. For example, if stimulus word is "sim" and the student says, "mis", only the "i" would be underlined, s <u>i</u> m, with a score of 1 because only the "i" was correct and in the correct place.

8. Insertions are not scored as incorrect. For example, if the stimulus word is "sim" and the student says "stim", the letters "s," "i," and "m" would be underlined and full credit would given for the word with no penalty for the insertion of /t/.

9. The student is not penalized for imperfect pronunciation due to dialect, articulation, or second language inferences. This is a professional judgment and should be based on the student's responses and any prior knowledge of their speech patterns. For example, a student may regularly substitute /th/ for /s/. If the stimulus word is "sim" and the student says "thim," the

letter "s" would be underlined and credit for a correct-letter sound correspondence would be given.

10. If a student skips an entire row, draw a line through the row and do not count the row in scoring.

11. If a student makes an error and corrects him/herself within 3 seconds, write "SC" above the letter and count it as correct.

12. Nonsense Word Fluency Pronunciation Key. Note: The letters "x" and "q" are not used. The letters "h," "w," "y," and "r" are used only in the initial position. The letters "c" and "g" are used only in the final position.

| Letter | Sound | Example |
|--------|-------|---------|
| a | /a/ | bat |
| e | /e/ | bet |
| i | /i/ | bit |
| o | /o/ | top |
| u | /u/ | hut |
| b | /b/ | bat |
| c | /k/ | bic |
| d | /d/ | dad |
| f | /f/ | fan |
| g | /g/ | pig |
| h | /h/ | hat |
| j | /j/ | jet |
| k | /k/ | can |
| l | /l/ | lot |
| m | /m/ | man |
| n | /n/ | not |
| p | /p/ | pan |
| r | /r/ | ran |
| s | /s/ | sat |
| t | /t/ | top |
| v | /v/ | van |
| w | /w/ | wet |
| y | /y/ | yak |
| z | /z/ | zipper |

sim        lut

University of Oregon
Dynamic Indicators of Basic Early Literacy Skills
<u>Nonsense Word Fluency</u>

<u>Probe 1</u>

| | | | | | |
|---|---|---|---|---|---|
| t o b | d o s | e t | t u f | k e j | __/14 |
| m u n | i k | s a f | n a f | m i d | __/14 |
| j a g | v o f | b i v | s e l | y i c | __/15 |
| l i v | h e f | z i s | j o m | v a j | __/15 |
| r a j | a k | k u j | r i t | h i k | __/14 |
| b u j | v o g | k a p | d a f | d o z | __/15 |
| s i g | z o g | m e b | k a g | l i n | __/15 |
| m u p | t i k | z o k | e g | f u b | __/14 |
| h o c | w i k | f u p | r e g | y e m | __/15 |
| t o j | m a m | e n | z e z | h i j | __/14 |
| z u z | f e z | d u t | n a s | w u s | __/15 |
| n o s | y e z | n e g | e k | j a l | __/14 |
| a k | v i b | i c | t a k | h u l | __/13 |
| k a n | h e z | p i v | a z | v u v | __/14 |
| t e j | w i v | p i k | f i f | k o j | __/15 |
| l e f | f e m | f o t | z i m | a d | __/14 |

Total: __/230

Revised: 04/17/99

Probe 1

| | | | | |
|---|---|---|---|---|
| tob | dos | et | tuf | kej |
| mun | ik | saf | naf | mid |
| jag | vof | biv | sel | yic |
| liv | hef | zis | jom | vaj |
| raj | ak | kuj | rit | hik |
| buj | vog | kap | daf | doz |
| sig | zog | meb | kag | lin |
| mup | tik | zok | eg | fub |
| hoc | wik | fup | reg | yem |
| toj | mam | en | zez | hij |
| zuz | fez | dut | nas | wus |
| nos | yez | neg | ek | jal |
| ak | vib | ic | tak | hul |
| kan | hez | piv | az | vuv |
| tej | wiv | pik | fif | koj |
| lef | fem | fot | zim | ad |

110

Revised: 04/17/99

# STATUS SHEET FOR SYNTACTIC STRUCTURES

DIRECTIONS:
1. Use this status sheet with a group of people who have worked with the student.
2. Carefully describe the settings and task you are thinking about while you fill out the sheet.
3. Filling out the sheet begins with the recognition of error (i.e. maladaptive) behavior. If the student makes an error, she doesn't have the skill so mark the category "NO". If the student doesn't make the error mark "YES". If you can't decide about the status of the category mark it "unsure"
4. Skills marked "YES" are considered PLOP. Those marked "NO" must be corrected, so teach the corresponding objective. For behaviors marked "UNSURE" employ a recommended **SLP** to get more information.

| IF THE STUDENT MAKES THIS ERROR: | THEN THIS IS THE PROBLEM: | AND THIS IS THE OBJECTIVE (without criteria): | DOES THE STUDENT HAVE THE SKILLS?: |
|---|---|---|---|
| Student omits noun/noun phrases or verb/verb phrases *or* student consistently fails to produce above. | 1. Noun/Noun phrase<br><br>2. Verb/Verb phrase | Student will produce (*by imitation, with prompts, or spontaneously*) sentences containing nouns/noun phases.<br><br>Student will produce (*by imitation, with prompts, or spontaneously*) sentences containing verb/verb phrases. | YES NO UNSURE |
| Student incorrectly uses quantity phrases or numbers to indicate more then one. *Ex. Many girl, three boy.* | 3. Regular plurals | Student will produce (*by imitation, with prompts, or spontaneously*) sentences containing regular plurals | YES NO UNSURE |
| Incorrectly uses nouns as predicate nouns or subjects. *Ex. It hit he. The car ran over he.* | 4. Subject pronouns | Student will produce (*by imitation, with prompts or spontaneously*) sentences containing subject pronouns | YES NO UNSURE |
| Student omits preposition and/or noun or pronoun object. *Ex. Girl go town. Boy sit chair.* | 5. Prepositional phrases | Student will produce (*by imitation, with prompts, or spontaneously*) sentences containing prepositional phrases. | YES NO UNSURE |
| Student vocabulary lacks descriptors and detail, no modifiers for nouns. *Ex. The dog silent. The cat.* | 6. Adjectives | Student will produce (*by imitation, with prompts, or spontaneously*) sentences containing adjectives | YES NO UNSURE |
| Student places the subject of the question before the helping verb. *Ex. I could do that?* | 7. Interrogative reversal form for questions | Student will produce (*by imitation, with prompts, or spontaneously*) questions containing interrogative forms. | YES NO UNSURE |

| | | | |
|---|---|---|---|
| Student omits pronouns that receive the action of the verb or follow prepositions as objects. *Ex. Him walked there. It's me.* | 8. Object pronouns | Student will produce *(by imitation, with prompts, or spontaneously)* sentences containing object pronouns. | YES NO UNSURE |
| Student uses double negatives to show negation of an action or description. *Ex. Don't never, hardly nobody, isn't never.* | 9. Negatives | Student will produce *(by imitation, with prompts, or spontaneously)* sentences containing proper negatives. | YES NO UNSURE |
| Omits or incorrectly uses am, is, are, was, where, be, been. *Ex. She looking. Boy peering.* | 10. Verb *to be* as a helping verb | Student will produce *(by imitation, with prompts, or spontaneously)* sentences using *to be* as a helping verb. | YES NO UNSURE |
| Student omits *to be* in sentences with predicate nouns or predicate adjectives and subjects. *Ex. That girl big. That boy large.* | 11. Verb *to be* as a linking verb | Student will produce *(by imitation, with prompts, or spontaneously)* sentences using *to be* as a linking verb. | YES NO UNSURE |
| When using the present tense of a verb as a noun, adjective or adverb in a sentence, the student omits the word *to*. *Ex. The girl wansa study. The boy wants ride bike.* | 12. Infinitives | Student will produce *(by imitation, with prompts, or spontaneously)* sentences containing infinitives. | YES NO UNSURE |
| Student uses incorrect form, or omits determiners (a, an, the, that, this, these, and those) in sentence. *Ex. This kinds are bad.* | 13. Determiners | Student will produce *(by imitation, with prompts, or spontaneously)* sentences containing determiners. | YES NO UNSURE |
| Student omits words that join or connect words and/or phrases. *Ex. The girl(and) boy run (and) jump.* | 14. Coordinating conjunctions | Student will produce *(by imitation, with prompts, or spontaneously)* sentences containing coordinating conjunctions. | YES NO UNSURE |
| Student uses improper forms of words to establish possession or ownership. *Ex. The girls shoes. The boy eyes.* | 15. Possessive nouns and pronouns | Student will produce *(by imitation, with prompts, or spontaneously)* sentences containing possessive nouns and pronouns. | YES NO UNSURE |
| Noun and verb tense do not agree in phrases. *Ex. There goes the boys. The girl run to the store. There's is two of them.* | 16. Noun/Verb agreement | Student will produce *(by imitation, with prompts, or spontaneously)* sentences with noun/verb agreement. | YES NO UNSURE |

| | | | |
|---|---|---|---|
| When making comparisons with adjectives, student omits or uses the incorrect suffix ('er or 'est). *Ex. She's the smartest of the two. He's more smart.* | 17. Comparatives and superlatives | Student will produce *(by imitation, with prompts, or spontaneously)* sentences using comparatives and/or superlatives. | YES NO UNSURE |
| Student does not use the wh-structure to begin questions. *Ex. At the store you need?* | 18. Questions beginning with an interrogative pronoun. | Student will produce *(by imitation, with prompts, or spontaneously)* questions beginning with an interrogative pronoun. | YES NO UNSURE |
| Student omits –ed from regular verbs to signify past tense. Student uses improper form for irregular verbs in past tense. *Ex. Yesterday the girl look. The boy thinked she eated it.* | 19. Past tense of the verb | Student will produce *(by imitation, with prompts, or spontaneously)* sentences containing the correct past tense forms of verbs. | YES NO UNSURE |
| When describing something taking place in the future, student omits helping verbs (may, can, going to, will, should). *Ex. It happen tomorrow. She do it later.* | 20. Future aspect | When describing events of the future, student will produce *(by imitation, with prompts, or spontaneously)* sentences using future aspect helping verbs. | YES NO UNSURE |
| Student add's s to all nouns to signify plurality. *Ex. Mans, mouses, deers.* | 21. Irregular plurals | Student will produce *(by imitation, with prompts, or spontaneously)* sentences using correct forms of irregular plurals. | YES NO UNSURE |
| Student uses incorrect form of do (I/we/you/they do; he/she/it does; past tense did; have/has/had done). *Ex. She do it. We does it. He has did it.* | 22. Forms of do | Student will produce *(by imitation, with prompts, or spontaneously)* sentences containing the correct form of do. | YES NO UNSURE |
| Student omits helping verbs that add tense or intention to the action verb (has, have, had, would, should, could, might, must, ought, will, shall). *Ex. She ____ do it if she could.* | 23. Auxiliaries (Helping Verbs) | Student will produce *(by imitation, with prompts, or spontaneously)* sentences using the auxiliaries. | YES NO UNSURE |

| | | | |
|---|---|---|---|
| Student omits derivational endings (-or, -er, -ist, -ian) when changing verbs to nouns. *Ex. I am the paint of this picture.* | 24. Derivational endings which change verbs to nouns | Student will produce *(by imitation, with prompts, or spontaneously)* nouns from verbs by using derivational endings. | YES NO UNSURE |
| Student uses incorrect form of reflexive pronouns when reflecting back on nouns. *Ex. We did it ourself.* | 25. Reflexive pronouns | Student will produce *(by imitation, with prompts, or spontaneously)* sentences containing the correct form of reflexive pronouns. | YES NO UNSURE |
| Student omits or overuses qualifiers (very, much, more, most, less, least, too, so, etc.) to indicate when/why an action is carried out. *Ex. So then…. so then,,, so anyway…* | 26. Qualifiers | Student will produce *(by imitation, with prompts, or spontaneously)* sentences correctly using qualifiers. | YES NO UNSURE |
| Student omits or overuses coordinating conjunctions (and, but, or, nor, for , yet) to join clauses or simple sentences. *Ex. The fair was fun. The rides were fun. This summer we went to the zoo, and the beach, and the fair, and the pool and the park.* | 27. Coordinating conjunctions | Student will produce *(by imitation, with prompts, or spontaneously)* sentences, from simple sentences or clauses, using coordinating conjunctions. | YES NO UNSURE |
| Student omits (causing short, choppy sentences) or overuses (causing run-on sentences) conjunctions to relate clauses or simple sentences (after, before, because, if, since, so). *Ex. We went for a run. Then we went to a movie. Then we went to eat.; cuz…cuz…cuz…* | 28. Conjunctions commonly used to coordinate clauses | Student will produce *(by imitation, with prompts, or spontaneously)* complex sentences using conjunctions. | YES NO UNSURE |
| Student omits direct and indirect objects from sentences. *Ex. He gave (the girl) the cake.* | 29. Indirect and direct objects | Student will produce *(by imitation, with prompts, or spontaneously)* | YES NO UNSURE |

| | | | |
|---|---|---|---|
| Student uses the incorrect forms of adverbs to modify verbs, adjectives, and other adverbs. **Ex. She felt real good. I want to go, to.** | 30. Adverbs | Student will produce *(by imitation, with prompts, or spontaneously)* sentences using correct forms of adverbs to modify verbs, adjectives, and other adverbs. | YES NO UNSURE |
| Student omits "to" in infinitive phrases with subjects. **Ex. The girl wants him (to) play.** | 31. Infinitives with subjects | Student will produce *(by imitation, with prompts, or spontaneously)* sentences containing all parts of an infinitive phrases. | YES NO UNSURE |
| Student omits –ed or –ing on verbs preceding nouns used as adjectives. **Ex. She felt better after run laps.** | 32. Participles | Student will include *(by imitation, with prompts, or spontaneously)* correct forms of participles in sentences. | YES NO UNSURE |
| Student omits –ing from verbs used as nouns. **Ex. Walk is a healthy exercise** | 33. Gerunds | Student will produce *(by imitation, with prompts, or spontaneously)* gerunds in sentences. | YES NO UNSURE |
| Student overuses (in written communication) or omits passivity in communication. **Ex. The boy was saw in her company.** | 34. Passive voice | Student will produce *(by imitation, with prompts, or spontaneously)* sentences in the passive voice. | YES NO UNSURE |
| Student omits phrases, which indicate tense and intention. **Ex They (have been) studying diligently.** | 35. Complex verb forms-multiple auxiliaries | Student will produce *(by imitation, with prompts, or spontaneously)* sentences which are indicative of tense and intention. | YES NO UNSURE |
| Student omits relative adverb clauses (clauses preceded by where, when, or why) which modify the verb in the sentence. **Ex. The boy ran (when he was chased).** | 36. Relative adverb clauses | Student will produce *(by imitation, with prompts, or spontaneously)* sentences containing relative adverb clauses. | YES NO UNSURE |

| | | | |
|---|---|---|---|
| Student omits clauses (clauses preceded by which, that, or who) which act as adjectives in sentences;  Student creates agreement problems when using relative pronoun clauses. *Ex.  The boy (who was chased) ran away; The boy, that was chased, ran away.* | 37.  Relative pronoun clauses | Student will produce *(by imitation, with prompts, or spontaneously)* sentences, in agreement, containing relative pronoun clauses. | YES NO UNSURE |
| Student leaves action in a complex sentence incomplete or no conjunctions are used. *Ex.  While the girl was lifting weights.  The girl was lifting weights, the boy skied.* | 38.  Complex or subordinating conjunctions | Student will produce *(by imitation, with prompts, or spontaneously)* complete sentences using complex or subordinating conjunctions. | YES NO UNSURE |

# STATUS SHEET FOR COMMUNICATION/PRAGMATICS

**Directions:**

1.  Use this status sheet with a group of people who have worked with the student.
2.  Carefully describe the settings and task you are thinking about while you fill out the sheet.
3.  Judge each item of content for each type of behavior. If the student does seem to have the skill mark "YES." If the student doesn't seem to have the skill mark "NO." If you can't decide about the status mark it "UNSURE."
4.  Skills marked "YES" are considered PLEP. Those marked "NO" must be corrected, so convert them to an objective and teach.

| Behavior / Content | Receptive: The student recognizes and interprets | | | Expressive: The student expresses/uses… | | |
|---|---|---|---|---|---|---|
| **A. Executive Functions** | Yes ☐ | No ☐ | Unsure ☐ | Yes ☐ | No ☐ | Unsure ☐ |
| Plan ways to accomplish intent? | | | | | | |
| Monitor to see if intent is being met? | | | | | | |
| Recognize when a problem occurs? | | | | | | |
| Analyze problem for solution? | | | | | | |
| Recognize when assistance is needed? | | | | | | |
| Recognize resources for solution? | | | | | | |
| Seek appropriate help? | | | | | | |
| Adjust responses as result of analysis? | | | | | | |
| Recognize when intent is met? | | | | | | |
| Verify intent is met through alternative message? | | | | | | |
| Actively plan to incorporate new language skills into old? | | | | | | |
| **B. One-Way Communication** | Yes ☐ | No ☐ | Unsure ☐ | Yes ☐ | No ☐ | Unsure ☐ |
| 1. Wants | | | | | | |
| 2. Opinions | | | | | | |
| 3. Feelings | | | | | | |
| 4. Values | | | | | | |
| 5. Follows Directions | | | | | | |
| 6. Asks Questions | | | | | | |
| 7. Narrates | | | | | | |
| 8. States | | | | | | |
| 9. Sequences Events | | | | | | |
| 10. Subordinates Details | | | | | | |
| 11. Summarizes | | | | | | |
| 12. Describes | | | | | | |

| Behavior / Content | Receptive: The student recognizes and interprets | | | Expressive: The student expresses/uses… | | |
|---|---|---|---|---|---|---|
| 13.Compares and Contrasts | | | | | | |
| 14.Gives Instructions | | | | | | |
| 15. Explains | | | | | | |
| **C. Two-Way Communication** | Yes | No | Unsure | Yes | No | Unsure |
| 1.Considers the Listener | ☐ | ☐ | ☐ | ☐ | ☐ | ☐ |
| 2.Formulates Messages | | | | | | |
| 3.Participates in Discussions | | | | | | |
| 4.Uses Persuasion | | | | | | |
| 5.Resolves Differences | | | | | | |
| 6.Identifies Speaker's Biases | | | | | | |
| 7.Identifies Speaker's Assumptions | | | | | | |
| 8.Formulates Conclusions | | | | | | |
| **D. Nonverbal Communication** The student uses . . . | Yes | No | Unsure | Yes | No | Unsure |
| 1.Gestures | ☐ | ☐ | ☐ | ☐ | ☐ | ☐ |
| 2.Proximity | | | | | | |
| 3.Position | | | | | | |
| 4.Expression | | | | | | |
| 5.Eye Contact | | | | | | |

Source:Howell, K. W., Zucker, S. H. & Morehead, M. K. (2000b). Multilevel Academic Skills Inventory. Bellingham, WA: Applied Research and Development Center. To order contact the Student Co-op Bookstore, Western Washington University.
FAX (360) 650-2888. Phone (360) 650-3656.

| | | | |
|---|---|---|---|
| Student misidentifies or is unable to identify family members (in conversations about or in person) using their label. Ex. Mom, dad, grandma, grandpa, brother, sister.<br><br>Student uses unknown terminology when referring to family members in conversations without clarification. Ex. My moo-moo (grandma)… | 7. Family Members | Student will use common terminology, or clarify for listeners the meaning of terminology used, when describing family members | YES NO UNSURE |
| Student uses gestures to refer to objects around the home or uses incorrect terminology when referring to them. | 8. Home Objects | Student will label objects contained in and used in their homes. | YES NO UNSURE |
| When eating meals, student points to and makes demands to obtain desired food items | 9. Meals | During role play, student will use table etiquette (Ex. Please pass the ___) when attempting to obtain a desired food item | YES NO UNSURE |
| When referring to food or drink items, student points or uses incorrect terminology. | 10. Food and Drink | When shown a picture or packaging of common food items, student will label them using their appropriate names. | YES NO UNSURE |
| Student misidentifies colors and/or their significance. (Ex. Ignores orange sign signifying danger). | 11. Colors | When shown objects of different colors, student will label them appropriately by color. | YES NO UNSURE |
| | | When shown colored information or warning signs, student will identify their meanings. | YES NO UNSURE |
| Student omits words (adverbs) in sentences describing how, when, where, qualities, or quantities. (Ex. "John walked *slowly*" becomes "John walked"). | 12. Adverbs | Student will produce sentences using correct forms of adverbs to modify verbs, adjectives and other adverbs. | YES NO UNSURE |
| When speaking of occupations, student uses characteristics of jobs rather then their titles (Ex. "Then the guy who catches bad guys…"). | 13. Occupations | When shown pictures of individuals involved in employment tasks, student will identify their occupations. | YES NO UNSURE |
| Student ignores community indicators (Ex. Street signs, crosswalks, streetlights, community signs [hospital etc.]). | 14. Community | When shown pictures of community indicators, student will label and report their significance. | YES NO UNSURE |
| Student misidentifies or is unable to label grooming objects. | 15. Grooming Objects | In role play, student will label and identify functions of grooming objects. | YES NO UNSURE |
| Student misidentifies or identifies vehicles by verbalizing their sounds (Ex. "then we went in the vroom-vroom to the store). | 16. Vehicles | When shown pictures of various vehicles, student will label them and identify their function. | YES NO UNSURE |

B-3.3

# STATUS SHEET FOR SEMANTICS/VOCABULARY

DIRECTIONS:
1. Use this status sheet with a group of people who have worked with the student.
2. Carefully describe the settings and task you are thinking about while you fill out the sheet.
3. Filling out the sheet begins with the recognition of error (i.e. maladaptive) behavior. If the student makes an error, she doesn't have the skill so circle "NO" for that category. If the student doesn't is correct circle "YES". If you can't decide about the status of the category, or if the student doesn't display the skill, mark it "Unsure"
4. Skills with "YES" circles represent the student's PLOP. Those circled "NO" must be corrected, so teach the corresponding objective. For behaviors rated "UNSURE" employ a recommended **SLP** to get more information.

| IF THE STUDENT MAKES THIS ERROR: | THEN THIS IS THE PROBLEM: | AND THIS IS THE OBJECTIVE: [without the criteria] | DOES THE STUDENT HAVE THE SKILLS?: |
|---|---|---|---|
| | **BASIC VOCABULARY** | | |
| Student misidentifies or is unable to name body parts. | 1.   Body Parts | Student will name and/or identify the functions of (*designated*) body parts. | YES NO UNSURE |
| Student misidentifies or is unable to name items of clothing. | 2.   Clothing | Student will name and/or identify the functions of {*designated*} pieces of clothing | YES NO UNSURE |
| Student misidentifies, misuses, or is unable to name classroom objects. | 3.   Classroom Objects | Student will name and/or identify functions of {*designated*} classroom objects. | YES NO UNSURE |
| Student uses the passive or singular forms of verbs to signify action. Ex. I am hope for rain. | 4.   Action Verbs | In conversation, student will use the action form of verbs to signify movement/action. | YES NO UNSURE |
| Student misidentifies or is unable to name animals or insects. | 5.   Animals and Insects | Student will name and identify facts related to (*designated*) (animals &/or insects). | YES NO UNSURE |
| Student misidentifies or is unable to describe outdoor events or words. | 6.   Outdoor Words | Student will name and describe properties of outdoor events or objects. | YES NO UNSURE |

B-3.3

| | | | |
|---|---|---|---|
| When paying for purchases, student miscounts money (Ex. Gives cashier $1.00 for a $10.00 item). | 17. Money | In role play, student will "pay" for items with the appropriate amount of money. | YES NO UNSURE |
| Student uses gender non-specific terms when referring to individuals (Ex. "That one over there [referring to a female classmate]). | 18. Gender | When shown pictures, student will identify individuals or groups using terminology appropriate to their gender. | YES NO UNSURE |
| Student mislabels objects, places, or people related to school (Ex. Refers to teachers as "that lady" or "that man," refers to school bus as "that big orange car"). | 19. School | When shown pictures of items related to school, student will accurately label them and identify their uses. | YES NO UNSURE |
| Student asks for playthings by pointing to and/or referring to them as things (Ex. Student points to ball and says "I want that thing"). | 20. Playthings | In role play, student will ask for play items using their labels. | YES NO UNSURE |
| Student asks for containers by pointing or using wrong name. | 21. Containers | Given various objects the student will correctly refer to containers by name. | YES NO UNSURE |
| Student misidentifies or is unable to label days of the week. Student often forgets or is unable to recall day specific events (Ex. "Today is Tuesday. What do we do every Tuesday?"[answer: Library]) | 22. Days of the Week | When shown a calendar, student will identify the current day and day specific events. | YES NO UNSURE |
| Student unable to identify which yearly events/holidays occur in which months(Ex. What month is your birthday in?). When asked for the date, student misidentifies the month. | 23. Months | Given a stimulus (verbal or paper) of yearly events/holidays, student will identify which month they occur in. When asked for the date, student will accurately identify the month | YES NO UNSURE YES NO UNSURE |
| Student misreads facial/body cues and mislabels emotions experienced by themselves or others. | 24. Emotions | In role play, student will accurately identify and label emotions of self and others. | YES NO UNSURE |
| Student misidentifies numbers in print or is unable to report numeric representations (Ex. "There are some kids in my class;" A lot of people live in my house). | 25. Numbers | {Upon request or while engaged in a play activity}, student will identify quantifies of items with numbers. | YES NO UNSURE |

121

| | | | |
|---|---|---|---|
| Student misidentifies upcoming celebrations and/or holidays or the length of time until their occurrence.<br><br>Student ruminates on one event or holiday throughout the year (Ex. Halloween is only 9 months away.)<br><br>Student unaware of the significance of holidays and/or celebrations. | 26. Celebrations and Holidays | Given a list of holidays and/or celebrations, student will identify when and the order in which they occur.<br><br>Given a list of holidays and/or celebrations, student will identify their significance. | YES NO UNSURE<br><br>YES NO UNSURE |
| When answering questions or making statements regarding objects placements, student confuses or omits spatial terminology (Ex. Student points to an item hanging from the ceiling and says "it's on top of my desk"). | 27. Spatial Concepts | Given a set of objects and verbal stimulus from instructor, student will model and identify spatial concepts. | YES NO UNSURE |
| When answering questions or making statements regarding how many student confuses and/or omits quantitative terminology, or uses quantitative terminology as an independent phrase (Ex. Student points to a box of crayons and says "I want please" or "some?"). | 28. Quantitative Concepts | Given a set of objects and verbal stimulus from instructor, student will model and identify quantitative concepts.<br><br>In role play, student will use quantitative concepts when answering "how many" questions. | YES NO UNSURE<br><br>YES NO UNSURE |
| When answering questions or making statements regarding when things occurred or are to occur, student omits or misuses temporal terminology (Ex. At the beginning of the school day student reports "We went to the movies tonight."). | 29. Temporal Concepts | In role play, student will answer questions and/or make statements using accurate temporal terminology. | YES NO UNSURE |
| Student misidentifies or is unable to identify shapes. | 30. Shapes | Shown stimulus' (pictures or objects) of various shapes, student will accurately identify them. | YES NO UNSURE |

| | | | |
|---|---|---|---|
| Student greets others inappropriately (i.e. interrupts conversations, yells across rooms, begins conversations immediately without saying hello, etc) and/or uses demanding terminology when attempting to acquire a desired item(s) (Ex. "Give me those crayons!"). | 31. Greetings and Polite Terms | In role play, student will greet others according to social rules (i.e. "Hello, how are you today"). | YES NO UNSURE |
| | | In role play, student will ask for desired items using socially appropriate means (i.e. saying please and thank-you). | YES NO UNSURE |
| Student cannot name or identify opposites | 32. Opposites | Student will correctly name or identify opposites. | YES NO UNSURE |
| Student does not correctly name or identify commonly used materials (e.g., paper, pencils, wood, glue). | 33. Materials | When shown examples the student will correctly name materials. | YES NO UNSURE |
| Student misidentifies or unable to identify sources of music or how they are used(Ex. Student asks teacher to play music but does not designate how [record player, tape, CD, instrument, etc]. *** | 34. Music | When shown stimulus' (pictures or objects) student will identify types of recording devices or instruments and how they are used | YES NO UNSURE |
| When shown or given basic tools (i.e. hammer, screwdriver, saw) student misidentifies or is unable to label them or their uses. *** | 35. Tools | When shown tools, student will label them and identify their use. Student will match tools to their appropriate use. | YES NO UNSURE |
| Student unable to or incorrectly categorizes items (objects or ideas) based on similar characteristics (Ex. When asked what category U.S. Grant, Gettysberg, the burning of Atlanta, and Abraham Lincoln fall under – student reports United States.). | 36. Categories | Given a set of objects or ideas, student will categorize them based on a pre-determined set of characteristics. | YES NO UNSURE |
| Student identifies partial or none of the 5 senses and their functions. Student uses one form of sense verbs for description (Ex. I hear music last night.). | 37. Verbs of the Senses | Student will label their senses. | YES NO UNSURE |
| | | Given a sense, student will identify its function. | YES NO UNSURE |
| | | During role play, student will use verbs of the senses for description of the situation. | YES NO UNSURE |

| | TOPICAL VOCABULARY | | |
|---|---|---|---|
| Student sits idly or retrieves incorrect materials when asked to prepare for reading. Student acts in a manner contrary to that requested by the instructor (Ex. Turns to page 15 instead of 25; Places finger on top of page rather then 1st full paragraph.). | 1. Reading Material Vocabulary | In role play, student will identify necessary materials for reading class. | YES NO UNSURE |
| | | Before reading, student will retrieve all necessary materials from desk. | YES NO UNSURE |
| Student has no prior experience in content area or incorrectly defines key vocabulary. Student makes errors directly related to content vocabulary presented (Ex. Student reports the United States is located on the equator). | 2. Content Area Vocabulary | Student will define key content area vocabulary for upcoming lessons and/or assignments. | YES NO UNSURE |
| Student reacts to idioms in a literal fashion or is unable to interpret their underlying meanings (Ex. When students attention appears to be elsewhere, teacher asks "are you out to lunch at?" Student reacts by saying "duh, I'm right here.") | 3. Idioms/Figurative Language | Given common idioms, student will define their meanings. | YES NO UNSURE |
| When words have multiple meanings, and are used in questions and/or directions, student requires further clarification. While communicating in writing, student frequently uses the incorrect form of a word (Ex. Teacher asks student to "wait" Student stares inquisitively at teacher and says "huh?"; Student writes "We went two the store.") | 4. Multiple Meaning of Words and Phrases | Given a passage, student will identify words with homonyms. | YES NO UNSURE |
| | | Given sentences containing words with multiple meanings, student will supply correct meaning. | YES NO UNSURE |
| Student ignores contextual cures and is unable to define previously unknown words. | 5. Influence of Context on Meaning | Given unknown words, student will use specified strategies (from text) to determine and supply meaning. | YES NO UNSURE |
| | | Student will use context to define specified words. | YES NO UNSURE |

Source: Howell, K. W., Zucker, S. H. & Morehead, M. K. (2000b). Multilevel Academic Skills Inventory. Bellingham, WA: Applied Research and Development Center. To order contact the Student Co-op Bookstore, Western Washington University.
FAX (360) 650-2888. Phone (360) 650-3656.

## Checklist of Language Content.

| I<br><br>Syntax | II<br>Semantics/<br>Vocabulary | III<br><br>Pragmatics |
|---|---|---|
| | **A. Basic Vocabulary** | **A. One-Way Communication** |
| 1. Noun Phrase | **1. Body Parts** | **1. Expresses Wants** |
| **2. Verb Phrase** | 2. Clothing | 2. Expresses Opinions |
| 3. Regular Plurals | **3. Classroom Objects** | **3. Expresses Feelings** |
| **4. Subject Pronouns** | 4. Action Verbs | 4. Expresses Values |
| 5. Prepositional Phrases | **5. Animals and Insects** | **5. Follows Directions** |
| **6. Adjectives** | 6. Outdoor Words | 6. Ask Questions |
| 7. Interrogative Reversals | **7. Family Members** | **7. Narrates Event** |
| **8. Object Pronouns** | 8. Home Objects | 8. States Main Idea |
| 9. Negatives | **9. Meals** | **9. Sequences Events** |
| **10. Verb *be* Auxiliary** | 10. Food and Drink | 10. Subordinates Details |
| 11. Verb be Copula | **11. Colors** | **11. Summarizes** |
| **12. Infinitives** | 12. Adverbs | 12. Describes |
| 13. Determiners | **13. Occupations** | **13. Compares and Contrasts** |
| **14. Conjunction *and*** | 14. Community | 14. Gives Instructions |
| 15. Possessives | **15. Grooming Objects** | **15. Explains** |
| **16. Noun/Verb Agreement** | 16. Vehicles | ***B. Two-Way Communication*** |
| 17. Comparatives | **17. Money** | **1. Considers the Listener** |
| **18. *Wh*- Questions** | 18. Gender | 2. Formulates Messages |
| 19. Past Tense | **19. School** | **3. Participates in Discussions** |
| **20. Future Aspect** | 20. Playthings | 4. Uses Persuasion |
| 21. Irregular Plurals | **21. Containers** | **5. Resolves Differences** |
| **22. Forms of *do*** | 22. Days of the Week | 6. Identifies Speaker's Biases |
| 23. Auxiliaries | **23. Months** | 7. Identifies Speaker's Assumptions |
| **24. Derivational Endings** | 24. Emotions | 8. Formulates Conclusions |
| 25. Reflexive Pronouns | **25. Numbers** | **C. Nonverbal Communication** |
| **26. Qualifiers** | 26. Celebrations and Holidays | 1. Gestures |
| 27. Conjunctions *and, but,* | **27. Spatial Concepts** | **2. Proximity** |
| 28. *or* | 28. Quantitative Concepts | 3. Position |

B-3.

| I<br>Syntax | II<br>Semantics/<br>Vocabulary | III<br>Pragmatics |
|---|---|---|
| 29.   Conjunctions | **29. Temporal Concepts** | **4. Expression** |
| **30.  Indirect and Direct** | 30. Shapes | 5. Eye Contact |
| 31.  Objects | **31. Greetings and<br>     Polite Terms** | *D. Executive<br>    Function* |
| **32.  Adverbs** | 32. Opposites | 1. Develops Intent |
| 33.  Infinitives with Subject | **33. Materials** | **2. Plans** |
| **34.  Participles** | 34. Music | 3. Monitors |
| 35.  Gerunds | **35. Tools** | **4. Identifies Problems** |
| **36.  Passive Voice** | 36. Categories | 5. Analyzes Problems |
| 37.  Complex Verb Forms | **37. Verbs of the Senses** | **6. Recognizes Needed<br>    Assistance** |
| **38.  Relative Adverb Clauses** | *B. Topical Vocabulary* | 7. Recognizes Solutions |
| 39.  Relative Pronoun | **1. Reading Material** | **8. Seeks Help** |
| **40.  Clauses** | 2. Content Area | 9. Adjusts Message |
| 41.  Complex Conjunctions | **3. Technical** | **10. Uses Alternative Messages** |
| | 4. Idioms/Figurative Language | 11. Incorporates New<br>    Language Skills |
| | **5. Multiple Meaning of Words** | |
| | 6. Influence of Context on<br>   Meaning | **12. Attributes Events** |
| | | 13. Reflects |
| | | **14. Speculates** |
| | | 15. Regulates |
| | | **16. Repairs Communications** |

Source: Howell, K. W., Zucker, S. H. & Morehead, M. K. (2000b). Multilevel Academic Skills Inventory. Bellingham, WA: Applied Research and Development Center. To order contact the Student Co-op Bookstore, Western Washington University. Fax (360) 650-2888. Phone (360) 650-3656. Reprinted with permission.

B-3.5

*Analysis of Communication.*

**Directions:** Beginning with the column on the right, judge the quality of usage for each communication skill. If use is inadequate, mark it "NO," then move to the condition(s) found to the left. Criteria should take into account the context of usage. Mark items YES, NO, or UNSURE.

| Analysis of Communication | Identify Correct Example | Produce after Model | Produce after Prompt | Produce in Familiar Content | Produce with Strangers |
|---|---|---|---|---|---|
| A. One-Way Communication | | | | | |
| 1. Expresses Wants | | | | | |
| 2. Expresses Opinions | | | | | |
| 3. Expresses Feelings | | | | | |
| 4. Expresses Values | | | | | |
| 5. Follows Directions | | | | | |
| 6. Ask Questions | | | | | |
| 7. Narrates Event | | | | | |
| 8. States Main Idea | | | | | |
| 9. Sequences Events | | | | | |
| 10. Subordinates Details | | | | | |
| 11. Summarizes | | | | | |
| 12. Describes | | | | | |
| 13. Compares and Contrasts | | | | | |
| 14. Gives Instructions | | | | | |
| 15. Explains | | | | | |
| B. Two-Way Communication | | | | | |
| 1. Considers the Listener | | | | | |
| 2. Formulates Messages | | | | | |
| 3. Participates in Discussions | | | | | |
| 4. Uses Persuasion | | | | | |
| 5. Resolves Differences | | | | | |
| 6. Identifies Speaker's Biases | | | | | |
| 7. Identifies Speaker's Assumptions | | | | | |
| 8. Formulates Conclusions | | | | | |
| C. Nonverbal Communication | | | | | |
| 1. Gestures | | | | | |
| 2. Proximity | | | | | |
| 3. Position | | | | | |
| 4. Expression | | | | | |
| 5. Eye Contact | | | | | |

Source: Howell, K. W., Zucker, S. H. & Morehead, M. K. (2000b). Multilevel Academic Skills Inventory. Bellingham, WA: Applied Research and Development Center. To order contact the Student Co-op Bookstore, Western Washington University. Fax (360) 650-2888. Phone (360) 650-3656. Reprinted with permission.

B-3.7

# Table of Specifications for Syntactic Structures

This table includes a list of syntactic structures (down the vertical axis), and a sequence or student display across the top.

- Each square in the table is an intersection of content and behavior/conditions. Therefore, each square represents an objective (CAP in this domain should approach 100% accuracy—"100%," "95%," or "9 out of 10 attempts are correct").
- The syntax column does <u>not</u> present an absolute sequence (although the skills at the top tend to be more basic than those at the bottom). The display sequence at the top <u>is</u> meant to provide a progression of student response. Usually, for each separate skill, those squares in column A are the first you would teach and C are the last.
- Other display conditions and behaviors could be added to calibrate the sequence according to each individual student's needs.
- Objectives for particular students should be selected according to their present level of performance.
- On the table, write the dates on which each student enters a square and then moves out of it; this will allow you to monitor progress.

| Syntactic Structures | (A) Imitates Sentences Including the Content While Working 1:1 | (B) Produces Content in Sentences with Prompts or in Controlled Settings | (C) Produces the Content Within Spontaneous Sentences (Across Settings) |
|---|---|---|---|
| 1. Noun/noun phrase | | | |
| 2. Verb/verb phrase | | | |
| 3. Regular plurals | | | |
| 4. Subject pronouns | | | |
| 5. Prepositional phrases | | | |
| 6. Adjectives | | | |
| 7. Interrogative reversal form for questions | | | |
| 8. Object pronouns | | | |
| 9. Negatives | | | |
| 10 Verb to be as a helping verb | | | |
| 11 Verb to be as a linking verb | | | |
| 12 Infinitives | | | |
| 13 Determiners | | | |
| 14 Coordinating conjunctions | | | |
| 15 Possessive nouns and pronouns | | | |
| 16 Noun/verb agreement | | | |
| 17 Comparatives and superlatives | | | |
| 18 Questions beginning with an interrogative pronoun | | | |
| 19 Past tense of the verb | | | |
| 20 Future aspect | | | |
| 21 Irregular plurals | | | |
| 22 Forms of do | | | |
| 23 Auxiliaries (helping verbs) | | | |
| 24 Derivational endings which change verbs to nouns | | | |
| 25 Reflexive pronouns | | | |
| 26 Qualifiers | | | |
| 27 Coordinating conjunctions | | | |

| Syntactic Structures | (A) Imitates Sentences Including the Content While Working 1:1 | (B) Produces Content in Sentences with Prompts or in Controlled Settings | (C) Produces the Content Within Spontaneous Sentences (Across Settings) |
|---|---|---|---|
| 28 Conjunctions commonly used to coordinate clauses | | | |
| 29 Conjunctions commonly used to coordinate clauses | | | |
| 30 Indirect and direct objects | | | |
| 31 Adverbs | | | |
| 32 Infinitives with subjects | | | |
| 33 Participles | | | |
| 34 Gerunds | | | |
| 35 Passive voice | | | |
| 36 Complex verb forms— multiple auxiliaries | | | |
| 37 Relative adverb clauses | | | |
| 38 Relative pronoun clauses | | | |
| 39 Complex or subordinating conjunctions | | | |

## Setting Observation.

| Opportunity to Learn Language | Yes | No |
|---|---|---|
| 1. Is the presentation understandable—semantics and syntactic structure at correct level? | —— | —— |
| 2. Is the presentation meaningful—linked to prior knowledge or interest of students? | —— | —— |
| 3. Is there visual support for verbal input—pictures, graphs, role playing, objects, gestures, etc.? | —— | —— |
| 4. Is the student given frequent opportunities to respond? | | |
| 5. Is there monitoring for understanding? | —— | —— |
| 6. Are corrections linked to critical attributes of skill and to meaningfulness? | —— | —— |
| 7. Are there multiple models (peers and teachers) available? | —— | —— |
| 8. Is the classroom structured to increase frequency of communications? | —— | —— |
| 9. Do peers and teacher have strategies for engaging a shy student who would remain silent if given choice? | —— | —— |
| 10. Are peers and teacher comfortable communicating with all students or do they look away or move away when some students initiate contact? | —— | —— |
| 11. If student is acquiring English as a second language, is the primary language and culture of the student valued? | —— | —— |
| 12. Is there collaboration with other classes, activities, and the home to ensure focus, quality, and frequency of opportunity? | —— | —— |
| 13. Is the teacher responsive to student contributions? | —— | —— |
| 14. Do class discussions typically revolve around a theme? | —— | —— |
| 15. Do TIES descriptors relate to this class's: | | |
|     Clarity of instructions? | —— | —— |
|     Checking understanding? | —— | —— |
|     Class climate? | —— | —— |
|     Teacher expectation? | —— | —— |
|     Motivational strategies? | —— | —— |
|     Student understanding? | —— | —— |

# Analytic Scales for Writing.

Directions: Rate the student 1-5 in the following categories, as applicable.

| Narrative | Story-Idea | Organization-Cohesion | Convention-Mechanics |
|---|---|---|---|
| **5** | **5** | **5** | **5** |
| • Includes accurate facts and backs them up with argument or citations when necessary | • Includes characters | • Overall story is organized into a beginning, a middle, and an end | • Sentence structure generally is accurate |
| • Delineates the message and any expected response in a clear and logical fashion | • Delineates a plot | • Events are linked and cohesive | • Spelling does not hinder readability |
| • Contains ideas required to address the topic | • Contains original ideas | • Sentences are linked, often containing some transitions to help with organization (finally, then, next, etc.) | • Sometimes contain dialogue |
| • Illustrates a balance between detail and efficiency | • Contains some detail | | • Handwriting is legible |
| • Uses technical vocabulary correctly | • Word choice | | • Punctuation does not affect readability too much |
| • Contains descriptors (adverbs and adjectives) which are derivatives of the purpose and audience | • Contains descriptors (adverbs and adjectives) and colorful, infrequently used, and/or some long words | | • Word usage generally is correct <br> • (s.v.o./homophone/s-v agreement) |
| • Cause and effect relationships as well as relative importance are clear | | | |
| **4** | **4** | **4** | **4** |
| • Includes assertions and facts that may be disputed without support | • Includes characters, but they are not original, often coming from movies | • Story has somewhat of a beginning, middle, and an end | • Sentence structure generally is accurate but not as good as 5 |
| • Messages and responses are included but may not be presented clearly and/or logically | • Delineates a plot, although it is not as clear as 5 | • Events seem somewhat random, but some organization exists | • Spelling does not hinder readability too much |
| • Sentence complexity is compatible with intent and audience | • Contains some original ideas but is fairly predictable | • Sample may contain some transitions to help with organization: finally, then, next, etc. | • Sometimes contains dialogue |
| • Is missing some important ideas, or includes some unnecessary information | • Contains some detail | • Story often contains too many events, disrupting cohesion | • Handwriting is legible |
| • Details are not always presented in an effective way | • Includes descriptors (adverbs and adjectives) | | • Punctuation does not affect readability too much |
| • Includes descriptors (adverbs and adjectives) that are repetitious or out of alignment with purpose and audience | • Word choice: contains some descriptors (adverbs and adjectives) and some colorful, infrequently used, and/or long words | | • Word usage generally is correct <br> • (s.v.o./homophone/s-v agreement) |
| • Some omission and/or misuse of technical vocabulary | | | |

| Narrative 3 | Story-Idea 3 | Organization-Cohesion 3 | Convention-Mechanics 3 |
|---|---|---|---|
| • Presents facts that do not need to be provided (the audience already knows them) | • Characters are predictable and undeveloped | • Somewhat of a plot exists but story may still lack a beginning, middle, or an end | • Sentence structure has a few problems |
| • The information provided to support the message is insufficient and/or poorly sequenced | • Plot is somewhat haphazard | • Events are somewhat random | • Spelling is somewhat of a problem |
| • Very few ideas are included and some important ideas are missing while unimportant ideas may be included | • May or may not contain original ideas | • Often lacks transitions | • May use dialogue but does not punctuate it correctly |
| • Details are presented in a confusing way, or omitted | • Lacks detail | • Sometimes lacks referents | • Handwriting is legible |
| • Some technical terms are used incorrectly | • Word choice is somewhat predictable, only sometimes contains descriptors (adverbs and adjectives) | | • Punctuation is fair |
| • Descriptors are out of alignment with message | | | • Problems sometimes occur with word usage (s.v.o./homophone/s-v agreement) |
| 2 | 2 | 2 | 2 |
| • Few facts are present and factual errors are common | • Includes few if any characters | • Plot lacks organization into a beginning, middle and an end | • Sentence structure makes story difficult to read |
| • The message is not developed and/or its accuracy is questionable | • Plot is not developed or apparent | • Events are random, lacking in cohesion | • Spelling makes it difficult to read |
| • Ideas are trivial | • Contains virtually no original ideas | • Lacks transitions | • May use dialogue but does not punctuate it correctly |
| • Little detail is provided | • Detail is significantly absent | • Often lacks referents | • Handwriting is not very legible |
| • Technical vocabulary, while attempted, is generally used incorrectly | • Events are very predictable | • Punctuation is inconsistent and problematic | |
| • Few adverbs or adjectives are used to clarify or describe important points | • Word choice is predictable, lacking descriptors (adverbs and adjectives) | | • Word usage is problematic (s.v.o./homophone/s-v agreement) |

| Narrative 1 | Story-Idea 1 | Organization-Cohesion 1 | Convention-Mechanics 1 |
|---|---|---|---|
| • Factual content is filled with inaccuracies | • Includes few if any characters | • Plot is virtually nonexistent | • Sentence structure is problematic |
| • Writing distorts the message and confuses the audience; it is random ("stream of consciousness") | • Plot is nonexistent | • Events are few and random | • Spelling makes it extremely difficult to read |
| • The ideas are trivial, redundant, and/or hackneyed | • Contains no original ideas | • Lacks transitions | • Handwriting is illegible, making it extremely difficult to decode |
| • No detail | • Detail is significantly absent | • Lacks referents | • Punctuation is virtually nonexistent |
| • Technical vocabulary is missing | • Events are few and predictable | | • Word usage is problematic (s.v.o./homophone/s-v agreement) |
| • Descriptors are missing | • Lacks descriptors (adverbs and adjectives) | | |

Based on "Analyzing Student Writing to Develop Instructional Strategies," by G. Tindal and J. Hasbrouck, 1991, Learning Disabilities Research & Practice, 6, (4), p. 239.

## Status Sheet Interview/Observation of Writing Process and Product

### THE WRITING PROCESS

| Planning | EXPLAIN | | | EMPLOY | | |
|---|---|---|---|---|---|---|
| Did the writer define a purpose or establish an intent before beginning to write? | yes | no | unsure | yes | no | unsure |
| Did the writer develop a list of content items appropriate to purpose or intent? | yes | no | unsure | yes | no | unsure |
| Did the writer formulate a drawing, model, map, or outline (plan) to structure content appropriate to purpose or intent? | yes | no | unsure | yes | no | unsure |
| Did the writer use the plan as a basis for writing the first draft? | yes | no | unsure | yes | no | unsure |

| Reviewing | EXPLAIN | | | EMPLOY | | |
|---|---|---|---|---|---|---|
| During the writing of the draft(s) does the writer go back and read what was written to check on development and structure? | yes | no | unsure | yes | no | unsure |

| Revision | EXPLAIN | | | EMPLOY | | |
|---|---|---|---|---|---|---|
| Is there evidence in the drafts to indicate that the writer made changes to accomplish purpose/obtain intent? | yes | no | unsure | yes | no | unsure |

### THE WRITING PRODUCT

| Structure | EXPLAIN | | | EMPLOY | | |
|---|---|---|---|---|---|---|
| Is there an early sentence to focus the reader on the writer's intent or purpose? | yes | no | unsure | yes | no | unsure |
| Are the subtopics and/or events arranged in a recognizable order? | yes | no | unsure | yes | no | unsure |

| Cohesion | EXPLAIN | | | EMPLOY | | |
|---|---|---|---|---|---|---|
| Do all the sentences relate to the writer's intent or purpose? | yes | no | unsure | yes | no | unsure |
| Is there an apparent order in the presentation of the sentences? | yes | no | unsure | yes | no | unsure |
| Does the writer make use of organizing words and devices? | yes | no | unsure | yes | no | unsure |
| Does the final sentence provide an appropriate ending/conclusion? | yes | no | unsure | yes | no | unsure |
| Does the writer make use of transitional words and devices? | yes | no | unsure | yes | no | unsure |

# Writing Sample Summary.

| Error Category | Type of Condition | | | |
|---|---|---|---|---|
| | Copy | Dictation | Story Starter | Assignment |
| | Total Letters____ | Total Letters____ | Total Letters____ | Total Letters____ |
| | Rate____ | Rate____ | Rate____ | Rate____ |
| Number Letters **formed** incorrectly % | | | | |
| Number Letters **spelled** incorrectly % | | | | |
| Number Words **capitalized** incorrectly % | | | | |
| Number Words **punctuated** incorrectly % | | | | |
| Total errors | | | | |
| Total accuracy | | | | |

## CORRECT SENTENCE

The squirrel, or one of its band, ate Norvic's cinnamon bun.

## INCORRECT SENTENCE

the squrrul or one of its band atte novics cinamon bun

| Spelling | Raw Scores | Proportion of Corrects |
|---|---|---|
| ʌʌ ʌʌʌ ʌ ʌ ʌʌ ʌʌʌ ʌʌ ʌʌʌ ʌʌʌʌ ʌʌ ʌ ʌʌ ʌʌʌʌ ʌʌʌ ʌ ʌʌ ʌʌʌ <br> the squrrul or one of its band atte novics cinamon bun <br>    v v                    v              v | 41 Correct <br> 5 Errors | 90% |
| **Capitalization** <br> the squrrul or one of its band atte novics cinamon bun <br> v                            v | 0 Correct <br> 2 Errors | 0% |
| **Punctuation** <br> the squrrul or one of its band atte novics cinamon bun <br>        v              v          v              v | 0 Correct <br> 4 Errors | 0% |

Scoring a writing sample.

Student _____ Grade _____ Date _____

Task _____ Evaluator _____

TIMED/UNTIMED          COPY(NEAR/FAR)/MEMORY          TOTAL NO. OF LETTERS _____

| 1. ALIGNMENT | 2. RELATIVE SIZE | 3. RELATIVE SPACING | 4. PROPORTION OF PARTS | 5. INCONSISTENT STYLE | 6. INCONSISTENT MODE | 7. INCONSISTENT SLANT | 8. CLOSED LOOPS | 9. STRAIGHT & CURVED LINES |
|---|---|---|---|---|---|---|---|---|
| Ya X ↘ K | cat ↕ ca | ca t ↕ ↔ | bird ↑ ↑ r d | bird cursive | birD ↑ cap | cat / / / | cut ↑ a | cat ↖ ↗ |
|  |  |  |  |  |  |  |  |  |

*Handwriting errors.*

136

# Punctuation Status Sheet
## (Exhibit: 11.8)

Directions (only do this for content where problems exist):

✓ Report the number of opportunities for each error.
✓ Report the number of errors.
✓ Report % of accuracy.
✓ Report status
✓ Teach skills marked 'No'
✓ Do additional assessment to check skills marked 'Unsure'

Summarize your results by using the SBD model (see part A-1-e.1).

| | Opportunities | Errors | % Accuracy | Status Yes No Unsure |
|---|---|---|---|---|
| **Capitalization** | | | | |
| First word in sentence | | | | |
| Name of person | | | | |
| Title | | | | |
| Days of week | | | | |
| Month | | | | |
| Street names | | | | |
| Towns, cities, states, countries | | | | |
| Personal pronoun "I" | | | | |
| Buildings, companies, products | | | | |
| Geographical names | | | | |
| Family relationships used for name | | | | |
| First word of quotation | | | | |
| Pronouns | | | | |
| Other | | | | |
| **Period** | | | | |
| End of sentence | | | | |
| Initials and abbreviations | | | | |
| **Question Mark** | | | | |
| End of sentence | | | | |
| **Exclamation point** | | | | |
| Exclamatory sentence | | | | |
| Emphasis | | | | |
| **Comma** | | | | |
| Items in a series | | | | |
| Month, year | | | | |
| Day, month | | | | |
| City, state | | | | |
| **Direct address** | | | | |
| After year in sentence | | | | |
| After state or country in sentence | | | | |
| After introductory word in sentence | | | | |
| Before conjunction joining independent clause | | | | |
| Surround appositive | | | | |
| Set off dependent clause | | | | |
| Set off adverbial clause | | | | |
| After greeting and closing in letters | | | | |

| | Opportunities | Errors | % Accuracy | Status Yes No Unsure |
|---|---|---|---|---|
| **Apostrophe** | | | | |
| Contraction | | | | |
| Possessions | | | | |
| **Semicolon** | | | | |
| Separation of series | | | | |
| Other | | | | |
| **Colon** | | | | |
| Salutation of letter | | | | |
| Expression of time | | | | |
| Appositives | | | | |
| Other | | | | |
| **Hyphen** | | | | |
| Compound word or phrase | | | | |
| Prefix when base is capitalized | | | | |
| Other | | | | |
| **Quotation Marks** | | | | |
| Direct quotations | | | | |
| Single within direct | | | | |
| Block quotations (no marks) | | | | |
| Dialogue | | | | |
| Titles | | | | |
| Words used as words | | | | |
| Foreign words | | | | |
| Special use words | | | | |
| **Parentheses** | | | | |
| Interruptions | | | | |
| Technical information within a text | | | | |
| Author comment | | | | |
| **Underline/Bold/Italic** | | | | |
| Titles | | | | |
| Stress | | | | |
| **Dash** | | | | |
| Interruptions | | | | |
| **Notation in text** | | | | |
| Numbers/bullets | | | | |

## Phonetic Spelling Strategy

1.  Word reproduction: Given words dictated one at a time by the examiner, the student will correctly repeat each word with 100% accuracy taking no more than 5 seconds per word.

2.  Word sorting: Given written words, and words dictated one at a time by the examiner, the student will correctly repeat each word and compare it with the printed version to sort the words into "Sounds like it's spelled" or "Doesn't sound like it's spelled" categories. CAP: 100% accuracy.

3.  Word sorting: Given written words, and words dictated one at a time by the examiner, the student will correctly repeat each word and compare it with the printed version. He will then identify (point, circle, name letter(s)) any portions of the word that are not spelled as they are sounded. CAP: 100% accuracy.

4.  Word sorting: Given words dictated one at a time by the examiner, the student will correctly repeat each word and sort it into "Sounds like it's spelled" or "Doesn't sound like it's spelled" categories. He will then list those words, or portions of words, for which the phonetic spelling strategy cannot be completely applied. CAP: 100% accuracy.

5.  Letter isolation: Given words dictated one at a time by the examiner, the student will correctly say each word with an obvious pause between letters and/or morphemes. This will be done with 100% accuracy taking no more than 5 seconds per word.

6.  Sound isolation: Given non-morpheme clusters/syllables, dictated one at a time, the student will correctly say each sounded phoneme with an obvious pause between sounds. This will be done with 100% accuracy taking no more than 5 seconds per cluster/syllable.

7.  Sound morphograph correspondence: Given morphograph sounds (phonemes) dictated one at a time by the examiner, the student will correctly say/write the letters (graphemes) in the morphograph. This will be done with 100% accuracy taking no more than 5 seconds per sound.

8.  Sound single-symbol correspondence: Given mixed (single letter or morphographs) sounds (phonemes) dictated one at a time by the examiner, the student will correctly say/write the letters (graphemes) that make each sound. This will be done with 100% accuracy taking no more than 5 seconds per sound.

9.  Operational knowledge; Given the directions to do so, the student will correctly say and describe all of the steps necessary to phonetically spell unknown words. This will be done with 100% accuracy taking no more than 15 seconds. The answer is:
    - ✓ Repeat words
    - ✓ Recognize words that are not spelled like they sound (phonetic spelling strategy cannot be applied to all portions of the word)
    - ✓ Isolate syllables in words
    - ✓ Isolate sounds in syllables
    - ✓ Say letters for morphograph sound
    - ✓ Say letter for sound

B-5.1

# Status Sheet: Basic Math Concepts

Directions: Circle item as "Yes", "Maybe" or "No" to describe the student's status..

| GIVEN THIS ITEM | IF THE STUDENT MAKES THIS KIND OF ERROR | THEN THIS IS THE CONCEPTUAL PROBLEM |
|---|---|---|
| If a child sees that his parents read a lot, will that help him learn to read? | Error: No, the kid has to be the one reading.<br>Correct: Yes, it provides a model and raises the value of the task. | 40. Cause-and-effect<br><br>Yes  Maybe  No |
| If some remedial readers are also having trouble with math, should we teach them math to improve their reading? | Error: Sure, if both things happen at the same time it's a good bet one is causing the other.<br>Correct: No, low math and low reading are probably caused by something else. | 39. Correlation<br><br>Yes  Maybe  No |
| I flipped a coin and got 'heads' 3 times in a row. If the odds are supposed to be 50/50, how could I do that? | Error: You must be really good at flipping coins!<br><br>Correct: What is true of large samples of items may not always be apparent when examining a few items. | 38. Representatives<br><br>Yes  Maybe  No |
| "What is the probability of getting 'heads' when I flip this coin?" | Error: It depends on how many times you flip it.<br><br>Correct: 50-50 | 37. Probability<br><br>Yes  Maybe  No |
| "How likely are two people in a room to have the same birthday?" | Error: 50-50<br><br>Correct: It depends on how many people there are and how they were selected to be in the room. | 36. Chance and coincidence<br><br>Yes  Maybe  No |
| Would the answer to 710 + 50 be closer to 700, 800, or 900? | Error: 700 or 900<br><br>Correct: 800 | 35. Estimation<br><br>Yes  Maybe  No |
| $252 \div 9 = 28$<br>"Show me how you would check this answer." | Error: $252 \times 9 = 2268$<br><br>Correct: $28 \times 9 = 252$ | 34. Algorithms for checking problems<br><br>Yes  Maybe  No |
| 1. 44  2. $\frac{3}{8} \div \frac{5}{8} =$<br>$\times$ 22 | Error: 44  $\frac{3}{8} \div \frac{5}{8} = 1$ r2<br>$\times 22$  8 8  0<br>88<br>Correct:<br>1. 44  2. $\frac{3}{8} \div \frac{5}{8} = \frac{3}{8} \times \frac{8}{5}$<br>$\times$ 22<br>88<br>88  $\frac{24}{40} = \frac{12}{20} = \frac{6}{10} = \frac{3}{5}$<br>968 | 33. Algorithms (procedures)<br><br>Yes  Maybe  No |

139

| | | |
|---|---|---|
| There are 5 children in the math group. Today 4 are absent. How many are present? | Error: $\quad 4 - 5 =\quad$ or $\quad\begin{array}{r}4 \\ -5\end{array}$ <br><br> Correct: $5 - 4 =\quad$ or $\quad\begin{array}{r}5 \\ +4\end{array}$ | 32. Set up equation <br> This is a 1-step problem. (In a 2- or more step problem a critical concept would involve which step to complete first as well as how to set up each step.) <br><br> Yes   Maybe   No |
| Thad has 7 miles to walk to get home. He walks 4 days a week. How many miles does he walk in 4 days? | Error: $\quad 7 - 4 =$ <br> $\quad 7 + 4 =$ <br> $\quad 4 \div 4 =$ <br><br> Correct: $4 \times 7 =$ | 31. Select operation <br><br> Yes   Maybe   No |
| Kris catches 14 lobsters and releases 3 because they are too small. Kathy catches 9 and keeps them all. Jack notices that 5 are "in berries" (carrying eggs). How many lobsters do they have? | Error:   a. $\begin{array}{r}14 \\ -\ 3\end{array}$    $\begin{array}{r}11 \\ +9\end{array}$ <br><br> b. $\begin{array}{r}14 \\ -\ 9\end{array}$    $\begin{array}{r}5 \\ +3\end{array}$ <br><br> c. $\begin{array}{r}14 \\ +\ 3\end{array}$    $\begin{array}{r}17 \\ +17\end{array}$ <br><br> Correct: 5 is irrelevant | 30. Irrelevant information <br><br> Yes   Maybe   No |
| Howard and Tom play racquetball 3 days a week. Howard wins 2 of every 3 games they play. Howard is 5'11" tall and Tom is 6'. Tom weighs 150 pounds. How much does Howard weigh? | Error: $\dfrac{x}{5'11"} = \dfrac{6}{150}$ <br><br> Correct: Can't tell. There is not enough information. | 29. Missing information <br><br> Yes   Maybe   No |
| $1.7 \underline{\quad} 1.8 \quad \dfrac{1}{4} = .\underline{\quad}?$ | Error: $1.7 \geq 1.8 \quad \dfrac{1}{4} = .75$ <br><br> Correct: <br> $1.7 \leq 1.8 \qquad \dfrac{1}{4} = \dfrac{4}{4}$ | 28. Decimals <br><br> Yes   Maybe   No |
| $\dfrac{3}{8} \div \dfrac{5}{8} = \dfrac{3}{8} \times \underline{\quad}$ | Error: $\dfrac{3}{8} \div \dfrac{5}{8} = \dfrac{3}{8} \times \dfrac{5}{8}$ <br><br> Correct: $\dfrac{3}{8} \div \dfrac{5}{8} = \dfrac{3}{8} \times \dfrac{8}{5}$ | 27. Inverse of fractions <br><br> Yes   Maybe   No |
| $\dfrac{5}{8} + \dfrac{1}{2} = \underline{\quad}$ | Error: $\dfrac{5}{8} + \dfrac{1}{2} = \dfrac{6}{10}$ <br><br> Correct: $\dfrac{5}{8} + \dfrac{1}{2} = 1\dfrac{1}{8}$ | 26. Mixed numbers <br><br> Yes   Maybe   No |
| $\dfrac{1}{2} = \dfrac{?}{4} \quad \dfrac{2}{4} = \dfrac{?}{8}$ | Error: $\dfrac{1}{2} = \dfrac{3}{4} \quad \dfrac{2}{4} = \dfrac{6}{8}$ <br><br> Correct: $\dfrac{1}{2} = \dfrac{2}{4} \quad \dfrac{2}{4} = \dfrac{4}{8}$ | 25. Equivalent fractions <br><br> Yes   Maybe   No |

| | | |
|---|---|---|
| $1 = \dfrac{?}{2} = \dfrac{?}{3} = \dfrac{?}{4}$ | Error: $\quad 1 = \underline{1/2\ 1/3\ 1/4}$<br><br>Correct: $\quad 1 = \underline{2/2\ 3/3\ 4/4}$ | 24. Fraction equal to "one"<br><br>Yes    Maybe    No |
| $\dfrac{1}{2} + \dfrac{1}{4} = \underline{\quad}$ | Error: $\quad \dfrac{1}{2} + \dfrac{1}{4} = \underline{2/6}$<br><br>Correct: $\quad \dfrac{1}{2} + \dfrac{1}{4} = \underline{3/4}$ | 23. Common denominator<br><br>Yes    Maybe    No |
| $1 \times 4 = \underline{?}$<br><br>$4 \div 1 = \underline{?}$ | Error: $\quad 1 \times 4 = \underline{1}$<br>$\phantom{Error: \quad} 4 \div 1 = \underline{1}$<br><br>Correct: $\ 1 \times 4 = \underline{\ 4}$<br>$\phantom{Correct: \ } 4 \div 1 = \underline{\ 4}$ | 22. Unity<br><br>Yes    Maybe    No |
| $17 \div 4 = 4r\underline{?}$ | Error: $17 \div 4 = \underline{4r\ 2.5}$<br><br>Correct: $17 \div 4 = \underline{4\ r1}$ | 21. Remainders<br><br>Yes    Maybe    No |
| $10 \times 6 = 60$<br>$(2 \times 5) + (10 \times 5) = \underline{?}$ | Error:<br>$10 \times 6 = 600$<br>$(2 \times 5) + (10 \times 5) = 510$<br><br>Correct:<br>$10 \times 6 = 60$<br>$(2 \times 5) + (10 \times 5) = \underline{\ 60}$ | 20. Distributive property<br><br>Yes    Maybe    No |
| $\begin{array}{ccc} 8 & 8 & 8= \\ \underline{\times 1} & \underline{\times 0} & 1 \end{array}$ | Error: $\begin{array}{cccc} 8 & 8 & = \dfrac{8}{1} & = 1 \\ \underline{\times 1} & \underline{\times 0} & & 1 \\ 1 & 8 & & \end{array}$<br><br>Correct:<br>$\begin{array}{cccc} 8 & 8 & & \dfrac{8}{1} = 8 \\ \underline{\times 1} & \underline{\times 0} & = & 1 \\ 8 & 0 & & \end{array}$ | 19. Multiplication/Division by 1 and 0<br><br>Yes    Maybe    No |
| $2 + 2 + 2 = \underline{?}$ | Error: $\quad 8 + 2$ or<br>$\phantom{Error: \quad} 1 + 2$ or<br>$\phantom{Error: \quad} 2 + 2$<br>Correct:<br>$2 + 2 + 2 = \underline{4 + 2}$ | 18. Associative property<br><br>Yes    Maybe    No |

| | | |
|---|---|---|
| x x x + x x = _?_ | Error: a. x x    b. x   (c.   x)<br>    x x      x<br>    x x      x<br>          x<br><br>Correct:<br>x x x + x x = x x<br>             x<br>            x x | 17 Set seperation |
| x x x + x x = _?_ | Error: a. x x    b. x   (c.   x)<br>    x x      x<br>    x x      x<br>          x<br>Correct:<br>x x x + x x = x x<br>             x<br>            x x | 16. Union of sets<br><br>Yes   Maybe   No |
| Circle the set of ▲'s<br>x ▲ ▲ ▲ x<br>x ▲ x   x x | Error:<br>Cirlce the set of ▲'s<br>x ▲ ▲ ▲ x<br>x ▲ x   x x<br><br>Correct:<br>Cirlce the set of ▲'s<br>x ▲ ▲ ▲ x<br>x ▲ x   x x | 15. Sets<br><br>Yes   Maybe   No |
| ___ + ___ = 8.<br>___ - ___ = 8.<br>___ × ___ = 8.<br>___ ÷ ___ = 8. | Error:<br>_5_ + _4_ = 8.<br>_24_ - _17_ = 8.<br>_2_ × _6_ = 8.<br>_16_ ÷ _8_ = 8.<br><br>Correct:<br>_5_ + _3_ = 8<br>_24_ - _16_ = 8<br>_2_ × _4_ = 8<br>_16_ ÷ _2_ = 8 | 14. Equality<br><br>Yes   Maybe   No |
| 763 is equal to<br>__ hundreds<br>__ tens<br>__ ones | Error:<br>_6_ hundreds _3_ tens _7_ ones<br><br>Correct:<br>_7_ hundreds _6_ tens _3_ ones | 13. Expanded notation<br><br>Yes   Maybe   No |
| "Write this number"<br>_7_ hundreds<br>_0_ tens<br>_3_ ones | Error: 700, 111<br><br>Correct: 703 | 12. Zero as a place holder<br><br>Yes   Maybe   No |

| | | |
|---|---|---|
| $\begin{array}{ccc} 27 & 20 & ? \\ +11 = & +\ ? & +1 \\ \hline & 30\ + & 8\ =\ ? \end{array}$ | Error: $\begin{array}{ccc} 27 & 20 & 9 \\ +11 = & +\ 1 & +1 \\ \hline & 21\ + & 8 = 29 \end{array}$<br><br>Correct: $\begin{array}{ccc} 27 & 20 & 7 \\ +11 = & +10 & +1 \\ \hline & 30\ + & 8 = 38 \end{array}$ | 11.  Place Value<br><br>Yes   Maybe   No |
| 7 tens and 8 ones can be written as __ tens and 18 ones | Error:<br>9 tens and 18 ones<br><br>Correct:<br>6 tens and 18 ones | 10.  Regrouping<br><br>Yes   Maybe   No |
| $\begin{array}{cccc} 2 & 2 & 2 \\ +2 & -2 & \times 2 & 2 \div 2 = \end{array}$ | Error:<br>$\begin{array}{cccc} 2 & 2 & 2 \\ +2 & -2 & \times 2 & 2 \div 2 = 4 \\ \hline 0 & 4 & 1 \end{array}$<br>Correct:<br>$\begin{array}{cccc} 2 & 2 & 2 \\ +2 & -2 & \times 2 & 2 \div 2 = 1 \\ \hline 4 & 0 & 4 \end{array}$ | 9. Addition, Subtraction, multiplication, division<br><br>Yes   Maybe   No |
| Read these numbers"<br>14   87   172 | Error: "one-four, eight-seven, one-seven and two"<br><br>Correct:  "Fourteen, eighty-seven, one hundred seventy-two" | 8.  Multi-digit numbers<br><br>Yes   Maybe   No |
| $+, -, \times, \div, =, <, >$ | Error:<br>$+$ = divide    $-$ = dash<br>$\times$ = X     $\div$ = add<br>$<$ = more than $>$ = less than<br>$=$ = similar to<br><br><br>Correct:<br>$+$ = add    $-$ = subtract<br>$\times$ = multiply  $\div$ = divide<br>$<$ = less than  $>$ = greater<br>$=$ = equals     than | 7. Mathematical symbols, terminology and notation<br><br><br><br>Yes   Maybe   No |
| "Draw lines from each    to three 0's<br>0<br>0<br>  0<br>0<br>0<br>  0<br>0<br>0 | Error:       Correct: | 6. One to many correspondence<br><br>Yes   Maybe   No |
| "Draw a line from each    to one 0"<br>0<br>0 | Error:       Correct: | 5. One-to-one correspondence |

| | | |
|---|---|---|
| 0<br>0<br>0<br>  0<br>0<br>0 | | Yes    Maybe    No |
| "Circle 7 x's"<br><br>x x x x x x<br>x x x x x x | Error:<br><br><br><br>Correct:<br><br> | Numeral values<br><br><br>Yes    Maybe    No |
| "Write this number"<br>9 thousands<br>7 hundreds<br>6 tens<br>3 ones | Error: 9, 763<br>Correct:<br>9000<br>  700<br>    60<br>     3 | 3.   Groups of 1's, 10's, 100's,<br>      1,000's<br><br>Yes    Maybe    No |
| "Count the x's"<br><br>x x x x x | Error: 5<br><br>Correct:  "1, 2, 3, 4, 5," | 2.  Cardinal numbers<br>     (especially "0")<br><br>Yes    Maybe    No |
| " Place these numbers in<br>sequence"<br><br>12  7  18 | Error:  18, 7, 12<br><br>Correct: 7, 12, 18 | 1.   Number order<br><br><br>Yes    Maybe    No |

*Source:* Adapted from G.G. bitter, J.M. Englehart, and J. Wiedbe, *One Step at a Time,* St. Paul: EMC Corp., 1977; and K.W. Howell, S.H. Zucker, and M.K. Morehead, *Multilevel Academic Survey Test.* San Antonio, TX: The Psychological Corp. 1985.

# Tables of Specifications for Computation and Application

| Prerequisite Objectives. | Identity | Accuracy | Mastery | Automatic | MASI | Local Curriculum Level |
|---|---|---|---|---|---|---|
| **Reading Number Words** Numbers in word form | | 23a | | | | |
| **Vocabulary** Computational Vocabulary | | 22a | | | | |
| **Symbols** Computational Notation | | 21a | | | | |
| **Place Value** Expanded Notation (0–9, 0–20, 0–100) | | 20a | | | | |
| Value of Zero in multidigit numbers up to 1000 | | 16a | | | | |
| 1000's, 100's, 10's, and/or 1's | 15i | 15a | | | | |
| **Sets** Intersect numerical sets | | 19a | | | | |
| Remainder of separation of sets | 10i | | | | | |
| Sum of union of sets | 9i | | | | | |
| Elements in subsets | | 8a | | | | |
| Sets to numbers | 7i | | | | | |
| Elements in sets | | 6a | 6m | | | |
| Equal and unequal sets | | | | | | |
| Sets having the most (least) | | 2a | | | | |
| **Counting** Skip count | | 18a | | | | |
| Arranging three numbers in sequence (0–10, 10 or greater) | | 13a | 13m | | | |
| Counting forward and backward | | 12a | 12m | | | |
| Supplying previous or next number | | 11a | 11m | | | |
| Reciting Numbers (0–10, 10 or greater) | | 4a | 4m | | | |
| One-to-one correspondence | | 1a | | | | |
| **Rounding** Round numbers to nearest tens and/or hundreds place | | 17a | | | | |

| | Identity | Accuracy | Mastery | Automatic | MASI | Local |
|---|---|---|---|---|---|---|
| | | | | | | Curriculum Level |
| **Writing Digits** | | | | | | |
| Digits (1–100) | | 14a | 14m | | | |
| **Reading Numbers** | | | | | | |
| Numbers (0–10, 10 or greater) | 5i | 5a | 5m | | | |
| | | | | | | |
| ***Addition Objectives.*** | | | | | | |
| Placement Test | | | | | | |
| Adding mixed addition problems | | | | 9p | | |
| Regrouping and No Regrouping | | | | | | |
| Two or more addends with two or more digits | | 8a | | 9p | 3–4 | |
| Two two-digit addends | | 7a | | 9p | 3 | |
| Regrouping | | | | | | |
| One-digit addend to two-digit addend | | 5a | 5m | 9p | 2 | |
| No Regrouping | | | | | | |
| Two two-digit addends | | 6a | | 9p | 2 | |
| One-digit addend to two-digit addend | | 4a | | 9p | 2 | |
| Three or more one-digit addends in a column | | 3a | | 9p | 2 | |
| Zero | | | | | | |
| Adding zero or 1 to one-digit addend | | 2a | | 9p | 1 | |
| Facts | | | | | | |
| Addition facts (0–20) | 1i | 1a | 1m | 9p | 1 | |
| | | | | | | |
| ***Subtraction Objectives.*** | | | | | | |
| Placement Test | | | | | | |
| Mixed subtraction problems | | | | 8p | | |
| Regrouping and No Regrouping | | | | | | |
| Two- or more-digit numbers from a three- or more-digit number | | 7a | | 8p | 4 | |
| Regrouping | | | | | | |
| Two-digit numbers from a two-digit number | | 6a | 6m | 8p | 3 | |
| One-digit numbers from a two-digit number | | 4a | 4m | 8p | 2 | |

| | Identity | Accuracy | Mastery | Automatic | MASI | Local |
|---|---|---|---|---|---|---|
| | | | | | Curriculum Level | |
| **No Regrouping** | | | | | | |
| Two-digit numbers from a two-digit number | | 5a | | 8p | 2 | |
| One-digit numbers from a two-digit number | 2i | 2a | 2m | 8p | 1 | |
| **Zero** | | | | | | |
| Two-digit numbers ending in zero from a two-digit number | | 3a | | 8p | 2 | |
| **Facts** | | | | | | |
| Subtraction facts (0–20) | 1i | 1a | 1m | 8p | 1 | |
| | | | | | | |
| ***Multiplication Objective.*** | | | | | | |
| **Placement Test** | | | | | | |
| Mixed multiplication problems | | | | 9p | | |
| **Squaring** | | | | | | |
| Squares of numbers (0–12) | 8i | 8a | 8m | 9p | 8 | |
| **Regrouping and No Regrouping** | | | | | | |
| Two or more digits by two or more digits | | 7a | | 9p | 4–5 | |
| Two-digit numbers by a two-digit number | | 4a | 4m | 9p | 4 | |
| **Place Value** | | | | | | |
| Multidigit problems with zeros | | 6a | | 9p | 4 | |
| Multiply by 1, 10, 100, 1000 | | 5a | | 9p | 5 | |
| **Regrouping** | | | | | | |
| Two-digit number by a one-digit number | | 3a | 3m | 9p | 4 | |
| **No Regrouping** | | | | | | |
| Two-digit number by a one-digit number | | 2a | 2m | 9p | 4 | |
| **Facts** | | | | | | |
| Multiplication facts (0–10) | 1i | 1a | 1m | 9p | 4 | |
| | | | | | | |
| ***Division Objectives.*** | | | | | | |
| **Placement Test** | | | | | | |
| Mixed division problems | | | | 8p | | |
| **Square Root** | | | | | | |
| Square root of a number in which the answer is 0–12 | 7i | 7a | 7m | 8p | 8 | |

|  | Identity | Accuracy | Mastery | Automatic | MASI | Local |
|---|---|---|---|---|---|---|
|  |  |  |  |  | Curriculum Level |  |
| **Place Value** |  |  |  |  |  |  |
| Two- or more-digit number with zero |  | 6a |  | 8p | 5 |  |
| Two- or more-digit number by 1, 10, 100, 1000 |  | 5a |  | 8p | 5 |  |
| **Remainder and No Remainder** |  |  |  |  |  |  |
| Two- or more-digit number by a one- or two-digit number |  | 4a |  | 8p | 4 |  |
| **Remainder** |  |  |  |  |  |  |
| Two-digit number by a one-digit number (one- or two-digit answer) |  | 3a | 3m | 8p | 4 |  |
| **No Remainder** |  |  |  |  |  |  |
| Two-digit number by a one-digit number (two-digit answer) |  | 2a | 2m | 8p | 4 |  |
| **Facts** |  |  |  |  |  |  |
| Division facts (0–10) | 1i | 1a | 1m | 8p | 4 |  |
| ***Fraction Objectives.*** |  |  |  |  |  |  |
| **Placement Test** |  |  |  |  |  |  |
| Mixed fraction problems |  |  |  | 25p | 6 |  |
| **Dividing** |  |  |  |  |  |  |
| Mixed number by another mixed number |  | 24a |  | 25p | 6 |  |
| Whole numbers by fractions |  | 23a |  | 25p | 6 |  |
| Fractions with conversions |  | 22a |  | 25p | 6 |  |
| Fractions with cancellation |  | 21a |  | 25p | 6 |  |
| **Multiplying** |  |  |  |  |  |  |
| Mixed Numbers with conversions |  | 20a |  | 25p | 6 |  |
| Conversions to simplest form |  | 19a |  | 25p | 6 |  |
| **Adding and Subtracting** |  |  |  |  |  |  |
| Mixed numbers without common factors between uncommon denominators (conversion) |  | 18a |  | 25p | 6 |  |
| No common factors between uncommon denominators (conversion) |  | 17a |  | 25p | 6 |  |
| Common factors between uncommon denominators (conversion) |  | 16a |  | 25p | 6 |  |

| | Identity | Accuracy | Mastery | Automatic | MASI | Local |
|---|---|---|---|---|---|---|
| | | | | | Curriculum Level | |
| Common factors between uncommon denominators (conversion) | | 15a | | 25p | 6 | |
| Mixed numbers (conversion) | | 14a | | 25p | 6 | |
| Fractions with common denominators | | 13a | | 25p | 5 | |
| Mixed numbers (no conversion) | | 12a | | 25p | 5 | |
| With add and subtract fractions | | 11a | | 25p | 5 | |
| Converting<br>Mixed numbers into mixed numbers with improper fractions | | 10a | | 25p | 5 | |
| Improper fraction to a whole or a mixed number | | 9a | | 25p | 6 | |
| Fractions to simplest form | | 8a | | 25p | 5 | |
| Equivalence<br>Equivalent fractions | | 7a | | 25p | 5 | |
| Fractions equal to 1 | | 4a | | 25p | 5 | |
| Least Common Denominator<br>Least common denominator of two simple fractions | 6i | 6a | | 25p | 5 | |
| Sets<br>Denominator sets | | 5a | | 25p | 2 | |
| Matching fractions to subdivided objects | 3i | | | 25p | 1–2 | |
| Subdivide sets and/or objects | | 1a | | 25p | 1 | |
| Reading Fractions<br>Fractions | | 2a | | 25p | 2 | |
| | | | | | | |
| ***Decimal, Ratio, Percent Objectives.***<br>Placement Test<br>Mixed decimal, ratio, percent problems | | | | 12p | | |
| Ratios<br>Ratio sentences | | 11a | | 12p | 8 | |
| Rounding<br>Nearest tenth, hundredth, thousandth | | 10a | | 12p | 8 | |
| Computing Decimals<br>Dividing decimals, with one to four decimal places | | 9a | | 12p | 7 | |

| | Identity | Accuracy | Mastery | Automatic | MASI | Local |
|---|---|---|---|---|---|---|
| | | | | | | Curriculum Level |
| Multiply decimal with one to four decimal places | | 8a | | 12p | 7 | |
| Add and Subtract decimals with one to four decimal places | | 7a | | 12p | 7 | |
| Converting<br>Fraction to percent | | 6a | 6m | 12p | 8 | |
| Percent to fraction | | 5a | 5m | 12p | 8 | |
| Decimal to percent | 4a | | 12p | 8 | | |
| Fraction to decimal | | 3a | | 12p | 7 | |
| Reading Fractions and Percents<br>Fraction and Percents | | 2a | | 12p | 4 | |
| Reading Place Value<br>Decimals | | 1a | | 12p | 4 | |

**Time and Temperature Objectives.**

| | Identity | Accuracy | Local |
|---|---|---|---|
| | | | Curriculum Level |
| Knowledge<br>Seasons | | 10a | |
| Temperature Units | | 9a | |
| Months of the year | | 8a | |
| Days of the week | | 7a | |
| Seconds, minutes, hours, days, weeks, months, years, decades, centuries | | 6a | |
| Tools<br>Temperatures | | 5a | |
| Calendar | | 4a | |
| Time | | 3a | |
| Uses of a clock, watch, calendar, thermometer | | 2a | |
| Name clock, watch, calendar, thermometer | | 1a | |

| | Identity | Accuracy | Local |
|---|---|---|---|
| **Money Objectives.** | | Curriculum Level | |
| **Knowledge** | | | |
| Checkbook record and balance | | 11a | |
| Checks for bills | | 10a | |
| Change due—purchases over $1 and less than $20 | | 9a | |
| Change due—purchases less than $1 | | 8a | |
| Symbols for money | 7i | 7a | |
| Value of coins and currency | | 6a | |
| Names of coins and currency | | 5a | |
| **Tools** | | | |
| Four operation calculator | | 4a | |
| **Vocabulary** | | | |
| Budget vocabulary | | 3a | |
| Banking vocabulary | | 2a | |
| Money vocabulary | | 1a | |
| **Geometry Objectives: Plane and Solid.** | | | |
| **Knowledge** | | | |
| Calculating volume of a cube, rectangular prism, cone, and cylinder | 7i | 7a | |
| Calculating the area of a square, rectangle, triangle, and circle | 6i | 6a | |
| Calculating the perimeter of a polygon, square, rectangle, and circle | 5i | 5a | |
| **Vocabulary** | | | |
| Meanings of perimeter, surface area, square units, cubic units, volume, circumference | | 4a | |
| Meanings of length, width, height, diameter, radius, degree, base | 3i | 3a | |
| Meanings of line, line segment, ray, angle, arc, point | 2i | 2a | |
| Meaning of circle, square, rectangle, triangle, trapezoid, parallelogram, pentagon, hexagon, octagon, cone, cylinder, oval | 1i | 1a | |

| | Identity | Accuracy | Local |
|---|---|---|---|
| **Metric Measurement Objectives:** *Linear, Weight, and Capacity.* | | Curriculum Level | |
| Knowledge | | | |
| Abbreviations for weight units (gram, kilogram, centigram, decigram, decagram, milligram, hectogram) | | 11a | |
| Abbreviations for capacity units (centiliter, milliliter, decaliter, hectoliter, decaliter, liter) | | 10a | |
| Abbreviations for linear units (millimeter, kilometer, hectometer, centimeter, decameter, decimeter, meter) | | 9a | |
| Meanings of metric prefix (milli-, centi-, deci-, deca-, hecto-, kilo-) | | 8a | |
| Tools | | | |
| Measure to nearest correct unit— millimeter, centimeter | | 7a | |
| Match linear tool to task (ruler, meterstick, tape measure, degree protractor, and rolling meter counter) | 6i | | |
| Capacity tool for task— milliliter, liter | 5i | | |
| Weight tool for task variety of scales | 4i | | |
| Vocabulary | | | |
| Key vocabulary for weight measurement | 3i | 3a | |
| Key vocabulary for liquid and dry measurement | 2i | 2a | |
| Key vocabulary for linear measurement | 1i | 1a | |
| **Customary Measurement Objectives:** *Linear, Weight, and Capacity.* | | | |
| Knowledge | | | |
| Abbreviations for weight units (ounces, pounds, tons) | | 13a | |
| Abbreviations for capacity units (teaspoon, tablespoon, cup, pint, quart, gallon) | | 12a | |
| Abbreviations for linear units (inch, foot, yard) | | 11a | |

| | Identity | Accuracy | Local |
|---|---|---|---|
| | | | Curriculum Level |
| Weight unit equivalents (ounces, pounds, tons) | | 10a | |
| Capacity unit equivalents (teaspoons, cups, pints, quarts, gallons) | | 9a | |
| Linear unit equivalents (inches, feet, yards, miles) | | 8a | |
| Tools | | | |
| Measure to the nearest correct unit using a ruler, yardstick, degree protractor, tape measure, and rolling yard measure | | 7a | |
| Match linear tool to task | 6i | | |
| Match capacity tool to task | 5i | | |
| Match weight tool to task | 4i | | |
| Vocabulary | | | |
| Key vocabulary to weight measurement | 3i | 3a | |
| Key vocabulary for liquid and dry measurement | 2i | 2a | |
| Key vocabulary for linear measurement | 1i | 1a | |
| | | | |
| ***Problem Solving Objectives.*** | | | |
| Apply Knowledge | | | |
| Check solution to problems using functional algorithm | | 7a | |
| Estimate correct answer to word problems | | 6a | |
| Correct equation to solve word problems | 5i | | |
| Missing information in word problems | | 4a | |
| Essential and nonessential information | | 3a | |
| Restating in own words | | 2a | |
| Vocabulary | | | |
| Match operation name to key vocabulary words and phrases | | 1a | |

# SPECIFICATIONS FOR MATHEMATICS

This is a comprehensive list of computation and application objectives.

## Objectives

These objectives are presented by operation (e.g., addition, subtraction) and content (e.g., time, measurement). The objectives with the smallest numbers are taught first. In some cases there will be multiple objectives for the same operation. If an objective has the letter **m** attached to it, it is a mastery objective specifying rate criteria. If the objective has the letter **a**, it is an accuracy objective. Both **a** and **m** objectives require the student to produce correct answers. Objectives with an **i** require identification of the correct answer. The **i** objectives always have accuracy criteria; **i** objectives are easiest and m objectives are hardest.

| Content | Number | Objective (Mastery CAP is in rate per minute) |
|---|---|---|
| **Prerequisites** | | |
| Reading Number Words | 23a | Read numbers in word form. Accuracy CAP 100%. |
| Vocabulary 100%. | 22a | Demonstrate knowledge of computational vocabulary. Accuracy CAP |
| Symbols 100%. | 21a | Demonstrate knowledge of computational notation. Accuracy CAP |
| Place Value Accuracy CAP 100%. | 20a | Demonstrate knowledge of expanded notation (0–9, 0–20, 0–100). |
| Sets | 19a | Intersect numerical sets. Accuracy CAP 100%. |
| Counting | 18a | Skip count. Accuracy CAP 100%. |
| Rounding 100%. | 17a | Round numbers to nearest ten's and/or hundred's place. Accuracy CAP |
| Place Value CAP 100%. | 16a | Supply the value of zero in multi-digit numbers up to 1000. Accuracy |
| Place Value Accuracy CAP 100%. | 15a | Supply the number of 1000s, 100s, 10s, and/or 1s in a multi-digit number. |
| Place Value | 15i | Identify the digit holding the place of 1000s, 100s, 10s, and/or 1s in multi-digit numbers. Accuracy CAP 100%. |
| Writing Digits | 14m | Write digits (1–100). Mastery CAP: 100 correct with zero errors. |
| Writing Digits | 14a | Write digits (1–100). Accuracy CAP 100%. |
| Counting 50 correct with zero errors. | 13m | Arrange three numbers in sequence (0–10, 10 or greater). Mastery CAP: |
| Counting 100%. | 13a | Arrange three numbers in sequence (0–10, 10 or greater). Accuracy CAP |
| Counting | 12m | Rote count (forward and backward from one number to another). Mastery CAP: 100 correct with zero errors. |
| Counting | 12a | Rote count (forward and backward from one number to another). Accuracy CAP 100%. |
| Counting | 11m | Supply previous or next number. Mastery CAP: 100 correct with zero errors. |
| Counting | 11a | Supply previous or next number. Accuracy CAP 100%. |
| Sets | 10i | Identify remainder of separation of sets. Accuracy CAP 100%. |
| Sets | 9i | Identify sum of union sets (0–20). Accuracy CAP 100%. |
| Sets | 8a | Count the elements in subsets. Accuracy CAP 100%. |
| Sets | 7i | Match sets to numbers. Accuracy CAP 100%. |

B-5.3

Objectives, continued

| Content | Number | Objective (Mastery CAP is in rate per minute) |
|---|---|---|
| Sets | 6m | Count the elements in sets. Mastery CAP: 50 elements counted with zero errors. |
| Sets | 6a | Count the elements in sets. Accuracy CAP 100%. |
| Reading Numbers | 5m | Read numbers (0–10, 10 or greater) from probe sheet. Mastery CAP: 100 numbers correct with zero errors. |
| Reading Numbers | 5a | Read numbers (0–10, 10 or greater) from untimed probe sheet. Accuracy CAP 100%. |
| Reading Numbers | 5i | Identify numbers (0–10, 10 or greater). Accuracy CAP 100%. |
| Counting | 4m | Recite numbers (0–10, 10 or greater). Mastery CAP: 100 correct with zero errors. |
| Counting | 4a | Recite numbers (0–10, 10 or greater). Accuracy CAP 100%. |
| Sets | 3a | Identify equal and unequal sets. Accuracy CAP 100%. |
| Sets | 2a | Identify which sets have the most (least). Accuracy CAP 100%. |
| Counting | 1a | Indicate one-to-one correspondence between figures. Accuracy CAP 100%. |

**Addition**

| | | |
|---|---|---|
| | 9p | Placement Test. Add mixed addition problems. Accuracy CAP 100%. |
| Regrouping and No Regrouping | 8a | Add two or more addends with two or more digits with or without regrouping. Accuracy CAP 100%. |
| Regrouping and No Regrouping | 7a | Add two two-digit addends with or without regrouping. Accuracy CAP 100%. |
| No Regrouping | 6a | Add two two-digit addends without regrouping. Accuracy CAP 100%. |
| Regrouping | 5m | Add one-digit addend to two-digit addend with regrouping. Mastery CAP: 70 digits correct with zero errors. |
| Regrouping | 5a | Add one-digit addend to two-digit addend with regrouping. Accuracy CAP 100%. |
| No Regrouping | 4a | Add one-digit addend to two-digit addend without regrouping. Accuracy CAP 100%. |
| No Regrouping | 3a | Add three or more one-digit addends in a column. Accuracy CAP 100%. |
| Zero | 2a | Add zero or 1 to one-digit addend. Accuracy CAP 100%. |
| Facts | 1m | Addition facts (0–20). Mastery CAP: 80 digits correct with zero errors. |
| Facts | 1a | Addition facts (0–20). Accuracy CAP 100%. |
| Facts | 1i | Identify answers to addition facts (0–20). Accuracy CAP 100%. |

**Subtraction**

| | | |
|---|---|---|
| | 8p | Placement test. Subtract mixed subtraction problems. Accuracy CAP 100%. |
| Regrouping and No Regrouping | 7a | Subtract a two- or more-digit number from a three- or more-digit number with or without regrouping. Accuracy CAP 100%. |
| Regrouping | 6m | Subtract a two-digit number from a two-digit number with regrouping. Mastery CAP: 40 digits correct with zero errors. |
| Regrouping | 6a | Subtract a two-digit number from a two-digit number with regrouping. Accuracy CAP 100%. |
| No Regrouping | 5a | Subtract a two-digit number from a two-digit number without regrouping. Accuracy CAP 100%. |

Objectives, continued

| Content | Number | Objective (Mastery CAP is in rate per minute) |
|---|---|---|
| Regrouping | 4m | Subtract a one-digit number from a two-digit number with regrouping. Mastery CAP: 60 digits correct with zero errors. |
| Regrouping | 4a | Subtract a one-digit number from a two-digit number with regrouping. Accuracy CAP 100%. |
| Zero | 3a | Subtract a two-digit number ending in zero from a two-digit number ending in zero. Accuracy CAP 100%. |
| No Regrouping | 2m | Subtract a one-digit number from a two-digit number without regrouping. Mastery CAP: 70 digits correct with zero errors. |
| No Regrouping | 2a | Subtract a one-digit number from a two-digit number without regrouping. Accuracy CAP 100%. |
| No Regrouping | 2i | Identify answers to problems in which a one-digit number is subtracted from a two-digit number without regrouping. Accuracy CAP 100%. |
| Facts | 1m | Subtraction facts (0–20). Mastery CAP: 80 digits correct with zero errors. |
| Facts | 1a | Subtraction facts (0–20). Accuracy CAP 100%. |
| Facts | 1i | Identify answers to subtraction facts (0–20). Accuracy CAP 100%. |

## Multiplication

| Content | Number | Objective (Mastery CAP is in rate per minute) |
|---|---|---|
| | 9p | Placement Test. Multiply mixed multiplication problems. Accuracy CAP 100%. |
| Squaring | 8m | Produce squares of numbers (0–12). Mastery CAP: 40 digits correct with zero errors. |
| Squaring | 8a | Produce squares of numbers (0–12). Accuracy CAP 100%. |
| Squaring | 8i | Identify squares of numbers (0–12). Accuracy CAP 100%. |
| Regrouping and No Regrouping | 7a | Multiply a number containing two or more digits by another number containing two or more digits with or without regrouping. Accuracy CAP 100%. |
| Place Value | 6a | Multiply multi-digit problems with zeros as place holders. Accuracy CAP 100%. |
| Place Value | 5a | Multiply by 1, 10, 100, 1000. Accuracy CAP 100%. |
| Regrouping and No Regrouping | 4m | Multiply a two-digit number by a two-digit number with or without regrouping. Mastery CAP: 40 digits correct with zero errors. |
| Regrouping and No Regrouping | 4a | Multiply a two-digit number by a two-digit number with or without regrouping. Accuracy CAP 100%. |
| Regrouping | 3m | Multiply a two-digit number by a one-digit number with regrouping. Mastery CAP: 30 digits correct with zero errors. |
| Regrouping | 3a | Multiply a two-digit number by a one-digit number with regrouping. Accuracy CAP 100%. |
| No Regrouping | 2m | Multiply a two-digit number by a one-digit number without regrouping. Mastery CAP: 40 digits correct with zero errors. |
| No Regrouping | 2a | Multiply a two-digit number by a one-digit number without regrouping. Accuracy CAP 100%. |
| Facts | 1m | Multiplication facts (0–10). Mastery CAP: 80 digits correct with zero errors. |
| Facts | 1a | Multiplication facts (0–10). Accuracy CAP 100%. |
| Facts | 1i | Identify answers to multiplication facts (0–10). Accuracy CAP 100%. |

B-5.3

Objectives, continued

| Content | Number | Objective (Mastery CAP is in rate per minute) |
|---|---|---|
| **Division** | | |
| | 8p | Placement test. Divide mixed division problems. Accuracy CAP 100%. |
| Square Root | 7m | Produce the square root of a number in which the answer is 0–12. Mastery CAP: 40 digits correct with zero errors. |
| Square Root | 7a | Produce the square root of a number in which the answer is 0–12. Accuracy CAP 100%. |
| Square Root | 7i | Identify the square root of a number in which the answer is 0–12. Accuracy CAP 100%. |
| Place Value | 6a | Divide a two- or more-digit number with zero as a place holder to get answers with or without remainders. Accuracy CAP 100%. |
| Place Value | 5a | Divide a two- or more-digit number by 1, 10, 100, 1000 to get answers without decimals. Accuracy CAP 100%. |
| Remainder and No Remainder | 4a | Divide a two- or more-digit number by a one- or two-digit number to get to an answer with or without a remainder. Accuracy CAP 100%. |
| Remainder | 3m | Divide a two-digit number by a one-digit number to get a one- or two-digit answer with a remainder. Mastery CAP: 40 digits correct with zero errors. |
| Remainder | 3a | Divide a two-digit number by a one-digit number to get a one- or two-digit answer with a remainder. Accuracy CAP 100%. |
| No Remainder | 2m | Divide a two-digit number by a one-digit number to get a two-digit answer without a remainder. Mastery CAP: 40 digits correct with zero errors. |
| No Remainder | 2a | Divide a two-digit number by a one-digit number to get a two-digit answer without a remainder. Accuracy CAP 100%. |
| Facts | 1m | Division facts (0–10). Mastery CAP: 80 digits correct with zero errors. |
| Facts | 1a | Division facts (0–10). Accuracy CAP 100%. |
| Facts | 1i | Identify answers to division facts (0–10). Accuracy CAP 100%. |
| **Fractions Objectives** | | |
| | 25p | Placement test. Produce answers to mixed fraction problems. Accuracy CAP 100%. |
| Dividing | 24a | Divide a mixed number by another mixed number with conversion. Accuracy CAP 100%. |
| Dividing | 23a | Divide whole numbers by fractions. Accuracy CAP 100%. |
| Dividing | 22a | Divide fractions with conversion. Accuracy CAP 100%. |
| Dividing | 21a | Divide fractions with cancellation. Accuracy CAP 100%. |
| Multiplying | 20a | Multiply two mixed numbers with conversion. Accuracy CAP 100%. |
| Multiplying | 19a | Multiply fractions with conversion to simplest form. Accuracy CAP 100%. |
| Adding and Subtracting | 18a | Add and subtract mixed numbers without common factors between uncommon denominators (conversion required). Accuracy CAP 100%. |
| Adding and Subtracting | 17a | Add and subtract fractions without common factors between uncommon denominators (conversion required). Accuracy CAP 100%. |
| Adding and Subtracting | 16a | Add and subtract fractions with common factors between uncommon denominators (conversion required). Accuracy CAP 100%. |

Objectives, continued

| Content | Number | Objective (Mastery CAP is in rate per minute) |
|---|---|---|
| Adding and Subtracting | **15a** | Add and subtract fractions with common factors between uncommon denominators (no conversion required). Accuracy CAP 100%. |
| Adding and Subtracting | **14a** | Add and subtract mixed numbers with common denominators (conversion required). Accuracy CAP 100%. |
| Adding and Subtracting | **13a** | Add and subtract fractions with common denominators (conversion required). Accuracy CAP 100%. |
| Adding and Subtracting | **12a** | Add and subtract mixed numbers with common denominators (no conversion required). Accuracy CAP 100%. |
| Adding and Subtracting | **11a** | Add and subtract fractions with common denominators (no conversion required). Accuracy CAP 100%. |
| Converting | **10a** | Convert (rename) mixed numbers into improper fractions. Accuracy CAP 100%. |
| Converting | **9a** | Convert (rename) an improper fraction to a whole or a mixed number. Accuracy CAP 100%. |
| Converting | **8a** | Convert (rename) fractions to simplest form. Accuracy CAP 100%. |
| Equivalence | **7a** | Produce equivalent fractions. Accuracy CAP 100%. |
| Least Common Denominator | **6a** | Produce the least common denominator of two simple fractions. Accuracy CAP 100%. |
| Least Common Denominator | **6i** | Identify the least common denominator of two simple fractions. Accuracy CAP 100%. |
| Sets | **5a** | Locate intersection of denominator sets. Accuracy CAP 100%. |
| Equivalence | **4a** | Produce fractions equal to 1. Accuracy CAP 100%. |
| Sets | **3i** | Identify fractions (simplest form) by matching them to subdivided objects. Accuracy CAP 100%. |
| Reading Fractions | **2a** | Read fractions. Accuracy CAP 100%. |
| Sets | **1a** | Subdivide sets and/or objects. Accuracy CAP 100%. |

**Decimals, Ratios, and Percents**

| | | |
|---|---|---|
| | **12p** | Placement test. Answer mixed decimal, ratio, and percent problems. Accuracy CAP 100%. |
| Ratio | **11a** | Complete ratio sentences. Accuracy CAP 100%. |
| Rounding | **10a** | Round decimals to nearest tenth, hundredth, and thousandth. Accuracy CAP 100%. |
| Computing Decimals | **9a** | Divide decimals having one to four decimal places. Accuracy CAP 100%. |
| Computing Decimals | **8a** | Multiply decimals having one to four decimal places. Accuracy CAP 100%. |
| Computing Decimals | **7a** | Add and subtract decimals having one to four decimal places. Accuracy CAP 100%. |
| Converting | **6m** | Convert a fraction to a percent. Mastery CAP 100%. |
| Converting | **6a** | Convert a fraction to a percent. Mastery CAP 100%. |
| Converting | **5m** | Convert a percent to a fraction. Mastery CAP 100%. |
| Converting | **5a** | Convert a percent to a fraction. Accuracy CAP 100%. |
| Converting | **4a** | Convert a decimal to a percent. Accuracy CAP 100%. |
| Converting | **3a** | Convert a fraction to a decimal. Accuracy CAP 100%. |
| Reading Fractions and Percents | **2a** | Read fractions and percents. Accuracy CAP 100%. |
| Reading Place Value | **1a** | Read decimals in tenths, hundredths, and thousandths. Accuracy CAP 100%. |

B-5.3

Objectives, continued

| Content | Number | Objective (Mastery CAP is in rate per minute) |
|---|---|---|
| **Time and Temperature** | | |
| Knowledge | 10a | Name the seasons. Accuracy CAP 100%. |
| Knowledge | 9a | Know Fahrenheit or Celsius temperature units. Accuracy CAP 100%. |
| Knowledge | 8a | Name the months of the year. Accuracy CAP 100%. |
| Knowledge | 7a | Name the days of the week. Accuracy CAP 100%. |
| Knowledge | 6a | Know equivalent units: seconds, minutes, hours, days, weeks, months, years, decades, centuries. Accuracy CAP 100%. |
| Tools | 5a | Read temperatures. Accuracy CAP 100%. |
| Tools | 4a | Use a calendar. Accuracy CAP 100%. |
| Tools | 3a | Tell time. Accuracy CAP 100%. |
| Tools | 2a | Describe uses of time-and-temperature tools: clock, watch, calendar, thermometer. Accuracy CAP 100%. |
| Tools | 1a | Name clock, watch, calendar, thermometer. Accuracy CAP 100%. |
| | | |
| **Money** | | |
| Knowledge | 11a | Enter credit and debit in checkbook record and balance. Accuracy 100%. |
| Knowledge | 10a | Write checks for bills. Accuracy CAP 100%. |
| Knowledge | 9a | Determine the change due for purchases costing more than $1 and less than $20. Accuracy CAP 100%. |
| Knowledge | 8a | Determine the change due, using the fewest possible coins, for purchases costing less than $1. Accuracy CAP 100%. |
| Knowledge | 7a | Know symbols for money. Accuracy CAP 100%. |
| Knowledge | 7i | Identify symbols for money. Accuracy CAP 100%. |
| Knowledge | 6a | Know values of coins and currency. Accuracy CAP 100%. |
| Knowledge | 5a | Know names of coins and currency. Accuracy CAP 100%. |
| Tools | 4a | Use four-operation calculator to solve knowledge problems. Accuracy CAP 100%. |
| Vocabulary | 3a | Know budget vocabulary. Accuracy CAP 100%. |
| Vocabulary | 2a | Know banking vocabulary. Accuracy CAP 100%. |
| Vocabulary | 1a | Know money vocabulary. Accuracy CAP 100%. |
| | | |
| **Geometry: Plane and Solid** | | |
| Knowledge | 7a | Produce formulas for calculating the volume of a cube, a rectangular prism, a cone, and a cylinder. Accuracy CAP 100%. |
| Knowledge | 7i | Identify formulas for calculating the volume of a cube, a rectangular prism, a cone, and a cylinder. Accuracy CAP 100%. |
| Knowledge | 6a | Produce formulas for calculating the area of a square, a rectangle, a triangle, and a circle. Accuracy CAP 100%. |
| Knowledge | 6i | Identify formulas for calculating the area of a square, a rectangle, a triangle, and a circle. Accuracy CAP 100%. |
| Knowledge | 5a | Produce formulas for calculating the perimeter of a polygon, a square, a rectangle, and a circle. Accuracy CAP 100%. |
| Knowledge | 5i | Identify formulas for calculating the perimeter of a polygon, a square, a rectangle, and a circle. Accuracy CAP 100%. |
| Vocabulary | 4a | Produce formula vocabulary meanings: perimeter, surface area, square units, cubic units, volume, circumference. Accuracy CAP 100%. |

B-5.3

Objectives, continued

| Content | Number | Objective (Mastery CAP is in rate per minute) |
|---|---|---|
| Vocabulary | 3a | Produce dimensions vocabulary meanings: length, width, height, diameter, radius, degree, base. Accuracy CAP 100%. |
| Vocabulary | 3i | Identify dimensions vocabulary meanings: length, width, height, diameter, radius, degree, base. Accuracy CAP 100%. |
| Vocabulary | 2a | Produce elements-of-shapes vocabulary meanings: line, line segment, ray, angle, arc, point. Accuracy CAP 100%. |
| Vocabulary | 2i | Identify elements-of-shapes vocabulary meanings: line, line segment, ray, angle, arc, point. Accuracy CAP 100%. |
| Vocabulary | 1a | Produce geometric-shapes vocabulary meanings: circle, square, rectangle, triangle, trapezoid, parallelogram, pentagon, hexagon, octagon, cone, cylinder, oval. Accuracy CAP 100%. |
| Vocabulary | 1i | Identify geometric-shapes vocabulary meanings: circle, square, rectangle, triangle, trapezoid, parallelogram, pentagon, hexagon, octagon, cone, cylinder, oval. Accuracy CAP 100%. |

**Metric Measurement: Linear, Weight, and Capacity**

| Content | Number | Objective (Mastery CAP is in rate per minute) |
|---|---|---|
| Knowledge | 11a | Produce abbreviations for weight units: gram, kilogram, centigram, decigram, decagram, milligram, hectogram. Accuracy CAP 100%. |
| Knowledge | 10a | Produce abbreviations for capacity units: centiliter, milliliter, deciliter, hectoliter, decaliter, liter. Accuracy CAP 100%. |
| Knowledge | 9a | Produce abbreviations for linear units: millimeter, kilometer, hectometer, centimeter, decameter, decimeter, meter. Accuracy CAP 100%. |
| Knowledge | 8a | Produce meanings of metric prefixes: milli-, centi-, deci-, deca-, hecto-, kilo-. Accuracy CAP 100%. |
| Tools | 7a | Use measuring tools to measure to nearest correct unit: millimeter, centimeter. Accuracy CAP 100%. |
| Tools | 6i | Match linear tool to task: ruler, meterstick, tape measure, degree protractor, and rolling meter counter. Accuracy CAP 100%. |
| Tools | 5i | Identify capacity tool for task: milliliter, liter. Accuracy CAP 100%. |
| Tools | 4i | Identify weight tool for task: variety of scales. Accuracy CAP 100%. |
| Vocabulary | 3a | Produce meaning of key vocabulary for weight measurement: heavy, heavier, heaviest, light, lighter, lightest, weight. Accuracy CAP 100%. |
| Vocabulary | 3i | Identify meaning of key vocabulary for weight measurement: heavy, heavier, light, lighter. Accuracy CAP 100%. |
| Vocabulary | 2a | Produce meaning of key vocabulary for liquid and dry measurement: full, fuller, fullest, empty, emptier, emptiest, more, less. Accuracy CAP 100%. |
| Vocabulary | 2i | Identify meaning of key vocabulary for liquid and dry measurement: full, fuller, fullest, empty, more, less. Accuracy CAP 100%. |
| Vocabulary | 1a | Produce meaning of key vocabulary for linear measurement: height, width, depth, length, long, longer, longest, short, shorter, shortest, deep, deeper, deepest, high, higher, highest, tall, taller, tallest, narrow, narrower, narrowest, wide, wider, widest, shallow, distance. Accuracy CAP 100%. |
| Vocabulary | 1i | Identify meaning of key vocabulary for linear measurement: long, longer, longest, shorter, deepest, taller, narrow, wider. Accuracy CAP 100%. |

Objectives, continued

| Content | Number | Objective (Mastery CAP is in rate per minute) |
|---|---|---|

**Customary Measurement: Linear, Weight, and Capacity**

| | | |
|---|---|---|
| Knowledge | 13a | Produce abbreviations for weight units: ounces, pounds, tons. Accuracy CAP 100%. |
| Knowledge | 12a | Produce abbreviations for capacity units: teaspoon, cup, pint, quart, gallon. Accuracy CAP 100%. |
| Knowledge | 11a | Produce abbreviations for linear units: inch, foot, yard. Accuracy CAP 100%. |
| Knowledge | 10a | Produce weight unit equivalents: ounces, pounds, tons. Accuracy CAP 100%. |
| Knowledge | 9a | Produce capacity unit equivalents: teaspoons, tablespoons, cups, pints, quarts, and gallons. Accuracy CAP 100%. |
| Knowledge | 8a | Produce linear unit equivalents: inches, feet, yards, miles. Accuracy CAP 100%. |
| Tools | 7a | Measure to nearest correct unit ($1/8$ in., $1/4$ in., $1/2$ in., foot, yard), using the following tools: ruler, yardstick, degree protractor, tape measure, and rolling yard measure. Accuracy CAP 100%. |
| Tools | 6i | Match linear tool to task: ruler, yardstick, degree protractor, rolling yard measure, tape measure. Accuracy CAP 100%. |
| Tools | 5i | Match capacity tool to task: teaspoon, tablespoon, cup, pint, quart, and gallon. Accuracy CAP 100%. |
| Tools | 4i | Match weight tool to task: ounces, pounds, tons. Accuracy CAP 100%. |
| Vocabulary | 3a | Produce meaning of key vocabulary for weight measurement: heavy, heavier, heaviest, light, lighter, lightest weight. Accuracy CAP 100%. |
| Vocabulary | 3i | Identify meaning of key vocabulary for weight measurement: heavy, heavier, light, lighter. Accuracy CAP 100%. |
| Vocabulary | 2a | Produce meaning of key vocabulary for liquid and dry measurement: full, fuller, fullest, empty, emptier, emptiest, more, less. Accuracy CAP 100%. |
| Vocabulary | 2i | Identify meaning of key vocabulary for liquid and dry measurement: full, fuller, fullest, empty, more, less. Accuracy CAP 100%. |
| Vocabulary | 1a | Produce meaning of key vocabulary for linear measurement: height, width, depth, length, long, longer, longest, short, shorter, shortest, deep, deeper, deepest, high, higher, highest, tall, taller, tallest, narrow, narrower, narrowest, wide, wider, widest, shallow, distance. Accuracy CAP 100%. |
| Vocabulary | 1i | Identify meaning of key vocabulary for linear measurement: long, longer, longest, shorter, deepest, taller, narrow, wider. Accuracy CAP 100%. |

**Problem Solving**

| | | |
|---|---|---|
| Apply Knowledge | 7a | Check solution to problems using functional algorithm. Accuracy CAP 100%. |
| Apply Knowledge | 6a | Estimate correct answer to word problems. Accuracy CAP 100%. |
| Apply Knowledge | 5i | Identify correct equation to solve word problems. Accuracy CAP 100%. |
| Apply Knowledge | 4a | Recognize missing information in word problems. Accuracy CAP 100%. |
| Apply Knowledge | 3a | Recognize essential and non-essential information in word problems. Accuracy CAP 100%. |
| Apply Knowledge | 2a | Restate word problems in own words. Accuracy CAP 100%. |
| Vocabulary | 1a | Match operation name to key vocabulary words and phrases. Accuracy CAP 100%. |

# COMPUTATION ANALYSIS

This appendix contains a list of all computation items appearing on the survey tests found in Howell (et. al. 2000a). Next to the item numbers you will find the objective for that item and a list of subskills.

The prerequisite column in this grid contains the objective numbers of subskills selected in conformity with the standards set down in the "Rules for Developing Assumed Causes." When a student fails an item on the survey test, these prerequisites should be checked. The prerequisites in the table are those most likely to lead to instructionally relevant teaching decisions.

The basic assumption of the task analysis model is that any task is composed of a task strategy and a set of essential subtasks. If a student cannot complete a task, it is assumed that she lacks an essential subskill or cannot carry out the strategy. Strategies are the procedures by which the subtasks are combined to produce the task. In mathematics these strategies are referred to as algorithms, although the term strategy should connote more than a series of operational steps. Strategies are the organizational devices that teachers teach to students so they can pull operational knowledge and subtask knowledge together for task completion. No matter how good the instruction is, a student cannot carry out a strategy if he cannot carry out the subtasks that the strategy is to combine. Similarly, a student who can carry out all essential subtasks in isolation must know the strategy for organizing them in order to succeed at a task. An evaluator first needs to find out if a student can do a task. Next, he/she needs to check the student's use of subtasks and strategies. Here are the closest subtasks for Fraction Objective 20a:

"Multiply two mixed numerals on an untimed probe sheet with 100% accuracy."

Task-Specific Subskills.

A. Multiplying fractions with conversion to simplest form (Fraction Objective 19a)
B. Multiplication facts (Multiplication Objective 1m)
C. Converting mixed numbers into mixed numbers with improper fractions (Fraction Objective 10a)
D. Producing the least common denominator of two simple fractions (Fraction Objective 6a)

If a student cannot pass objective 20a, then the evaluator should check the subskills of 20a, beginning with those listed. If the student passes the subskills, the assumption is that he cannot use the strategy. If a teacher is teaching at the correct level of difficulty, she has verified subskill adequacy and is teaching strategies.

**Computation Analysis**

| Survey Test Item | Full Objective | Prerequisites from Appendix 12.3.A |
|---|---|---|
| **Addition** | | |
| 1–3 | 1a. Addition facts (0–20), Accuracy CAP 100%. | add 1i, pre 5m, pre 9i, p 7i, p 21a, r 12m |
| | 1m. Addition facts (0–20), Mastery CAP 80 digits correct with zero errors. | add 1a, pre 14m, pre 9i, pre 7i, pre 12m |
| 4–5 | 2a. Add zero or __ to one-digit addend, Accuracy CAP 100%. | add 1m, add 1a, add 9i, pre 7i |
| 6–7 | 3a. Add three or more one-digit addends in a column, Accuracy CAP 100%. | add 2a, add 1m |
| 8–9 | 4a. Add one-digit addend to two-digit addend without regrouping, Accuracy CAP 100%. | 3a, Add 2a 1m |
| 10–11 | 5a. Add one-digit addend to two-digit addend with regrouping, Accuracy CAP 100%. | 3a add 1m 1a 2a |

**Computation Analysis, continued**

| Survey Test Item | Full Objective | Prerequisites from Appendix 12.3.A |
|---|---|---|
| | 5m. Add one-digit addend to two-digit addend with regrouping, Mastery CAP is 70 digits correct with zero errors. | add 5a, add 4a, add 3a, add 1m |
| 12–14 | 6a. Add two-digit addends without regrouping, Accuracy CAP 100%. | add 4a, add 3a, add 1m |
| 15–17 | 7a. Add two-digit addends with or without regrouping, Accuracy CAP 100%. | add 6a, add 5m, add 1m |
| 18–20 | 8a. Add two or more addends with three or more digits with or without regrouping, Accuracy CAP 100%. | add 7a, add 6a, add 5m, add 1m |

**Subtraction**

| Survey Test Item | Full Objective | Prerequisites from Appendix 12.3.A |
|---|---|---|
| 1–5 | 1a. Subtraction facts (0–20), Accuracy CAP 100%. | subtraction 1i<br>prereq. 14m<br>prereq. 10i |
| | 1m. Subtraction facts (0–20), Mastery CAP is 80 digits correct with zero errors. | subtraction 1a<br>prereq. 10i<br>prereq. 7i |
| 6 | 2a. Subtract a one-digit number from a two-digit number without regrouping, Accuracy CAP 100%. | subtraction 2i<br>subtraction 1m |
| | 2m. Subtract a one-digit number from a two-digit number without regrouping, Mastery CAP is 70 digits correct with zero errors. | subtraction 2a<br>subtraction 1m |
| 7–9 | 3a. Subtract a two-digit number ending in zero from a two-digit number ending in zero, Accuracy CAP 100%. | subtraction 2m<br>subtraction 1m |
| 10–12 | 4a. Subtract a one-digit number from a two-digit number with regrouping. | subtraction 2m<br>subtraction 1m |
| | 4m. Subtract a one-digit number from a two-digit number with regrouping, Mastery CAP is 60 digits correct with zero errors. | subtraction 4a<br>subtraction 3a<br>subtraction 2m<br>subtraction 1m |
| 13–15 | 5a. Subtract a two-digit number from a two-digit number without regrouping, Accuracy CAP 100%. | subtraction 2m<br>subtraction 1m |
| 16–17 | 6a. Subtract a two-digit number from a two-digit number with regrouping, Accuracy CAP 100%. | subtraction 5a<br>subtraction 4m<br>subtraction 1m |
| 16–17 | 6m. Subtract a two-digit number from a two-digit number with regrouping, Mastery CAP is 40 digits correct with zero errors. | subtraction 6a<br>subtraction 5a<br>subtraction 4m<br>subtraction 1m |
| 18–20 | 7a. Subtract a two-or-more-digit number from a three-or-more-digit number with or without regrouping, Accuracy CAP 100%. | subtraction 6m<br>subtraction 6a<br>subtraction 5a<br>subtraction 4m |

**Multiplication**

| Survey Test Item | Full Objective | Prerequisites from Appendix 12.3.A |
|---|---|---|
| 1–3 | 1a. Multiplication facts (0–10), Accuracy CAP 100%. | division 1a<br>multiplication 1i<br>addition 1a<br>prerequisite 18a |

| | | |
|---|---|---|
| | 1m. Multiplication facts (0–10), Mastery CAP is 80 digits correct with zero errors. | multiplication 1a<br>division 1m<br>addition 1m |
| 4–5 | 2a. Multiply a two-digit number by a one-digit number without regrouping, Accuracy CAP 100%. | multiplication 1m and 1a<br>division 1m<br>addition 1m |
| | 2m. Multiply a two-digit number by a one-digit number without regrouping, Mastery CAP 40 digits correct with zero errors. | multiplication 2a<br>multiplication 1m |
| 6–7 | 3a. Multiply a two-digit number by a one-digit number with regrouping, Accuracy CAP 100%. | multiplication 2m<br>multiplication 1m |
| | 3m. Multiply a two-digit number by a one-digit number with regrouping, Mastery CAP 30 digits correct with zero errors. | multiplication 3a<br>multiplication 2m<br>multiplication 1m |
| 8–9 | 4a. Multiply a two-digit number by a two-digit number with or without regrouping, Accuracy CAP 100%. | multiplication 3m<br>multiplication 2m<br>multiplication 1m |
| | 4m. Multiply a two-digit number by a two-digit number with or without regrouping, Mastery CAP 40 digits correct with zero errors. | multiplication 4a<br>multiplication 3m<br>multiplication 1m |
| 10–12 | 5a. Multiply by 1, 10, 100, 1000, Accuracy CAP 100%. | division 5a<br>multiplication 4m<br>multiplication 1m |
| 13–15 | 6a. Multiply multi-digit problems with zeros as placeholders, Accuracy CAP 100%. | division 6a<br>multiplication 5a<br>multiplication 5m<br>multiplication 1m |
| 16–18 | 7a. Multiply a number containing two or more digits by another containing two or more digits with or without regrouping, Accuracy CAP 100%. | multiplication 6a<br>multiplication 4m<br>multiplication 3m<br>multiplication 1m |
| 19–20 | 8a. Produce squares of numbers (0–12), Accuracy CAP 100%. | division 7a<br>multiplication 8i<br>multiplication 1m |
| | Mastery CAP 40 digits correct with zero errors. | multiplication 8a<br>multiplication 1m |

**Division**

| | | |
|---|---|---|
| 1–5 | 1a. Division facts (0–10), Accuracy CAP 100%. | division 1i<br>multiplication 1a<br>subtraction 1a |
| | 1m. Division facts (0–10), Mastery CAP 80 digits correct with zero errors. | division 1a<br>multiplication 1m<br>subtraction 1m |
| 6–8 | 2a. Divide a two-digit number by a one-digit number to get a two-digit answer without a remainder, Accuracy CAP 100%. | division 1m<br>multiplication 1m<br>subtraction 1m |
| | 2m. Divide a two-digit number by a one-digit number to get a two-digit answer without a remainder, Mastery CAP 40 digits correct with zero errors. | division 2a<br>division 1m |
| 9–10 | 3a. Divide a two-digit number by a one-digit number to get a one- or two-digit answer with a remainder, Accuracy CAP 100%. | division 2m<br>division 1m |
| | 3m. Divide a two-digit number by a one-digit number to get a one- or two-digit | division 3a<br>division 2m |

B-5.4

## Computation Analysis, continued

| Survey Test Item | Full Objective | Prerequisites from Appendix 12.3.A |
|---|---|---|
| | answer with a remainder, Mastery CAP 40 digits correct. | division 1m |
| 11–12 | 4a. Divide a two-or-more-digit number to get an answer with or without a remainder, Accuracy CAP 100%. | multiplication 4a<br>division 3m<br>division 1m<br>prerequisite 17a |
| 13–15 | 5a. Divide a two-or-more-digit number by 1, 10, 100, 1000 to get answers without decimals, Accuracy CAP 100%. | multiplication 5a<br>division 3m<br>division 1m<br>prerequisite 17a |
| 16–18 | 6a. Divide a two-or-more-digit number with zero as a place holder to get answers with or without remainders, Accuracy CAP 100%. | division 4a<br>division 3m<br>division 1m<br>prerequisite 16a<br>prerequisite 17a |
| 19–20 | 7a. Produce the square root of a number in which the answer is 0–12, Accuracy CAP 100%. | multiplication 8a<br>division 7i<br>division 1m |
| | 7m. Produce the square root of a number in which the answer is 0–12, Mastery CAP 40 digits correct with zero errors. | multiplication 8m<br>division 7a<br>division 1m |

165

# SURVEY-LEVEL TESTING

**Test 1: Addition Objective 1m**

Practice Items:

| 7 | 10 | 3 | 5 |
|---|----|---|---|
| + 7 | + 2 | +17 | + 5 |
| *16* | *12* | *20* | *10* |

| | | | | | | | | | | | | |
|---|---|---|---|---|---|---|---|---|---|---|---|---|
| 16 | 20 | 7 | 12 | 9 | 1 | 2 | 0 | 15 | 9 | 3 | 17 | Digit count (21) |
| + 2 | + 0 | + 2 | + 6 | + 1 | + 8 | +18 | +10 | + 5 | + 7 | + 6 | + 1 | |
| *18* | *20* | *9* | *18* | *10* | *9* | *20* | *10* | *20* | *16* | *9* | *18* | |
| | | | | | | | | | | | | Facts 11–20 |
| 8 | 11 | 15 | 1 | 17 | 8 | 1 | 3 | 3 | 4 | 2 | 10 | |
| + 4 | + 9 | + 4 | + 8 | + 2 | + 5 | + 6 | +17 | + 3 | +16 | + 5 | +10 | |
| *12* | *20* | *19* | *9* | *19* | *13* | *7* | *20* | *6* | *20* | *7* | *20* | (41) |
| | | | | | | | | | | | | Facts 0–10 |
| 8 | 6 | 14 | 13 | 2 | 19 | 1 | 10 | 4 | 2 | 14 | 4 | |
| +11 | + 9 | + 5 | + 7 | + 4 | + 0 | + 8 | + 6 | +11 | + 7 | + 3 | + 9 | |
| *19* | *15* | *19* | *20* | *6* | *19* | *9* | *16* | *15* | *9* | *17* | *9* | (61) |
| | | | | | | | | | | | | Facts 0–10 |
| 7 | 0 | 5 | 0 | 3 | 4 | 18 | 5 | 2 | 12 | 9 | 1 | |
| +13 | +19 | + 1 | +20 | +17 | + 5 | + 1 | + 2 | + 3 | + 5 | + 0 | +19 | |
| *20* | *19* | *6* | *20* | *20* | *9* | *19* | *7* | *5* | *17* | *9* | *20* | (80) |
| | | | | | | | | | | | | Facts 0–20 |
| 8 | 20 | 3 | 10 | 1 | 14 | 8 | 19 | 4 | 7 | 12 | 2 | |
| + 5 | + 0 | +15 | +10 | +13 | + 5 | + 0 | + 1 | + 5 | + 2 | + 4 | + 9 | |
| *13* | *20* | *18* | *20* | *14* | *19* | *8* | *20* | *9* | *9* | *16* | *11* | (101) |
| | | | | | | | | | | | | Facts 0–10 |
| 10 | 5 | 18 | 6 | 9 | 16 | 7 | 4 | 2 | 6 | 0 | 14 | |
| +10 | + 6 | + 2 | +12 | + 1 | + 2 | +11 | + 1 | +17 | + 3 | + 9 | + 3 | |
| *20* | *11* | *20* | *18* | *10* | *18* | *18* | *5* | *19* | *9* | *9* | *17* | (122) |
| *Facts 0–10* | *Facts 0–10* | *Facts 11–20* | *Facts 11–20* | *Facts 0–10* | *Facts 11–20* | *Facts 11–20* | *Facts 0–10* | *Facts 11–20* | *Facts 0–10* | *Facts 0–10* | *Facts 11–20* | |

*Objective: Addition facts (0–10). Mastery CAP: 80 digits correct with zero errors.*

*Source:* From Howell, K. W., Zucker, S. H., & Morehead, M. K. (2000b) *Multilevel Academic Skills Inventory.* Reprinted with permission.

B-5.5

**Test 2: Subtraction Objective 1m**

Practice Items:

| 10 | 17 | 19 | 9 |
|---|---|---|---|
| − 7 | − 8 | −12 | − 2 |
| 3 | 9 | 7 | 7 |

| | | | | | | | | | | | | | | Digit count |
|---|---|---|---|---|---|---|---|---|---|---|---|---|---|---|
| 12 | 2 | 19 | 6 | 16 | 3 | 13 | 1 | 20 | 10 | 15 | 4 | 11 | 0 | |
| −10 | − 2 | − 5 | − 5 | − 3 | − 3 | − 6 | − 1 | − 9 | − 8 | − 9 | − 1 | − 8 | − 0 | |
| 2 | 0 | 14 | 1 | 13 | 0 | 7 | 0 | 11 | 2 | 6 | 3 | 3 | 0 | Facts (16) 0–10 |
| 7 | 17 | 10 | 15 | 9 | 13 | 5 | 19 | 8 | 14 | 7 | 13 | 6 | 14 | |
| − 3 | −12 | − 9 | − 4 | − 6 | − 8 | − 2 | −13 | − 1 | − 3 | − 5 | −11 | − 5 | − 9 | |
| 4 | 5 | 1 | 11 | 3 | 5 | 3 | 6 | 7 | 11 | 2 | 2 | 1 | 5 | Facts (32) 11–20 |
| 17 | 1 | 20 | 0 | 18 | 9 | 20 | 4 | 12 | 2 | 20 | 3 | 15 | 8 | |
| −14 | − 0 | − 8 | − 0 | −11 | − 2 | −10 | − 4 | −10 | − 1 | −16 | − 2 | −13 | − 4 | |
| 3 | 1 | 12 | 0 | 7 | 7 | 10 | 0 | 2 | 1 | 4 | 1 | 2 | 4 | Facts (48) 0–10 |
| 3 | 18 | 9 | 13 | 5 | 11 | 7 | 15 | 10 | 17 | 7 | 12 | 1 | 19 | |
| − 1 | −10 | − 2 | − 3 | − 2 | −10 | − 2 | −12 | − 6 | − 5 | − 7 | − 8 | − 1 | −12 | |
| 2 | 8 | 7 | 10 | 3 | 1 | 5 | 3 | 4 | 12 | 0 | 4 | 0 | 7 | Facts (64) 11–20 |
| 12 | 2 | 16 | 3 | 16 | 4 | 14 | 0 | 18 | 5 | 11 | 6 | 16 | 8 | |
| − 8 | − 0 | −12 | − 0 | − 4 | − 3 | − 3 | − 0 | −10 | − 5 | − 7 | − 0 | − 9 | − 3 | |
| 4 | 2 | 4 | 3 | 12 | 1 | 11 | 0 | 8 | 0 | 4 | 6 | 7 | 5 | Facts (80) 0–10 |
| 4 | 15 | 0 | 20 | 8 | 17 | 2 | 18 | 9 | 19 | 6 | 14 | 0 | 11 | |
| − 1 | − 3 | − 0 | −12 | − 4 | − 6 | − 1 | −13 | − 6 | − 7 | − 2 | − 3 | − 0 | − 1 | |
| 3 | 12 | 0 | 8 | 4 | 11 | 1 | 5 | 3 | 12 | 4 | 11 | 0 | 10 | Facts (99) 11–20 |
| 16 | 5 | 13 | 10 | 18 | 9 | 15 | 7 | 12 | 6 | 11 | 5 | 17 | 2 | |
| − 9 | − 3 | − 2 | − 0 | − 6 | − 2 | − 3 | − 1 | − 2 | − 3 | − 0 | − 5 | − 2 | − 0 | |
| 7 | 2 | 11 | 10 | 12 | 7 | 12 | 6 | 10 | 3 | 11 | 0 | 15 | 2 | Facts (120) 0–10 |

Facts 11–20  Facts 0–10  Facts 11–20  Facts 0–10  Facts 11–20  Facts 0–10  Facts 11–20  Facts 0–10  Facts 11–20  Facts 0–10  Facts 11–20  Facts 0–10  Facts 11–20

Objective: Subtraction facts (0–20). Mastery CAP: 80 digits correct with zero errors.

Source: From Howell, K. W., Zucker, S. H., & Morehead, M. K. (2000b) *Multilevel Academic Skills Inventory*. Reprinted with permission.

B-5.5

**Test 3: Multiplication Objective 1m**

Practice Items

| | | | |
|---|---|---|---|
| 4 ×3 = 12 | 3 ×7 = 21 | 9 ×8 = 72 | 5 ×6 = 30 |

| | | | | | | | | | | | | |
|---|---|---|---|---|---|---|---|---|---|---|---|---|
| 1 ×6 = 6 | 5 ×8 = 40 | 8 ×9 = 72 | 2 ×2 = 4 | 4 ×7 = 28 | 0 ×3 = 0 | 1 ×1 = 1 | 7 ×0 = 0 | 6 ×4 = 24 | 8 ×5 = 40 | 9 ×10 = 90 | 7 ×7 = 49 | |
| 8 ×10 = 80 | 3 ×6 = 18 | 8 ×8 = 48 | 9 ×9 = 81 | 7 ×2 = 14 | 6 ×7 = 42 | 2 ×3 = 6 | 4 ×1 = 4 | 5 ×0 = 0 | 3 ×4 = 12 | 5 ×5 = 25 | 2 ×10 = 20 | 7s |
| 3 ×5 = 15 | 1 ×10 = 10 | 4 ×6 = 24 | 7 ×8 = 56 | 3 ×9 = 27 | 6 ×2 = 12 | 5 ×7 = 35 | 9 ×3 = 27 | 6 ×1 = 6 | 4 ×0 = 0 | 9 ×4 = 36 | 3 ×5 = 15 | 10s |
| 4 ×4 = 16 | 7 ×5 = 35 | 0 ×10 = 0 | 6 ×6 = 36 | 2 ×8 = 16 | 6 ×9 = 54 | 9 ×2 = 18 | 8 ×7 = 56 | 7 ×3 = 21 | 9 ×1 = 9 | 1 ×0 = 0 | 4 ×4 = 16 | 5s |
| 6 ×0 = 0 | 5 ×4 = 20 | 6 ×5 = 30 | 5 ×10 = 50 | 7 ×6 = 42 | 3 ×8 = 24 | 1 ×9 = 9 | 5 ×2 = 10 | 2 ×7 = 14 | 8 ×3 = 24 | 5 ×1 = 5 | 0 ×0 = 0 | 4s |
| 2 ×1 = 2 | 3 ×0 = 0 | 7 ×4 = 28 | 9 ×5 = 45 | 7 ×10 = 70 | 9 ×6 = 54 | 8 ×8 = 64 | 4 ×9 = 36 | 4 ×2 = 8 | 1 ×7 = 7 | 5 ×3 = 15 | 3 ×1 = 3 | 0s |
| 0s | 4s | 5s | 10s | 6s | 8s | 9s | 2s | 7s | 3s | 1s | 0s | |

Objective: Multiplication facts (0–10). Mastery CAP: 80 digits correct with zero errors.

Source: From Howell, K. W., Zucker, S. H., & Morehead, M. K. (2000b) Multilevel Academic Skills Inventory. Reprinted with permission.

168

## Test 4: Division Objective 1m

| Practice Items | | | | $2\overline{)4}$ | $3\overline{)12}$ | $6\overline{)24}$ | $8\overline{)16}$ |
|---|---|---|---|---|---|---|---|
| | | | | $^2$ | $^4$ | $^4$ | $^2$ |

| | | | | | | | | | Digit count |
|---|---|---|---|---|---|---|---|---|---|
| $5\overline{)25}$ $^5$ | $4\overline{)36}$ $^9$ | $7\overline{)49}$ $^7$ | $6\overline{)48}$ $^8$ | $2\overline{)2}$ $^1$ | $8\overline{)0}$ $^0$ | $9\overline{)9}$ $^1$ | $5\overline{)0}$ $^0$ | $1\overline{)1}$ $^1$ | (9) |
| $3\overline{)30}$ $^{10}$ | $5\overline{)45}$ $^9$ | $4\overline{)4}$ $^1$ | $7\overline{)63}$ $^9$ | $6\overline{)60}$ $^{10}$ | $2\overline{)8}$ $^4$ | $8\overline{)64}$ $^8$ | $9\overline{)64}$ $^6$ | $5\overline{)30}$ $^6$ | (20) |
| $1\overline{)9}$ $^9$ | $3\overline{)27}$ $^9$ | $5\overline{)35}$ $^7$ | $4\overline{)20}$ $^5$ | $7\overline{)56}$ $^8$ | $6\overline{)54}$ $^9$ | $2\overline{)6}$ $^3$ | $8\overline{)40}$ $^5$ | $9\overline{)81}$ $^9$ | 5s (29) |
| $10\overline{)90}$ $^9$ | $1\overline{)10}$ $^{10}$ | $3\overline{)21}$ $^7$ | $5\overline{)40}$ $^8$ | $4\overline{)16}$ $^4$ | $7\overline{)42}$ $^6$ | $6\overline{)6}$ $^1$ | $2\overline{)10}$ $^5$ | $8\overline{)16}$ $^2$ | 9s (39) |
| $9\overline{)27}$ $^3$ | $10\overline{)50}$ $^5$ | $1\overline{)2}$ $^2$ | $3\overline{)15}$ $^5$ | $5\overline{)20}$ $^4$ | $4\overline{)40}$ $^{10}$ | $7\overline{)35}$ $^5$ | $6\overline{)0}$ $^0$ | $2\overline{)14}$ $^7$ | 8s (49) |
| $8\overline{)24}$ $^3$ | $9\overline{)18}$ $^2$ | $10\overline{)30}$ $^3$ | $1\overline{)4}$ $^4$ | $3\overline{)9}$ $^3$ | $5\overline{)15}$ $^3$ | $4\overline{)32}$ $^8$ | $7\overline{)21}$ $^3$ | $6\overline{)6}$ $^1$ | 2s (58) |
| $2\overline{)16}$ $^8$ | $8\overline{)48}$ $^6$ | $9\overline{)36}$ $^4$ | $10\overline{)40}$ $^4$ | $1\overline{)3}$ $^3$ | $3\overline{)18}$ $^6$ | $5\overline{)10}$ $^2$ | $4\overline{)24}$ $^6$ | $7\overline{)28}$ $^4$ | 6s (67) |
| $6\overline{)18}$ $^3$ | $2\overline{)18}$ $^9$ | $8\overline{)56}$ $^7$ | $9\overline{)63}$ $^7$ | $10\overline{)80}$ $^8$ | $1\overline{)6}$ $^6$ | $3\overline{)24}$ $^8$ | $5\overline{)5}$ $^1$ | $4\overline{)28}$ $^7$ | 7s (76) |
| $7\overline{)14}$ $^2$ | $6\overline{)24}$ $^4$ | $2\overline{)20}$ $^{10}$ | $8\overline{)32}$ $^4$ | $9\overline{)45}$ $^5$ | $10\overline{)70}$ $^7$ | $1\overline{)5}$ $^5$ | $3\overline{)12}$ $^4$ | $5\overline{)50}$ $^{10}$ | 4s (87) |
| $4\overline{)8}$ $^2$ | $7\overline{)7}$ $^1$ | $6\overline{)30}$ $^5$ | $2\overline{)0}$ $^0$ | $8\overline{)72}$ $^9$ | $9\overline{)90}$ $^{10}$ | $10\overline{)20}$ $^2$ | $1\overline{)8}$ $^8$ | $3\overline{)6}$ $^2$ | 5s (96) |
| 7s | 6s | 2s | 8s | 9s | 10s | 1s | 3s | | |

Objective: Division facts (0–10). Mastery CAP: 80 digits correct with zero errors.

Source: From Howell, K. W., Zucker, S. H., & Morehead, M. K. (2000b) *Multilevel Academic Skills Inventory.* Reprinted with permission.

B-5.5

## Test 5: Addition Survey Test

| 1. (1,1)  | 2. (1,1)  | 3. (1,1)  | 4. (2,1)  | 5. (2,1)  |
|-----------|-----------|-----------|-----------|-----------|
| 8         | 13        | 5         | 1         | 0         |
| +7        | + 6       | +6        | +0        | +3        |
| 15        | 19        | 11        | 1         | 3         |

| 6. (3,2)  | 7. (3,2)  | 8. (4,2)  | 9. (4,2)  | 10. (5,2) |
|-----------|-----------|-----------|-----------|-----------|
| 7         | 9         | 64        | 43        | 32        |
| 2         | 3         | +2        | +5        | +8        |
| +2        | +4        | 66        | 48        | 40        |
| 11        | 16        |           |           |           |

| 11. (5,2) | 12. (6,2) | 13. (6,2) | 14. (6,2) | 15. (7,3) |
|-----------|-----------|-----------|-----------|-----------|
| 47        | 31        | 70        | 22        | 18        |
| + 9       | +24       | +19       | +53       | + 96      |
| 56        | 55        | 89        | 75        | 114       |

| 16. (7,3) | 17. (7,3) | 18. (8,3) | 19. (8,4) | 20. (8,4) |
|-----------|-----------|-----------|-----------|-----------|
| 95        | 48        | 569       | 4020      | 283       |
| +25       | +37       | 201       | + 689     | 21        |
| 120       | 85        | +877      | 4709      | +2764     |
|           |           | 1647      |           | 3068      |

## Test 6: Subtraction Survey Test

| 1. (1,1)  | 2. (1,1)  | 3. (1,1)  | 4. (1,1)  | 5. (1,1)  |
|-----------|-----------|-----------|-----------|-----------|
| 3         | 16        | 10        | 14        | 19        |
| −2        | − 7       | − 4       | − 5       | − 2       |
| 1         | 9         | 6         | 9         | 17        |

| 6. (2,2)  | 7. (3,2)  | 8. (3,2)  | 9. (3,2)  | 10. (4,2) |
|-----------|-----------|-----------|-----------|-----------|
| 68        | 50        | 40        | 60        | 80        |
| − 5       | −10       | −30       | −60       | − 5       |
| 63        | 40        | 10        | 0         | 75        |

| 11. (4,2) | 12. (4,2) | 13. (5,2) | 14. (5,2) | 15. (5,2) |
|-----------|-----------|-----------|-----------|-----------|
| 23        | 63        | 93        | 58        | 46        |
| − 6       | − 9       | −61       | −23       | −13       |
| 17        | 54        | 32        | 35        | 33        |

| 16. (6,3) | 17. (6,3) | 18. (7,4) | 19. (7,4) | 20. (7,4) |
|-----------|-----------|-----------|-----------|-----------|
| 53        | 64        | 8942      | 400       | 5906      |
| −29       | −27       | −5961     | −165      | − 248     |
| 24        | 37        | 2981      | 235       | 5658      |

*Source:* From Howell, K. W., Zucker, S. H., & Morehead, M. K. (2000b) *Multilevel Academic Skills Inventory.* Reprinted with permission.

B-5.5

## Test 7: Multiplication Survey Test

1. (1,4)
$$\begin{array}{r}2\\ \times 6\\ \hline 12\end{array}$$

2. (1,4)
$$\begin{array}{r}9\\ \times 5\\ \hline 45\end{array}$$

3. (1,4)
$$\begin{array}{r}8\\ \times 3\\ \hline 24\end{array}$$

4. (2,4)
$$\begin{array}{r}64\\ \times 7\\ \hline 448\end{array}$$

5. (2,4)
$$\begin{array}{r}24\\ \times 3\\ \hline 72\end{array}$$

6. (2,4)
$$\begin{array}{r}91\\ \times 1\\ \hline 91\end{array}$$

7. (3,4)
$$\begin{array}{r}18\\ \times 9\\ \hline 162\end{array}$$

8. (4,4)
$$\begin{array}{r}22\\ \times 86\\ \hline 1892\end{array}$$

9. (4,4)
$$\begin{array}{r}85\\ \times 63\\ \hline 5355\end{array}$$

10. (5,5)
$194 \times 10 = 1940$

11. (5,5)
$3 \times 1000 = 3000$

12. (5,5)
$100 \times 74 = 7400$

13. (6,4)
$$\begin{array}{r}102\\ \times 40\\ \hline 4080\end{array}$$

14. (6,4)
$$\begin{array}{r}40\\ \times 31\\ \hline 1240\end{array}$$

15. (6,5)
$$\begin{array}{r}7005\\ \times 26\\ \hline 182130\end{array}$$

16. (7,4)
$$\begin{array}{r}87\\ \times 25\\ \hline 2175\end{array}$$

17. (7,4)
$$\begin{array}{r}215\\ \times 48\\ \hline 10320\end{array}$$

18. (7,5)
$$\begin{array}{r}5684\\ \times 39\\ \hline 221676\end{array}$$

19. (8,8)
$5^2 = 25$

20. (8,8)
$12^2 = 144$

## Test 8: Division Survey Test

1. (1,4)
$2\overline{)4}$  quotient $2$

2. (1,4)
$7\overline{)56}$  quotient $8$

3. (1,4)
$9\overline{)54}$  quotient $6$

4. (1,4)
$10\overline{)90}$  quotient $9$

5. (1,4)
$8\overline{)32}$  quotient $4$

6. (2,4)
$3\overline{)72}$  quotient $24$

7. (2,4)
$5\overline{)80}$  quotient $16$

8. (2,4)
$7\overline{)91}$  quotient $13$

9. (3,4)
$5\overline{)23}$  quotient $.6$ , $4\ r\ 3$

10. (3,4)
$9\overline{)37}$  quotient $.11$ , $4\ r\ 1$

11. (4,4)
$7\overline{)169}$  quotient $.14$ , $24\ r\ 1$

12. (4,5)
$58\overline{)1209}$  quotient $.84$ , $20\ r\ 49$

13. (5,5)
$100\overline{)4200}$  quotient $42$

14. (5,5)
$10\overline{)1260}$  quotient $126$

15. (5,5)
$1\overline{)48}$  quotient $48$

16. (6,5)
$8\overline{)8500}$  quotient $.5$ , $1062\ r\ 4$

17. (6,5)
$31\overline{)1307}$  quotient $.16$ , $42\ r\ 5$

18. (6,5)
$15\overline{)306}$  quotient $.4$ , $20\ r\ 6$

19. (7,8)
$\sqrt{4}$  $2$

20. (7,8)
$\sqrt{121}$  $11$

*Source:* From Howell, K. W., Zucker, S. H., & Morehead, M. K. (2000b) *Multilevel Academic Skills Inventory.* Reprinted with permission.

## Test 9: Fractions Survey Test

1. (4,5)
$$1 = \frac{10}{10}$$

2. (8,5)
$$\frac{2}{8} = \frac{1}{4}$$

3. (9,5)
$$\frac{7}{3} = 2\frac{1}{3}$$

4. (13.5)
$$\frac{1}{8} + \frac{3}{8} = \frac{1}{2}$$

5. (14,6)
$$14\frac{8}{9} + 5\frac{5}{9} = 20\frac{4}{9}$$

6. (16,6)
$$\frac{7}{12} + \frac{1}{3} = \frac{11}{12}$$

7. (17,6)
$$\frac{3}{13} + \frac{1}{3} = \frac{22}{39}$$

8. (17,6)
$$\frac{3}{4} - \frac{2}{11} = \frac{25}{44}$$

9. (18,6)
$$\begin{array}{r} 1\frac{7}{10} \\ +2\frac{5}{6} \\ \hline 4\frac{8}{15} \end{array}$$

10. (18,6)
$$\begin{array}{r} 4\frac{2}{7} \\ +6\frac{3}{5} \\ \hline 10\frac{31}{35} \end{array}$$

11. (19,6)
$$\frac{5}{8} \times \frac{3}{4} = \frac{15}{32}$$

12. (19,6)
$$\frac{2}{3} \times \frac{1}{6} = \frac{1}{9}$$

13. (19,6)
$$\frac{3}{14} \times \frac{1}{1} = \frac{3}{14}$$

14. (20,6)
$$12\frac{3}{8} \times 4\frac{5}{6} = 59\frac{13}{16}$$

15. (20,6)
$$\frac{1}{3} \times 7\frac{1}{2} = 32\frac{1}{2}$$

16. (22,6)
$$\frac{2}{5} \div \frac{4}{9} = \frac{9}{10}$$

17. (22,6)
$$\frac{3}{4} \div \frac{5}{7} = 1\frac{1}{20}$$

18. (23,6)
$$11 \div \frac{1}{2} = 22$$

19. (23,6)
$$4 \div \frac{1}{7} = 28$$

20. (24,6)
$$8\frac{5}{8} \div 1\frac{1}{6} = 7\frac{11}{28}$$

21. (24,6)
$$7\frac{1}{3} \div 2\frac{3}{4} = 2\frac{2}{3}$$

## Test 10: Decimals, Ratios, Percents Survey Test

1. (3,7)
$$\frac{4}{9} = .444$$

2. (33,7)
$$\frac{5}{8} = .625$$

3. (4,8)
Convert to %
.7 = 70%

4. (4,8)
Convert to %
.016 = 1.6%

5. (5,8)
Convert to fraction
$$40\% = \frac{2}{5}$$

6. (5,8)
Convert to fraction
$$26\% = \frac{13}{50}$$

7. (6,8)
Convert to %
$$\frac{2}{8} = 25\%$$

8. (6,8)
Convert to %
$$\frac{3}{5} = 60\%$$

9. (7,7)
$$\begin{array}{r} 90.5 \\ -1.68 \\ \hline 88.82 \end{array}$$

10. (7,7)
$$\begin{array}{r} 813 \\ -13.9 \\ \hline 799.1 \end{array}$$

11. (7,7)
$$\begin{array}{r} 6.021 \\ +51.30 \\ \hline 57.321 \end{array}$$

12. (8,7)
$$\begin{array}{r} 16.2 \\ \times\ .40 \\ \hline 6.48 \end{array}$$

13. (8,7)
$$\begin{array}{r} .042 \\ \times\ .306 \\ \hline .012852 \end{array}$$

14. (8,7)
$$\begin{array}{r} 2.96 \\ \times\ .06 \\ \hline .1776 \end{array}$$

15. (9,7)
$$201\overline{)603}^{\ \ .3}$$

16. (9,7)
$$1.2\overline{).72}^{\ \ .6}$$

17. (10,8)
Round to the nearest hundredth
.1694 = .169

18. (10,8)
Round to the nearest tenth
.5096 = .51

19. (11,8)
Complete ratio
1:3 = 3:9

20. (11,8)
Complete ratio
2:8 = 4:16

Source: From Howell, K. W., Zucker, S. H., & Morehead, M. K. (2000b) *Multilevel Academic Skills Inventory.* Reprinted with permission.

## MATH SUMMARY

Student's Goal: Solve All Problems, Integrating Necessary Computation, Applications, and Problem-Solving Skills

Directions:

1.  Use the columns on the right to mark those items the student is expected (desired grade placement) to know and solve.
2.  Summarize the student's status on each applicable content area.

**Status:**

| Response Type: | Identify | Produce | | | No Pass | Pass |
|---|---|---|---|---|---|---|
| | | | | | Expected Curriculum Level | |
| **Standard:** | Accuracy | Accuracy | Mastery | Automatic | | |
| **Content:** | | | | | | |
| *Problem Solving* | | | | | | |
| Check work | | | | | | |
| Estimate answer | | | | | | |
| Work equation | | | | | | |
| Set up equation | | | | | | |
| Determine relevant information | | | | | | |
| Determine correct operations | | | | | | |
| **Content:** | | | | | | |
| *Measurement—Scaling:* | | | | | | |
| (specify metric or customary): | | | | | | |
| Vocabulary | | | | | | |
| Weight    Tools | | | | | | |
| Content | | | | | | |
| | | | | | | |
| Vocabulary | | | | | | |
| Volume    Tools | | | | | | |
| Content | | | | | | |
| | | | | | | |
| Vocabulary | | | | | | |
| Surface   Tools | | | | | | |
| Content | | | | | | |
| | | | | | | |
| Vocabulary | | | | | | |
| Linear    Tool | | | | | | |
| Content | | | | | | |
| | | | | | | |
| | | | | | | |
| | | | | | | |
| | | | | | | |

B-5.6

Status:

Expected
Curriculum Level

| Response Type: | | Identify | Produce | | | No Pass | Pass |
|---|---|---|---|---|---|---|---|
| **Standard:** | | Accuracy | Accuracy | Mastery | Automatic | | |
| **Content:** | | | | | | | |
| | Vocabulary | | | | | | |
| Money | Tools | | | | | | |
| | Content | | | | | | |
| | | | | | | | |
| | Vocabulary | | | | | | |
| Temperature | Tools | | | | | | |
| | Content | | | | | | |
| | | | | | | | |
| | Vocabulary | | | | | | |
| Time | Tools | | | | | | |
| | Content | | | | | | |
| | | | | | | | |
| **Content:** | | | | | | | |
| *Computation* | | | | | | | |
| + - / | Operations & Rational Numbers | | | | | | |
| | Ratios | | | | | | |
| | Percents | | | | | | |
| | Decimals | | | | | | |
| | Factions | | | | | | |
| | | | | | | | |
| **Content:** | | | | | | | |
| *Operations—Rational Numbers* | | | | | | | |
| ÷ | | | | | | | |
| X | | | | | | | |
| - | | | | | | | |
| + | | | | | | | |
| Operations-Whole Numbers | | | | | | | |
| ÷ | | | | | | | |
| X | | | | | | | |
| - | | | | | | | |
| + | | | | | | | |
| Basic Facts | | | | | | | |
| ÷ | | | | | | | |
| X | | | | | | | |
| - | | | | | | | |
| + | | | | | | | |

Source: From Howell, K. W., Zucker, S. H., & Morehead, M. K. (2000b) Multilevel Academic Skills Inventory.
Reprinted with permission.

B-5.7

# Applications Summary Checklist

| | | Identify Accuracy | Produce Accuracy | Mastery | Automatic | Appropriate Curriculum Level | |
|---|---|---|---|---|---|---|---|
| *Solve All Problems, Integrating Necessary Computation, Applications and Problem-Solving Skills* | | | | | | No Pass | Pass |
| Response Standard | | | | | | | |
| Applications-Integrate Subskills | | | | | | | |
| Measurement-Scaling | | | | | | | |
| Weight | Vocabulary Tools Content | | | | | | |
| Volume | Vocabulary Tools Content | | | | | | |
| Surface | Vocabulary Tools Content | | | | | | |
| Linear | Vocabulary Tools Content | | | | | | |
| Money | Vocabulary Tools Content | | | | | | |
| Temp | Vocabulary Tools Content | | | | | | |
| Time | Vocabulary Tools Content | | | | | | |

# Mathematics Tests

This section contains the following tests:

1. Addition facts

2. Subtraction facts

3. Multiplication facts

4. Division facts

5. Addition survey

6. Subtraction survey

7. Multiplication survey

8. Division survey

9. Fraction survey

10. Decimal/ratio/percent survey

Howell, K.W., Zucker, S.H. & Morehead, M.K. (2000). Multilevel Academic Skills Inventory. Bellingham, WA: Applied Research And Development Center. To order contact the Student Co-op Bookstore, Western Washington University. FAX (360) 650-2888. Phone (360) 650-3656.

| | | | | | |
|---|---|---|---|---|---|
| 16<br>+ 2 | 8<br>+ 4 | 8<br>+11 | 7<br>+13 | 8<br>+ 5 | 10<br>+10 |
| 20<br>+ 0 | 11<br>+ 9 | 6<br>+ 9 | 0<br>+19 | 20<br>+ 0 | 5<br>+ 6 |
| 7<br>+ 2 | 15<br>+ 4 | 14<br>+ 5 | 5<br>+ 1 | 3<br>+15 | 18<br>+ 2 |
| 12<br>+ 6 | 1<br>+ 8 | 13<br>+ 7 | 0<br>+20 | 10<br>+10 | 6<br>+12 |
| 9<br>+ 1 | 17<br>+ 2 | 2<br>+ 4 | 3<br>+17 | 1<br>+13 | 9<br>+ 1 |
| 1<br>+ 8 | 8<br>+ 5 | 19<br>+ 0 | 4<br>+ 5 | 14<br>+ 5 | 16<br>+ 2 |
| 2<br>+18 | 1<br>+ 6 | 1<br>+ 8 | 18<br>+ 1 | 8<br>+ 0 | 7<br>+11 |
| 0<br>+10 | 3<br>+17 | 10<br>+ 6 | 5<br>+ 2 | 19<br>+ 1 | 4<br>+ 1 |
| 15<br>+ 5 | 3<br>+ 3 | 4<br>+11 | 2<br>+ 3 | 4<br>+ 5 | 2<br>+17 |
| 9<br>+ 7 | 4<br>+16 | 2<br>+ 7 | 12<br>+ 5 | 7<br>+ 2 | 6<br>+ 3 |
| 3<br>+ 6 | 2<br>+ 5 | 14<br>+ 3 | 9<br>+ 0 | 12<br>+ 4 | 0<br>+ 9 |
| 17<br>+ 1 | 10<br>+10 | 4<br>+ 5 | 1<br>+19 | 2<br>+ 9 | 14<br>+ 3 |

*Add 1m*

Test 1

177

Test 2

**Subt 1m**

12  2  19  6  16  3  13  1  20  10  15  4  11  0
−10 −2 −5 −5 −7 −3 −6 −1 −9 −8 −9 −1 −8 −0

7  17 10 15  9  13  5  19  8  14  7  13  6  14
−3 −12 −9 −4 −6 −8 −2 −13 −1 −3 −5 −11 −5 −9

17  1  20  0  18  9  20  4  12  2  20  3  15  8
−14 −0 −8 −0 −11 −2 −10 −4 −10 −1 −16 −2 −13 −4

3  18  9  13  5  11  7  15  10 17 12  6  16 19
−1 −10 −2 −3 −2 −10 −2 −12 −6 −5 −8 −0 −9 −12

12  2  16  3  16  4  14  0  18  9  11  6  8
−8 −0 −12 −0 −4 −3 −3 −0 −10 −7 −7 −0 −3

4  15  0  20  8  17  2  18  9  19  6  14  5  17
−1 −3 −0 −12 −4 −6 −1 −13 −6 −7 −2 −3 −5 −2

16  5  13  10 18  9  15  7  12  6  11  5  11  2
−9 −3 −2 −0 −6 −2 −3 −1 −2 −3 −0 −5 −1 −0

Test 3    *Mult 1m*

$$\begin{array}{r}1\\\times 6\end{array}\qquad\begin{array}{r}8\\\times 10\end{array}\qquad\begin{array}{r}3\\\times 5\end{array}\qquad\begin{array}{r}4\\\times 4\end{array}\qquad\begin{array}{r}6\\\times 0\end{array}\qquad\begin{array}{r}2\\\times 1\end{array}$$

$$\begin{array}{r}5\\\times 8\end{array}\qquad\begin{array}{r}3\\\times 6\end{array}\qquad\begin{array}{r}1\\\times 10\end{array}\qquad\begin{array}{r}7\\\times 5\end{array}\qquad\begin{array}{r}5\\\times 4\end{array}\qquad\begin{array}{r}3\\\times 0\end{array}$$

$$\begin{array}{r}8\\\times 9\end{array}\qquad\begin{array}{r}6\\\times 8\end{array}\qquad\begin{array}{r}4\\\times 6\end{array}\qquad\begin{array}{r}0\\\times 10\end{array}\qquad\begin{array}{r}6\\\times 5\end{array}\qquad\begin{array}{r}7\\\times 4\end{array}$$

$$\begin{array}{r}2\\\times 7\end{array}\qquad\begin{array}{r}9\\\times 9\end{array}\qquad\begin{array}{r}7\\\times 8\end{array}\qquad\begin{array}{r}6\\\times 6\end{array}\qquad\begin{array}{r}5\\\times 10\end{array}\qquad\begin{array}{r}9\\\times 5\end{array}$$

$$\begin{array}{r}4\\\times 7\end{array}\qquad\begin{array}{r}7\\\times 2\end{array}\qquad\begin{array}{r}3\\\times 9\end{array}\qquad\begin{array}{r}2\\\times 8\end{array}\qquad\begin{array}{r}7\\\times 6\end{array}\qquad\begin{array}{r}7\\\times 10\end{array}$$

$$\begin{array}{r}0\\\times 3\end{array}\qquad\begin{array}{r}6\\\times 7\end{array}\qquad\begin{array}{r}6\\\times 2\end{array}\qquad\begin{array}{r}9\\\times 9\end{array}\qquad\begin{array}{r}3\\\times 8\end{array}\qquad\begin{array}{r}9\\\times 6\end{array}$$

$$\begin{array}{r}1\\\times 1\end{array}\qquad\begin{array}{r}2\\\times 3\end{array}\qquad\begin{array}{r}5\\\times 7\end{array}\qquad\begin{array}{r}9\\\times 2\end{array}\qquad\begin{array}{r}1\\\times 9\end{array}\qquad\begin{array}{r}8\\\times 8\end{array}$$

$$\begin{array}{r}7\\\times 0\end{array}\qquad\begin{array}{r}4\\\times 1\end{array}\qquad\begin{array}{r}9\\\times 3\end{array}\qquad\begin{array}{r}8\\\times 7\end{array}\qquad\begin{array}{r}5\\\times 2\end{array}\qquad\begin{array}{r}4\\\times 9\end{array}$$

$$\begin{array}{r}6\\\times 4\end{array}\qquad\begin{array}{r}5\\\times 0\end{array}\qquad\begin{array}{r}6\\\times 1\end{array}\qquad\begin{array}{r}7\\\times 3\end{array}\qquad\begin{array}{r}2\\\times 7\end{array}\qquad\begin{array}{r}4\\\times 2\end{array}$$

$$\begin{array}{r}8\\\times 5\end{array}\qquad\begin{array}{r}3\\\times 4\end{array}\qquad\begin{array}{r}4\\\times 0\end{array}\qquad\begin{array}{r}9\\\times 1\end{array}\qquad\begin{array}{r}8\\\times 3\end{array}\qquad\begin{array}{r}1\\\times 7\end{array}$$

$$\begin{array}{r}9\\\times 10\end{array}\qquad\begin{array}{r}5\\\times 5\end{array}\qquad\begin{array}{r}9\\\times 4\end{array}\qquad\begin{array}{r}1\\\times 0\end{array}\qquad\begin{array}{r}5\\\times 1\end{array}\qquad\begin{array}{r}5\\\times 3\end{array}$$

$$\begin{array}{r}7\\\times 7\end{array}\qquad\begin{array}{r}2\\\times 10\end{array}\qquad\begin{array}{r}3\\\times 5\end{array}\qquad\begin{array}{r}4\\\times 4\end{array}\qquad\begin{array}{r}0\\\times 0\end{array}\qquad\begin{array}{r}3\\\times 1\end{array}$$

179

5)25 4)36 7)49 6)48 2)2 8)0 9)9 5)0 1)1

3)30 5)45 4)4 7)63 6)60 2)8 8)64 9)54 5)30

1)9 3)27 5)35 4)20 7)56 6)54 2)6 8)40 9)81

10)90 1)10 3)21 5)40 4)16 7)42 6)6 2)10 8)16

9)27 10)50 1)2 3)15 5)20 4)40 7)35 6)0 2)14

8)24 9)18 10)30 1)4 3)9 5)15 4)32 7)21 6)6

.2)16 8)48 9)36 10)40 1)3 3)18 5)10 4)24 7)28

6)18 2)18 8)56 9)63 10)80 1)6 3)24 5)5 4)28

7)14 6)24 2)20 8)32 9)45 10)70 1)5 3)12 5)50

4)8 7)7 6)30 2)0 8)72 9)90 10)20 1)8 3)6

*Div 1m*

Test 4

180

```
   8        13         5         1         0
  +7        +6        +6        +0        +3
 ____      ____      ____      ____      ____


   7         9        64        43        32
   2         3       + 2       + 5       + 8
  +2        +4       ____      ____      ____
 ____      ____


  47        31        70        22        18
  +9       +24       +19       +53       +96
 ____      ____      ____      ____      ____


  95        48       569      4020       283
 +25       +37       201     + 689        21
 ____      ____     +877      ____      +2764
                    ____                 ____
```

Test 5

181

$$\begin{array}{r} 3 \\ -2 \\ \hline \end{array} \qquad \begin{array}{r} 16 \\ -7 \\ \hline \end{array} \qquad \begin{array}{r} 10 \\ -4 \\ \hline \end{array} \qquad \begin{array}{r} 14 \\ -5 \\ \hline \end{array} \qquad \begin{array}{r} 19 \\ -2 \\ \hline \end{array}$$

$$\begin{array}{r} 68 \\ -5 \\ \hline \end{array} \qquad \begin{array}{r} 50 \\ -10 \\ \hline \end{array} \qquad \begin{array}{r} 40 \\ -30 \\ \hline \end{array} \qquad \begin{array}{r} 60 \\ -60 \\ \hline \end{array} \qquad \begin{array}{r} 80 \\ -5 \\ \hline \end{array}$$

$$\begin{array}{r} 23 \\ -6 \\ \hline \end{array} \qquad \begin{array}{r} 63 \\ -9 \\ \hline \end{array} \qquad \begin{array}{r} 93 \\ -61 \\ \hline \end{array} \qquad \begin{array}{r} 58 \\ -23 \\ \hline \end{array} \qquad \begin{array}{r} 46 \\ -13 \\ \hline \end{array}$$

$$\begin{array}{r} 53 \\ -29 \\ \hline \end{array} \qquad \begin{array}{r} 64 \\ -27 \\ \hline \end{array} \qquad \begin{array}{r} 8942 \\ -5961 \\ \hline \end{array} \qquad \begin{array}{r} 400 \\ -165 \\ \hline \end{array} \qquad \begin{array}{r} 5906 \\ -248 \\ \hline \end{array}$$

Test 6

182

| ADDITION | | | | | |
|---|---|---|---|---|---|
| OBJECTIVE | ITEM | CURRICULUM LEVEL | EXPECTED PASS | PASS | DISCREPANCY |
| 8a | 20 | 4 | | | |
| 8a | 19 | 4 | | | |
| 8a | 18 | 3 | | | |
| 7a | 17 | 3 | | | |
| 7a | 16 | 3 | | | |
| 7a | 15 | 3 | | | |
| 6a | 14 | 2 | | | |
| 6a | 13 | 2 | | | |
| 6a | 12 | 2 | | | |
| 5a | 11 | 2 | | | |
| 5a | 10 | 2 | | | |
| 4a | 9 | 2 | | | |
| 4a | 8 | 2 | | | |
| 3a | 7 | 2 | | | |
| 3a | 6 | 2 | | | |
| 2a | 5 | 1 | | | |
| 2a | 4 | 1 | | | |
| 1a | 3 | 1 | | | |
| 1a | 2 | 1 | | | |
| 1a | 1 | 1 | | | |

| SUBTRACTION | | | | | |
| --- | --- | --- | --- | --- | --- |
| OBJECTIVE | ITEM | CURRICULUM LEVEL | EXPECTED PASS | PASS | DISCREPANCY |
| 7a | 20 | 4 | | | |
| 7a | 19 | 4 | | | |
| 7a | 18 | 4 | | | |
| 6a | 17 | 3 | | | |
| 6a | 16 | 3 | | | |
| 5a | 15 | 2 | | | |
| 5a | 14 | 2 | | | |
| 5a | 13 | 2 | | | |
| 4a | 12 | 2 | | | |
| 4a | 11 | 2 | | | |
| 4a | 10 | 2 | | | |
| 3a | 9 | 2 | | | |
| 3a | 8 | 2 | | | |
| 3a | 7 | 2 | | | |
| 2a | 6 | 2 | | | |
| 1a | 5 | 1 | | | |
| 1a | 4 | 1 | | | |
| 1a | 3 | 1 | | | |
| 1a | 2 | 1 | | | |
| 1a | 1 | 1 | | | |

$$2 \times 6$$

$$9 \times 5$$

$$8 \times 3$$

$$64 \times 7$$

$$24 \times 3$$

$$91 \times 1$$

$$18 \times 9$$

$$22 \times 86$$

$$85 \times 63$$

$$3 \times 1000 =$$

$$100 \times 74 =$$

$$102 \times 40$$

$$40 \times 31$$

$$194 \times 10 =$$

$$7005 \times 26$$

$$87 \times 25$$

$$215 \times 48$$

$$5684 \times 39$$

$$5^2 =$$

$$12^2 =$$

Test 7

$2\overline{)4}$ 

$7\overline{)56}$ 

$10\overline{)90}$ 

$8\overline{)32}$ 

$3\overline{)72}$ 

$5\overline{)80}$ 

$7\overline{)91}$ 

$9\overline{)54}$ 

$5\overline{)23}$ 

$9\overline{)37}$ 

$7\overline{)169}$ 

$58\overline{)1209}$ 

$100\overline{)4200}$ 

$10\overline{)1260}$ 

$1\overline{)48}$ 

$8\overline{)8500}$ 

$31\overline{)1307}$ 

$15\overline{)306}$ 

$\sqrt{4}$ 

$\sqrt{121}$

| | | MULTIPLICATION | | | |
|---|---|---|---|---|---|
| OBJECTIVE | ITEM | CURRICULUM LEVEL | EXPECTED PASS | PASS | DISCREPANCY |
| 8a | 20 | 8 | | | |
| 8a | 19 | 8 | | | |
| 7a | 18 | 5 | | | |
| 7a | 17 | 4 | | | |
| 7a | 16 | 4 | | | |
| 6a | 15 | 5 | | | |
| 6a | 14 | 4 | | | |
| 6a | 13 | 4 | | | |
| 5a | 12 | 5 | | | |
| 5a | 11 | 5 | | | |
| 5a | 10 | 5 | | | |
| 4a | 9 | 4 | | | |
| 4a | 8 | 4 | | | |
| 3a | 7 | 4 | | | |
| 2a | 6 | 4 | | | |
| 2a | 5 | 4 | | | |
| 2a | 4 | 4 | | | |
| 1a | 3 | 4 | | | |
| 1a | 2 | 4 | | | |
| 1a | 1 | 4 | | | |

| | | | DIVISION | | |
|---|---|---|---|---|---|
| OBJECTIVE | ITEM | CURRICULUM LEVEL | EXPECTED PASS | PASS | DISCREPANCY |
| 7a | 20 | 8 | | | |
| 7a | 19 | 8 | | | |
| 6a | 18 | 5 | | | |
| 6a | 17 | 5 | | | |
| 6a | 16 | 5 | | | |
| 5a | 15 | 5 | | | |
| 5a | 14 | 5 | | | |
| 5a | 13 | 5 | | | |
| 4a | 12 | 5 | | | |
| 4a | 11 | 4 | | | |
| 3a | 10 | 4 | | | |
| 3a | 9 | 4 | | | |
| 2a | 8 | 4 | | | |
| 2a | 7 | 4 | | | |
| 2a | 6 | 4 | | | |
| 1a | 5 | 4 | | | |
| 1a | 4 | 4 | | | |
| 1a | 3 | 4 | | | |
| 1a | 2 | 4 | | | |
| 1a | 1 | 4 | | | |

$1 = \dfrac{}{10}$

$\dfrac{2}{8} =$

$\dfrac{7}{3} =$

$\dfrac{1}{8} + \dfrac{3}{8} =$

$14\dfrac{8}{9} + 5\dfrac{5}{9} =$

$\dfrac{7}{12} + \dfrac{1}{3} =$

$\dfrac{3}{13} + \dfrac{1}{3} =$

$\dfrac{3}{4} - \dfrac{2}{11} =$

$\begin{array}{r} 1\dfrac{7}{10} \\ +2\dfrac{5}{6} \\ \hline \end{array}$

$\begin{array}{r} 4\dfrac{2}{7} \\ +6\dfrac{3}{5} \\ \hline \end{array}$

$\dfrac{5}{8} \times \dfrac{3}{4} =$

$\dfrac{2}{3} \times \dfrac{1}{6} =$

$\dfrac{3}{14} \times \dfrac{1}{1} =$

$12\dfrac{3}{8} \times 4\dfrac{5}{6} =$

$4\dfrac{1}{3} \times 7\dfrac{1}{2} =$

$\dfrac{2}{5} \div \dfrac{4}{9} =$

$\dfrac{3}{4} \div \dfrac{5}{7} =$

$11 \div \dfrac{1}{2} =$

$4 \div \dfrac{1}{7} =$

$8\dfrac{5}{8} \div 1\dfrac{1}{6} =$

$7\dfrac{1}{3} \div 2\dfrac{3}{4} =$

189

**Convert to %**

$.016 =$ _____ %

**Convert to %**

$\dfrac{3}{5} =$ _____ %

$$\begin{array}{r} 16.2 \\ \times\ .40 \\ \hline \end{array}$$

**Convert to %**

$.7 =$ _____ %

**Convert to %**

$\dfrac{2}{8} =$ _____ %

$$\begin{array}{r} 6.021 \\ +\,51.30 \\ \hline \end{array}$$

$1.2\overline{)\,.72\,}$

**Complete ratio**

_____ $:3 = 3:9$

**Complete ratio**

$2:8 = 4:$ _____

$\dfrac{5}{8} =$ -----

$$\begin{array}{r} 813 \\ -\,13.9 \\ \hline \end{array}$$

$$\begin{array}{r} 2.96 \\ \times\ .06 \\ \hline \end{array}$$

$2.01\overline{)\,.603\,}$

**Round to nearest tenth**

$.5096 =$

$\dfrac{4}{9} =$ -----

**Convert to fraction**

$26\% =$ _____

$$\begin{array}{r} .042 \\ \times\ .306 \\ \hline \end{array}$$

**Convert to fraction**

$40\% =$ _____

$$\begin{array}{r} 90.5 \\ -\,1.68 \\ \hline \end{array}$$

**Round to nearest hundredth**

$.1694 =$

190

| | | FRACTIONS | | | |
|---|---|---|---|---|---|
| OBJECTIVE | ITEM | CURRICULUM LEVEL | EXPECTED PASS | PASS | DISCREPANCY |
| 24a | 21 | 6 | | | |
| 24a | 20 | 6 | | | |
| 23a | 19 | 6 | | | |
| 23a | 18 | 6 | | | |
| 22a | 17 | 6 | | | |
| 22a | 16 | 6 | | | |
| 20a | 15 | 6 | | | |
| 20a | 14 | 6 | | | |
| 19a | 13 | 6 | | | |
| 19a | 12 | 6 | | | |
| 19a | 11 | 6 | | | |
| 18a | 10 | 6 | | | |
| 18a | 9 | 6 | | | |
| 17a | 8 | 6 | | | |
| 17a | 7 | 6 | | | |
| 16a | 6 | 6 | | | |
| 14a | 5 | 6 | | | |
| 13a | 4 | 5 | | | |
| 9a | 3 | 5 | | | |
| 8a | 2 | 5 | | | |
| 4a | 1 | 5 | | | |

**Directions:** All items on the survey tests are listed below. They are matched to objectives found in Appendix C of the text. The curriculum level at which each item is commonly taught is listed next to it (you will wish to change these if they are different at your school). If the student is currently assigned to a curriculum level at or above the level of a problem, then he/she is expected to pass it. Regardless of curriclum level, if the student has received instruction on an objective, he/she is also expected to pass it. Mark all items which you expect the student to pass with an X in the "Expected Pass" column before you give the test. Mark all items the student passed with an X in the "Pass" column. Mark any discrepancy between expected and actual performance with an X in the "Discrepancy" column. Total the discrepancies and transfer this total to the students IEP and/or record book. Specific-level testing may be required for objectives on which a discrepancy is noted.

| DECIMALS, RATIOS, PERCENTS | | | | | |
|---|---|---|---|---|---|
| OBJECTIVE | ITEM | CURRICULUM LEVEL | EXPECTED PASS | PASS | DISCREPANCY |
| 11a | 20 | 8 | | | |
| 11a | 19 | 8 | | | |
| 10a | 18 | 8 | | | |
| 10a | 17 | 8 | | | |
| 9a | 16 | 7 | | | |
| 9a | 15 | 7 | | | |
| 8a | 14 | 7 | | | |
| 8a | 13 | 7 | | | |
| 8a | 12 | 7 | | | |
| 7a | 11 | 7 | | | |
| 7a | 10 | 7 | | | |
| 7a | 9 | 7 | | | |
| 6a | 8 | 8 | | | |
| 6a | 7 | 8 | | | |
| 5a | 6 | 8 | | | |
| 5a | 5 | 8 | | | |
| 4a | 4 | 8 | | | |
| 4a | 3 | 8 | | | |
| 3a | 2 | 7 | | | |
| 3a | 1 | 7 | | | |

**Practice Item A**

Bud has 2 toy airplanes. Sis gives him 3 more. How many airplanes does Bud have all together?

a.
$$\begin{array}{r} 2 \\ -3 \\ \hline \end{array}$$

b.
$$\begin{array}{r} 4 \\ \times 8 \\ \hline \end{array}$$

c.
$$\begin{array}{r} 10 \\ \times 6 \\ \hline \end{array}$$

d.
$$\begin{array}{r} 3 \\ +2 \\ \hline \end{array}$$

193

**Practice Item B**

Jon has 10 comic books. Joe gives him 5 more. Jon sells 1. How many does Jon have left?

a.
$$\begin{array}{r} 10 \\ -1 \\ \hline \end{array}\quad\begin{array}{r} 5 \\ +1 \\ \hline \end{array}$$

b.
$$\begin{array}{r} 10 \\ -5 \\ \hline \end{array}$$

c.
$$\begin{array}{r} 10 \\ +5 \\ \hline \end{array}\quad\begin{array}{r} 15 \\ -1 \\ \hline \end{array}$$

d.
$$\begin{array}{r} 10 \\ \times 5 \\ \hline \end{array}\quad 1\overline{)50}$$

**2.** 45 children are standing up. 9 children sit down. How many children are left standing?

a. 45 + 9 =
b. 45 + 9 =
c. 9 × 45 =
d. 45 – 9 =

**Practice Item C**

Ed has 8 toy cars. He gives 2 to Ray. How many does he have left?

a. 6
b. 16
c. 4
d. 10

**3.** There are ten rows of desks. There are seven desks in each row. How many desks are there all together?

a.
$$\begin{array}{r} 10 \\ -7 \\ \hline \end{array}$$

b.
$$\begin{array}{r} 10 \\ +7 \\ \hline \end{array}$$

c.
$$\begin{array}{r} 10 \\ \times 7 \\ \hline \end{array}$$

d. 10 + 7

**Practice Item D**

Kim has 6 music books. She gives 4 to Lori and 1 to Linda. How many does she have left?

a. 11
b. 1
c. 24
d. 3

**4.** 5 boxes contain 500 tacks. How many tacks are in each box?

a. 500 + 5
b. 500 × 5
c. 500 – 5
d. 500 + 5

**1.** There are 12 red apples and 2 green apples. How many apples are there all together?

a. 2 – 12 =
b. 2 + 12 =
c. 12 × 2 =
d. 12 + 2 =

5. There are 40 students. 25% of the students have blue eyes. How many have blue eyes?

 a. $\begin{array}{r} 40 \\ +.25 \\ \hline \end{array}$

 b. $.25\overline{)40}$

 c. $\begin{array}{r} 40 \\ -.25 \\ \hline \end{array}$

 d. $\begin{array}{r} 40 \\ \times.25 \\ \hline \end{array}$

6. Colleen has 2 crayfish and Gary has 4 crayfish for the science project. On Tuesday, Albert brings them three more. On Wednesday, Robin brings them 5. How many crayfish do they have?

 a. $\begin{array}{r} 2 \\ +4 \\ \hline \end{array}\quad \begin{array}{r} 6 \\ +5 \\ \hline \end{array}$

 b. $\begin{array}{r} 4 \\ \times2 \\ \hline \end{array}\quad \begin{array}{r} 8 \\ \times5 \\ \hline \end{array}\quad 3\overline{)40}$

 c. $\begin{array}{r} 4 \\ +2 \\ \hline \end{array}\quad \begin{array}{r} 6 \\ -5 \\ \hline \end{array}$

 d. $\begin{array}{r} 2 \\ +4 \\ \hline \end{array}\quad \begin{array}{r} 6 \\ +3 \\ \hline \end{array}\quad \begin{array}{r} 9 \\ +5 \\ \hline \end{array}$

7. There are 40 desks in the 4th grade classroom. 2 desks are loaned to the 3rd grade classroom, 5 desks are loaned to the 6th grade classroom. How many desks are left in the 4th grade classroom?

 a. $\begin{array}{r} 40 \\ -2 \\ \hline \end{array}\quad \begin{array}{r} 38 \\ -5 \\ \hline \end{array}$

 b. $\begin{array}{r} 40 \\ +2 \\ \hline \end{array}\quad \begin{array}{r} 42 \\ +5 \\ \hline \end{array}$

 c. $\begin{array}{r} 40 \\ -4 \\ \hline \end{array}\quad \begin{array}{r} 36 \\ -2 \\ \hline \end{array}\quad \begin{array}{r} 34 \\ -3 \\ \hline \end{array}\quad \begin{array}{r} 29 \\ -5 \\ \hline \end{array}\quad \begin{array}{r} 24 \\ -6 \\ \hline \end{array}$

 d. $\begin{array}{r} 40 \\ -4 \\ \hline \end{array}\quad \begin{array}{r} 36 \\ -3 \\ \hline \end{array}\quad \begin{array}{r} 33 \\ -6 \\ \hline \end{array}$

8. There are 4 packages of pencils. Each package contains 5 pencils. There are 8 students, and three are boys. The pencils are to be divided equally among the girls. How many pencils will each girl get?

 a. $\begin{array}{r} 4 \\ \times5 \\ \hline \end{array}\quad \begin{array}{r} 8 \\ \times3 \\ \hline \end{array}\quad 20\overline{)24}$

 b. $\begin{array}{r} 4 \\ \times5 \\ \hline \end{array}\quad \begin{array}{r} 8 \\ -3 \\ \hline \end{array}\quad 5\overline{)20}$

 c. $\begin{array}{r} 5 \\ -4 \\ \hline \end{array}\quad \begin{array}{r} 8 \\ +3 \\ \hline \end{array}\quad 1\overline{)11}$

 d. $\begin{array}{r} 5 \\ \times4 \\ \hline \end{array}\quad 8\overline{)20}$

9. There are 30 pairs of scissors in the box. 10 are broken. Fifteen new pairs are given to the class. There are 5 art tables in the room. How many pairs of scissors that are not broken will each table get?

 a. $\begin{array}{r} 15 \\ -10 \\ \hline \end{array}\quad \begin{array}{r} 30 \\ +15 \\ \hline \end{array}\quad \begin{array}{r} 5 \\ +45 \\ \hline \end{array}\quad 5\overline{)50}$

 b. $\begin{array}{r} 30 \\ +10 \\ \hline \end{array}\quad 5\overline{)40}$

 c. $\begin{array}{r} 30 \\ -10 \\ \hline \end{array}\quad \begin{array}{r} 20 \\ +15 \\ \hline \end{array}\quad \begin{array}{r} 35 \\ \times5 \\ \hline \end{array}$

 d. $\begin{array}{r} 30 \\ -10 \\ \hline \end{array}\quad \begin{array}{r} 20 \\ +15 \\ \hline \end{array}\quad 5\overline{)35}$

10. 2% of the students were absent on Tuesday. 20% of those present brought a sack lunch and 75% of those present bought a hot lunch. The rest of the students fixed a lunch in their classroom. What percent of the students in school fixed a lunch in their classroom?

 a. $\begin{array}{r} 20\% \\ +75\% \\ \hline \end{array}\quad \begin{array}{r} 100\% \\ -95\% \\ \hline \end{array}$

 b. $\begin{array}{r} 2\% \\ 20\% \\ +75\% \\ \hline \end{array}\quad \begin{array}{r} 100\% \\ -97\% \\ \hline \end{array}$

 c. $\begin{array}{r} .20 \\ \times.02 \\ \hline \end{array}\quad \begin{array}{r} .20 \\ \times.75 \\ \hline \end{array}\quad .040\overline{)1500}$

 d. $\begin{array}{r} 75\% \\ \times20\% \\ \hline \end{array}\quad \begin{array}{r} 100\% \\ -15\% \\ \hline \end{array}$

194

11. There are 11 girls and 4 boys. How many children are there all together?

a. 14

b. 44

c. 15

d. 7

12. There are 42 pencils in a box. 7 pencils are given away. How many pencils are left?

a. 49

b. 6

c. 294

d. 35

13. There are 5 children on each team. There are 11 teams. How many children are there all together?

a. 55

b. 16

c. 6

d. 555

14. Students put the marbles from six packages into a jar. There were four hundred eighty marbles. How many marbles were there in each package?

a. 486

b. 474

c. 80

d. 2880

15. 1/3 of the 45 chairs are blue. How many blue chairs are there?

a. 90

b. 30

c. 25

d. 15

16. Herb had two pencils. Eleanor gave him 6 more pencils in the afternoon. The next day Jean gave him one pencil and Marilyn gave him two. How many pencils did Herb have?

a. 11

b. 6

c. 8

d. 5

Test 11.3

195

17. There are 25 lemons and 30 apples. Ten of the apples are large. There are 5 people. How many small apples will each person get if the small apples are shared equally?

a. 20

b. 6

c. 4

d. 11

18. Jack drank 1 glass of milk at each meal for 5 meals. Kathy drank 2 glasses of milk at each meal for 6 meals. Maggie drank 4 glasses of milk at each meal for 5 meals. All together, how many more glasses of milk did Kathy drink than Jack?

a. 7

b. 12

c. 2

d. 37

19. There are 138 red pencils and 162 blue pencils. There are 6 packages of paper with 200 sheets in each package. If the pencils and paper are divided equally, how many pencils and how many sheets of paper will 150 students receive?

a. 2 pencils, 1 sheet of paper

b. 2 pencils, 8 sheets of paper

c. 8 pencils, 2 sheets of paper

d. 20 pencils, 80 sheets of paper

20. There are 60 students in the band. 10% of the students are in the drum section. 1/2 of the drummers need new drums. How many students need new drums?

a. 6

b. 30

c. 20

d. 3

21. Lizzie went to the feed-and-grain store to buy food for her goat. She bought 2 sacks of grain for fifteen dollars. What was the price of one sack of grain?

a.
$$\frac{\$15.00}{+\ 2.}$$

b.
$$\frac{\$15.00}{\times\ 2}$$

c.
$$\frac{\$15.00}{-\ 2.}$$

d.
$$2\,)\overline{\$15.00}$$

22. Chris borrowed a five dollar bill from Donald. On the way to the zoo, he bought two sandwiches and three drinks. The price of one drink was $.45. The price of one sandwich was $1.25. How much change did Chris receive from the five dollar bill?

a.
$$\frac{\$1.25}{+\ .45}\qquad\frac{\$1.00}{+\ .80}$$

b.
$$\frac{\$.45}{\times\ 3}\qquad\frac{\$1.25}{\times\ 2}\qquad\frac{\$2.50}{+\ 1.35}\qquad\frac{\$5.00}{-\ 3.85}$$

c.
$$\frac{\$1.25}{+\ .45}\qquad\frac{\$5.00}{-\ 1.70}\qquad\frac{3}{\times 2}\qquad\frac{\$6.00}{-\ 3.30}$$

d.
$$\frac{\$.45}{\times\ 2}\qquad\frac{\$1.25}{\times\ 3}\qquad\frac{\$.90}{+\ 3.75}\qquad\frac{\$5.00}{-\ 4.65}$$

Test 11.4

196

23. Margo needs $45.00 to fix her bicycle. She earned $20.00. How much more money does she need?

a. $25.00

b. $15.00

c. $85.00

d. $ 2.25

24. Kenneth has five dollars in change. It costs a quarter to play a video game. How many games can he play if he saves half of his money for lunch?

a. 50

b. 25

c. 10

d. 100

25. It was 27°C when Gabby got up in the morning. By the time she walked to school, it was 31°C. How many degrees warmer had it gotten?

a.  $\begin{array}{r} 27° \\ +31° \\ \hline \end{array}$

b.  $\begin{array}{r} 31° \\ -27° \\ \hline \end{array}$

c.  $\begin{array}{r} 27° \\ \times31° \\ \hline \end{array}$

d.  $27° \overline{)31°}$

26. It was 72°F when Gabby got up in the morning. By the time she walked to school, it was 91°F. How many degrees warmer had it gotten?

a.  $\begin{array}{r} 72° \\ +91° \\ \hline \end{array}$

b.  $\begin{array}{r} 91° \\ -72° \\ \hline \end{array}$

c.  $\begin{array}{r} 72° \\ \times91° \\ \hline \end{array}$

d.  $72° \overline{)91°}$

27. Kim writes 3 new songs in January. During the rest of the year, she writes 2 songs a month. How many songs does she write a year?

a.  $\begin{array}{r} 1 \\ \times3 \\ \hline \end{array}$   $\begin{array}{r} 3 \\ \times2 \\ \hline \end{array}$   $\begin{array}{r} 6 \\ +0 \\ \hline \end{array}$

b.  $\begin{array}{r} 12 \\ -1 \\ \hline \end{array}$   $\begin{array}{r} 11 \\ \times2 \\ \hline \end{array}$   $\begin{array}{r} 3 \\ +22 \\ \hline \end{array}$

c.  $\begin{array}{r} 8 \\ -1 \\ \hline \end{array}$   $\begin{array}{r} 7 \\ +3 \\ \hline \end{array}$   $\begin{array}{r} 10 \\ +0 \\ \hline \end{array}$

d.  $\begin{array}{r} 14 \\ -1 \\ \hline \end{array}$   $\begin{array}{r} 13 \\ \times2 \\ \hline \end{array}$   $\begin{array}{r} 26 \\ +3 \\ \hline \end{array}$

28. Fred and Paula hiked to the Sapphire Mine with the Scouts. It was 9:30 in the morning when they started. The hike took two hours. What time was it when they arrived?

a. 7:30 A.M.

b. 11:30 A.M.

c. 11:30 P.M.

d. 11:00 A.M.

Test 11.5

29. Mary typed for 1 hr. and 30 min. on Thursday, 7 hrs. and 45 min. on Fri. and 4 hrs. and 45 min. on Sat. She rested for 20 minutes after she finished typing on Saturday. How many hours did she type?

a. 13 hr. 40 min.

b. 13 hr. 20 min.

c. 14 hr.

d. 12 hr. 140 min.

30. Eddie runs four kilometers each day. How many kilometers does he run in twelve days?

a.
$$\begin{array}{r} 12 \\ \times\ 4 \\ \hline \end{array}$$

b. $4\overline{)12}$

c.
$$\begin{array}{r} 12 \\ -\ 4 \\ \hline \end{array}$$

d. 1 km =
$$\begin{array}{r} 100 \\ \times\ 4 \\ \hline \end{array}$$

31. Katie was teaching Cliff and John how to fish. They wanted to catch 20 kg of trout for dinner for their friends. Cliff caught a fish which weighed 1100 g. John caught a fish which weighed 896 g. How many more g. of fish do they need to catch?

a.
$$\begin{array}{r} 1100 \\ +\ 896 \\ \hline \end{array}$$  1 kg =
$$\begin{array}{r} 1000 \\ \times\ 20 \\ \hline \end{array}$$
$$\begin{array}{r} 20000 \\ -\ 1996 \\ \hline \end{array}$$

b.
$$\begin{array}{r} 1100 \\ +\ 896 \\ \hline \end{array}$$
$$\begin{array}{r} 1996 \\ -\ 20 \\ \hline \end{array}$$

c.
$$\begin{array}{r} 1100 \\ +\ 896 \\ \hline \end{array}$$
$$\begin{array}{r} 1996 \\ +\ 20 \\ \hline \end{array}$$

d.
$$\begin{array}{r} 1100 \\ +\ 896 \\ \hline \end{array}$$  1 kg =
$$\begin{array}{r} 100 \\ \times\ 20 \\ \hline \end{array}$$
$$\begin{array}{r} 2000 \\ -\ 1996 \\ \hline \end{array}$$

32. Karna had 45 centimeters of ribbon. She wanted to cut it into 3 equal lengths. How long would each length be?

a. 42 cm

b. 135 cm

c. 15 cm

d. 55 cm

33. It takes two liters of huckleberries to make a cobbler. Bobbi picked one liter of huckleberries in the morning. Amy picked 750 ml the same day. How much must Jennifer and Joy pick together before there is enough to make a cobbler?

a.
$$\begin{array}{r} 750\ \text{ml} \\ +\quad 1 \\ \hline \end{array}$$
$$\begin{array}{r} 751\ \text{ml} \\ \times\quad 2 \\ \hline \end{array}$$

b.
$$\begin{array}{r} 750\ \text{ml} \\ \times\quad 1 \\ \hline \end{array}$$
$$\begin{array}{r} 750\ \text{ml} \\ +\quad 2 \\ \hline \end{array}$$

c. 1 liter =
$$\begin{array}{r} 1000 \\ +\ 750 \\ \hline \end{array}$$  1000ml × 2 =
$$\begin{array}{r} 2000 \\ -1750 \\ \hline \end{array}$$

d. 1 liter =
$$\begin{array}{r} 100 \\ +750 \\ \hline \end{array}$$  100 ml × 2 =
$$\begin{array}{r} 1750 \\ -\ 200 \\ \hline \end{array}$$

34. Eddie runs four miles each day. How many miles does he run in twelve days?

a.
$$\begin{array}{r} 12 \\ \times\ 4 \\ \hline \end{array}$$

b. $4\overline{)12}$

c.
$$\begin{array}{r} 12 \\ -\ 4 \\ \hline \end{array}$$

d. 1 m =
$$\begin{array}{r} 5280 \\ \times\quad 4 \\ \hline \end{array}$$
$$\begin{array}{r} 21120 \\ \times\quad 12 \\ \hline \end{array}$$

Test 11.6

198

35. Katie was teaching Cliff and John how to fish. They wanted to catch 20 lb. of trout for dinner for their friends. Cliff caught a fish which weighed 110 oz. John caught a fish which weighed 89 oz. John caught a more oz. of fish do they have to catch?

a.
```
  110      1 lb =  16    320
+  89            ×20    -199
```

b.
```
  110      199
+  89     - 20
```

c.
```
  110      199
+  89     + 20
```

d.
```
  110      1 lb =  20    199
+  89            × 8    -160
```

36. Karna had 45 inches of ribbon. She wanted to cut it into 3 equal lengths. How long would each length be?

a. 42 in

b. 135 in

c. 15 in

d. 48 in

37. It takes two quarts of huckleberries to make a cobbler. Bobbi picked one quart of huckleberries in the morning. Amy picked one pt. the same day. How much must Jennifer and Joy pick together before there is enough to make a cobbler?

a. 4 pt.

b. 3 pt.

c. 1 pt.

d. 5 pt.

38. Connie Ann is marking the edges of a square field with chalk. Each of the four edges of this square field measures 32 meters. How many meters will Connie Ann walk if she marks each side?

a.
```
 32
+ 4
```

b.
```
 32
× 4
```

c.
```
 4)32
```

d.
```
 32
- 4
```

39. Ellen is buying carpet for the living room in her new house. The living room is 18 feet by 20 feet. The dining room is 8 feet by 12 feet. She knows that there are 9 square feet in one square yard. How many square yards of carpet does she need for the living room?

a.
```
 18    12     38
+20   + 8   9)58
      +20
```

b.
```
 18    20     36
× 2   × 2   +40   9)76
```

c.
```
 18
+20   9)38
```

d.
```
 18
×20   9)360
```

40. Matthew and Randy varnished a floor that was 4 meters by 6 meters. They knew that the formula for surface area was length times width. What was the surface area they painted?

a. 10 square meters

b. 24 square meters

c. 20 square meters

d. 2 square meters

41. Howard is going to put a wire fence around a vegetable garden beside his house. He is putting another wire fence around a chicken yard behind his house. The vegetable garden is 3 meters by 2 meters and the chicken yard is 2 meters by 4 meters. The fence is sold by the meter. How many meters does he need?

a. 14

b. 48

c. 120

d. 22

42. Margaret and Mary Alice were going to fix a place for an ant colony to live. They decided to fill a glass tank with sand. The tank was 30 cm high, 20 cm wide and 40 centimeters long. They know that the formula for volume is length x width x height. What was the volume of the tank?

a. 1 m =    100 × 40 × 20 × 30 =

b. 30 + 20 + 40 =

c. 
$$\frac{40}{\times 20}\quad\frac{800}{\times 30}$$   2400 + 3 =

d. 40 × 20 × 30 =

43. Alvin and Joyce have 2 gardens which are shaped like a triangle. The base of each is 8 meters and the height is 10 meters. The fence is 2 meters high. What is the area of the two gardens?

a. $\frac{1}{2} \times 8 \times 2 =$    8 × 10 =

b. $\frac{1}{2} \times 8 \times 10 =$    40 × 2 =

c. 8 × 2 =    $\frac{1}{2}(16) \times 10 =$

d. 8 × 2 =    2 × 16 × 10 =

44. Darin wanted to find the circumference of a circle. He knew that the formula for the circumference of a circle is π d. He found that the diameter of the circle was 10 cm and he knew that π = 3.14. What was the circumference of the circle?

a. 13.14 cm

b. 6.86 cm

c. 31.4 cm

d. 314.0 cm

45. A paper cone is twelve cm high and ten cm across the top. How many cubic cm of fruit flavored silvered ice would two cones contain if they were filled only to the top?

a. 3768 cubic centimeters

b. 314 cubic centimeters

c. 628 cubic centimeters

d. 60 cubic centimeters

# Application Survey Summary

| Content | Item Type | | | | Content Subtotal |
| --- | --- | --- | --- | --- | --- |
| | select | | apply | | |
| | easy | hard | easy | hard | |
| Problem Solving | 1 | 6 | 11 | 16 | |
| | 2 | 7 | 12 | 17 | |
| | 3 | 8 | 13 | 18 | |
| | 4 | 9 | 14 | 19 | |
| | 5 | 10 | 15 | 20 | /20 |
| Money | 21 | 22 | 23 | 24 | /4 |
| Time & Temp. | 25/26 | 27 | 28 | 29 | /5 |
| Metric Meas. | 30 | 31 | 32 | 33 | /4 |
| Customary Meas. | 34 | 35 | 36 | 37 | /4 |
| Geometry I | 38 | 39 | 40 | 41 | /4 |
| Geometry II | 42 | 43 | 44 | 45 | /4 |
| Item Type Subtotal | /12 | /11 | /11 | /11 | Total /45 |

# APPLICATION SURVEY ERROR ANALYSIS TABLE

## SELECT

*The items below sample the student's skill in identifying/selecting the correct operation.*

### EASY PROBLEM SOLVING

1. Addition 1m
   a. Problem Solving 5i, 1a, Prerequisite 21a
   b. Correct Answer
   c. Problem Solving 5i
   d. Problem Solving 5i
2. Subtraction 4m
   a. Problem Solving 5i, 1a
   b. Problem Solving 5i, 1a
   c. Problem Solving 5i, 1a
   d. Correct Answer
3. Multiplication 1m
   a. Problem Solving 5i
   b. Problem Solving 5i
   c. Correct Answer
   d. Problem Solving 5i
4. Division 6a
   a. Correct Answer
   b. Problem Solving 5i, 6a
   c. Problem Solving 5i, 6a
   d. Problem Solving 5i, 6a
5. Decimals, Ratios, Percents 8a, 4a
   a. Problem Solving 5i, 6a, Decimals, Ratios, Percents 7a
   b. Problem Solving 5i, 6a
   c. Problem Solving 5i, 6a
   d. Correct Answer

### HARD PROBLEM SOLVING

6. Addition 1m
   a. Prerequisite 23a
   b. Problem Solving 5i
   c. Problem Solving 5i, Prerequisite 23a
   d. Correct Answer
7. Subtraction 4m
   a. Correct Answer
   b. Problem Solving 5i
   c. Problem Solving 3a, 5i
   d. Problem Solving 3a
8. Multiplication 1m, Subtraction 1m, Division 1m
   a. Problem Solving 5i
   b. Correct Answer
   c. Problem Solving 5i
   d. Problem Solving 3a, Prerequisite 23a
9. Subtraction 3a, Addition 6a, Division 1m
   a. Problem Solving 5i
   b. Prerequisite 23a
   c. Problem Solving 5i
   d. Correct Answer
10. Addition 6a, Subtraction 7a, Decimals, Ratios, Percents 4a, 7a
   a. Correct Answer
   b. Problem Solving 3a
   c. Problem Solving 3a, 5i
   d. Problem Solving 5i

## APPLY

*The items below sample the student's skill in applying the correct operation and computing the answer correctly*

### EASY PROBLEM SOLVING

11. Addition 1m
   a. Problem Solving 7a
   b. Problem Solving 5i, 6a
   c. Correct Answer
   d. Problem Solving 5i, 6a
12. Subtraction 4m
   a. Problem Solving 5i
   b. Problem Solving 5i, 6a
   c. Problem Solving 5i, 6a
   d. Correct Answer
13. Multiplication 2m
   a. Correct Answer
   b. Problem Solving 5i
   c. Problem Solving 5i
   d. Problem Solving 5i, 6a
14. Division 4a
   a. Problem Solving 5i
   b. Problem Solving 5i
   c. Correct Answer
   d. Problem Solving 5i
15. Fractions 20a
   a. Problem Solving 5i, 6a
   b. Problem Solving 5i, 6a
   c. Problem Solving 5i
   d. Correct Answer

### HARD PROBLEM SOLVING

16. Addition 1m
   a. Correct Answer
   b. Prerequisite 23a
   c. Problem Solving 5i
   d. Problem Solving 5i
17. Subtraction 3a, Division 1m
   a. Problem Solving 3a, 6a
   b. Problem Solving 3a, 5i
   c. Correct Answer
   d. Problem Solving 5i
18. Multiplication 1m, Subtraction 1m,
   a. Correct Answer
   b. Problem Solving 5i
   c. Problem Solving 5i
   d. Problem Solving 3a, 6a
19. Addition 8a, Multiplication 6a, Division 6a
   a. Problem Solving 5a
   b. Correct Answer
   c. Problem Solving 5i
   d. Problem Solving 5i, 6a
20. Decimals, Ratios, Percents, 5a, 6a, 8a
   a. Problem Solving 5i, 3a
   b. Problem Solving 5i, 6a, 3a
   c. Problem Solving 5i, 6a, 3a
   d. Correct Answer

# APPLICATION SURVEY ERROR ANALYSIS TABLE (cont'd.)

## SELECT

### EASY MONEY
21. Decimals, Ratios, Percents, 8a
    a. Problem Solving 5i
    b. Problem Solving 5i
    c. Decimals, Ratios, Percents 7a
    d. Correct Answer

### HARD MONEY
22. Decimals, Ratios, Percents, 7a, 8a
    a. Problem Solving 5i, Prerequisite 23a
    b. Correct Answer
    c. Problem Solving 5i
    d. Problem Solving 5i

### TIME & TEMPERATURE
25./26. Subtraction 6m
    a. Problem Solving 5i
    b. Correct Answer
    c. Problem Solving 5i
    d. Problem Solving 5i

### TIME & TEMPERATURE
27. Subtraction 1m, Multiplication 2m, Addition 4a
    a. Problem Solving 5i
    b. Correct Answer
    c. Problem Solving 5i
    d. Time & Temperature 6a

### METRIC MEASUREMENT
30. Multiplication 3m
    a. Correct Answer
    b. Problem Solving 5i
    c. Problem Solving 5i
    d. Problem Solving 5i

### METRIC MEASUREMENT
31. Addition 8a, Multiplication 5a, Subtraction 7a
    a. Correct Answer
    b. Problem Solving 5i, Metric Measurement 11a, 8a
    c. Problem Solving 5i, Metric Measurement 11a, 8a
    d. Problem Solving 5i, Metric Measurement 11a, 8a

## APPLY

### EASY MONEY
23. Subtraction 5a
    a. Correct Answer
    b. Problem Solving 6a, 7a
    c. Problem Solving 5i, 6a
    d. Problem Solving 5i, 6a

### HARD MONEY
24. Fractions 20a, Decimals, Ratios, Percents 8a
    a. Problem Solving 5i
    b. Problem Solving 5i
    c. Correct Answer
    d. Decimals, Ratios, Percents 9a, Problem Solving 6a

### TIME & TEMPERATURE
28. Addition 8a
    a. Problem Solving 5i
    b. Correct Answer
    c. Time & Temperature 3a
    d. Problem Solving 7a

### TIME & TEMPERATURE
29. Addition 8a
    a. Problem Solving 3a, Time & Temperature 6a
    b. Problem Solving 7a, Time & Temperature 6a
    c. Correct Answer
    d. Problem Solving 3a

### METRIC MEASUREMENT
32. Division 2m
    a. Problem Solving 5i
    b. Problem Solving 5i
    c. Correct Answer
    d. Problem Solving 5i

### METRIC MEASUREMENT
33. Addition 8a, Multiplication 5a, Subtraction 7a
    a. Problem Solving 5i, Metric Measurement 10a, 8a
    b. Problem Solving 5i, Metric Measurement 10a, 8a
    c. Correct Answer
    d. Metric Measurement 10a, 8a

# APPLICATION SURVEY ERROR ANALYSIS TABLE (cont'd.)

## SELECT

### EASY

**CUSTOMARY MEASUREMENT**

34. Multiplication 3m
   a. Correct Answer
   b. Problem Solving 5i
   c. Problem Solving 5i
   d. Problem Solving 3a, 4a

**GEOMETRY I**

38. Addition 4a
   a. Problem Solving 5i, Geometry 5a
   b. Correct Answer
   c. Problem Solving 5i, Geometry 5a
   d. Problem Solving 5i, Geometry 5a

**GEOMETRY II**

42. Multiplication 7a, 6a
   a. Problem Solving 5i
   b. Problem Solving 5i, Geometry 7a
   c. Problem Solving 5i, Geometry 7a
   d. Correct Answer

### HARD

**CUSTOMARY MEASUREMENT**

35. Addition 8a, Multiplication 4a, Subtraction 7a
   a. Correct Answer
   b. Problem Solving 5i, Customary Measurement 11a, 13a
   c. Problem Solving 5i, Customary Measurement 11a, 13a
   d. Problem Solving 5i, Customary Measurement 11a, 13a

**GEOMETRY I**

39. Multiplication 4m, Division 4a
   a. Problem Solving 5i, 3a, Geometry 6a
   b. Problem Solving 5i, 3a, Geometry 6a
   c. Problem Solving 5i, Geometry 6a
   d. Correct Answer

**GEOMETRY II**

43. Fractions 20a, Multiplication 7a, 6a, 5a
   a. Problem Solving 3a, 5i, Geometry 6a
   b. Correct Answer
   c. Problem Solving 3a, 5i, Geometry 6a
   d. Problem Solving 3a, 5i, Geometry 6a

## APPLY

### EASY

**CUSTOMARY MEASUREMENT**

36. Division 2a
   a. Problem Solving 5i
   b. Problem Solving 5i
   c. Correct Answer
   d. Problem Solving 5i

**GEOMETRY I**

40. Multiplication 1m
   a. Problem Solving 5i, Geometry 6a
   b. Correct Answer
   c. Problem Solving 5i, Geometry 6a
   d. Problem Solving 5i, Geometry 6a

**GEOMETRY II**

44. Decimals, Ratios, Percents 8a
   a. Problem Solving 5i, Geometry 5a
   b. Problem Solving 5i, Geometry 5a
   c. Correct Answer
   d. Decimals, Ratios, Percents 8a

### HARD

**CUSTOMARY MEASUREMENT**

37. Addition 1m, Multiplication 1m, Subtraction 1m
   a. Problem Solving 5i, Customary Measurement 12a
   b. Problem Solving 5i, Customary Measurement 12a
   c. Correct Answer
   d. Customary Measurement 12a

**GEOMETRY I**

41. Addition 1m
   a. Problem Solving 5i, Geometry 5a
   b. Problem Solving 5i, Geometry 5a
   c. Problem Solving 5i
   d. Correct Answer

**GEOMETRY II**

45. Decimals, Ratios, Percents 8a, Multiplication 8m, Fractions 22a
   a. Problem Solving 5i, Geometry 7a
   b. Problem Solving 5i, Geometry 7a
   c. Correct Answer
   d. Problem Solving 5i, Geometry 7a

# SPECIFIC LEVEL STATUS SHEET

DIRECTIONS:
1. Use this status sheet with a group of people who have worked with the student.
2. Carefully describe the settings and task you are thinking about while you fill out the sheet.
3. Filling out the sheet begins with the recognition of error (i.e. maladaptive) behavior. If the student makes an error mark the blank labeled "yes". If the student doesn't make the error mark it "no". If you can't decide about the error mark it "unsure"
4. Check each error.
5. Errors marked "yes" must be corrected, so teach the corresponding objective. Behaviors marked "no" indicate the student's current level of performance, they need not be taught (but should be noted as skill strengths). For behaviors marked "unsure" employ the corresponding **SLP** to get more information.

| IF THE STUDENT MAKES THIS ERROR: [does] | THEN THIS IS THE PROBLEM: [bold] | AND THIS IS THE OBJECTIVE (without criteria): [will] | DOES THE STUDENT HAVE THE SKILLS?: |
|---|---|---|---|
| Student identifies feelings which do not match their physical indicators or situation. *OR* Student is not able able to label what he is feeling. | **Personal (self control)** 1) Knows Own Feelings | In role play, student will recognize and state his/her feelings associated with different external events. | YES ☐  NO ☐  UNSURE ☐ |
| Student labels feelings but does not understand their significance or act in accordance with them | 2) Understands Own Feelings | When shown pictures depicting emotions, student will identify them. Student will use verbal/non-verbal means to express his feelings. | YES ☐  NO ☐  UNSURE ☐ |
| Student reacts to conflict in ways which may cause harm | 3) Deals with Conflicting Feelings | When encountering a situation which leads to conflicting feelings, the student will react by selecting options which are best in the long run and which reduce the conflict. | YES ☐  NO ☐  UNSURE ☐ |
| Student becomes confused/upset when once experienced feelings over an issue change. | 4) Recognizes Changing Feelings Due to Maturation | When confronted with a situation in which past feelings no longer exist or have changed, student will identify possible reasons. | YES ☐  NO ☐  UNSURE ☐ |
| Student interacts with others in ways that do not match their feelings | 5) Recognizes Another's Feelings | Shown a photograph or in a role play, student will correctly label feelings of others. | YES ☐  NO ☐  UNSURE ☐ |

| If the Student Makes This Error (does) | Then This Is the Problem: | And This Is the Objective (without criteria) (will) | Does the Student Have the Skills? | | |
|---|---|---|---|---|---|

**Personal (Self-Control)**

| If the Student Makes This Error (does) | Then This Is the Problem: | And This Is the Objective (without criteria) (will) | Yes | No | Unsure |
|---|---|---|---|---|---|
| Student makes statements/acts in a manner contradictory to other's known feelings. | 6. Shows understanding of another's feelings | Shown a photograph or in a role play, student will make statements in accordance to other's feelings. | ☐ | ☐ | ☐ |
| Student makes self-depreciating remarks related to his achievements. | 7. Rewards self | During role play, student will make positive remarks regarding achievements.<br><br>Student will reward self following achievements. | ☐ | ☐ | ☐ |
| Student seems to act impulsively and responds in ways that are not in his/her best interest. | 8. Uses self-control strategies | Student will employ (specified strategy) when presented with stressful situations. | ☐ | ☐ | ☐ |
| Student responds to consequences, related to his/her actions, in a negative manner.<br><br>Student often questions consequences related to his/her actions. | 9. Accepts consequences | In a role play situation, student will identify appropriate consequences for actions.<br><br>Student will accept consequences related to his actions. | ☐ | ☐ | ☐ |
| Student becomes agitated when not actively engaged in an activity. | 10. Deals with boredom | Student will choose and engage in an activity of individual choice when faced with a boredom situation. | ☐ | ☐ | ☐ |
| Student exhibits inappropriate behaviors (e.g., cussing, yelling, pouting) after losing. | 11. Deals with losing | Following activities involving competition, student will congratulate the (those) individual(s) who win. | ☐ | ☐ | ☐ |
| Student exhibits inappropriate behaviors when s(he) is not included in activities. | 12. Deals with being left out | Student will ask to be included in activities of choice and will identify viable alternatives to said activities. | ☐ | ☐ | ☐ |
| Student tries to "save face," making fun of or blaming other students for embarrassing situations. | 13. Deals with embarrassment | Student will respond to embarrassing situations by using one of several reactions he has generated and had approved by the teacher. | ☐ | ☐ | ☐ |

| | | | Yes | No | Unsure |
|---|---|---|---|---|---|
| Student gives up when faced with failure. | 14. Deals with failure | Student will accept assistance and continue to work after experiencing a failure. | ☐ | ☐ | ☐ |
| Student ignores and persists in his present behavior following the word "no." | 15. Accepts "no" | After hearing "no," student will discontinue his present behavior. | ☐ | ☐ | ☐ |
| Student implies/reports unfairness regarding the reasons for "no," or are unable to identify the rationale behind "no." | 16. Understands reasons for being told "no" | Student will identify and/or reiterate reasons for being told "no." | ☐ | ☐ | ☐ |
| | | Students will explain the rationale behind being told "no." | | | |
| Student primarily eats junk foods. | 17. Eats well | Student identifies rationale for eating healthy. | ☐ | ☐ | ☐ |
| | | Student identifies sources of appropriate nutrition. | | | |
| | | Student plans and follows a nutritious diet. | | | |
| Student is lethargic and sedentary. | 18 Exercises | Student identifies rationale for exercising. | ☐ | ☐ | ☐ |
| | | Student plans and incorporates physical activity in to each day's routine. | | | |
| Student frequently complains of not having enough time to complete assigned tasks, engage in enjoyed activities, etc. | 19. Manages time | Student will prepare and follow a daily schedule, incorporating all important activities of his/her day. | ☐ | ☐ | ☐ |
| Student complains of and appears frequently stressed. | 20. Relaxes | | Yes ☐ | No ☐ | Unsure ☐ |
| | (a) Muscle relaxation *(tightening and relaxing muscles)* | In a group setting, student will use the following relaxation techniques: | | | |
| Student utilizes maladaptive relaxation strategies (e.g., drinking, fighting). | (b) Deep breathing *(belly breathing)* | (a) muscle relaxation (b) counting backwards (c) deep breathing (d) positive imagery (e) meditation | | | |
| | (c) Counting backwards *(from a preselected number)* | When faced with an identified stressor, student will utilize relaxation techniques. | | | |
| | (d) Positive imagery (e) Meditation | | | | |

| If the Student Makes This Error (does) | **Then This Is the Problem:** | And This Is the Objective (without criteria) (will) | Does the Student Have the Skills? | | |
|---|---|---|---|---|---|
| | **Personal (Self-Control)** | | | | |
| Student often attributes incompetancies or outside negative variables/actions to inner, unchangeable characteristics. | 21. Eliminates distorted thinking<br>(a) identifies feelings triggered by distorted thoughts<br>(b) identifies distorted thoughts<br>(c) refutes distorted thoughts<br>(d) stops distorted thoughts | The student will<br>(a) identify feelings triggered by distorted thoughts<br>(b) identify distorted thoughts<br>(c) refute distorted thoughts<br>(d) stop distorted thoughts | Yes ☐ | No ☐ | Unsure ☐ |
| Student surrounds self with individuals who make depreciating remarks and/or engage in maladaptive behaviors. | 22. Maintains supportive environment | In a role play, student will identify characteristics of friends.<br><br>Student will identify people in his/her life to turn to for support. | Yes ☐ | No ☐ | Unsure ☐ |
| Student refuses assistance from family and/or friends.<br><br>Student spends most time alone. | 23. Maintains a support group | When faced with a negative situation during role play, student will appropriately solicit assistance/advice.<br><br>Student will choose a peer buddy each day. | Yes ☐ | No ☐ | Unsure ☐ |
| | **Interpersonal** | | | | |
| When student enters a new situation/group, he/she automatically begins talking. | 1. Introduces self | In role play, students will introduce themselves to unknown individuals. | Yes ☐ | No ☐ | Unsure ☐ |
| Student's speech is disjointed and follows no clear train of thought. | 2. Makes clear statements | Student will plan and make clear, concise statements. | Yes ☐ | No ☐ | Unsure ☐ |
| Student uses aggressive "you" blaming language (e.g., "it's your fault I got an 'F' on my spelling test). | 3. Uses "I" messages | In role play, student will use "I" messages in conversation (e.g., "I feel sad when I don't pass my spelling tests"). | Yes ☐ | No ☐ | Unsure ☐ |
| Student waits for others to begin speaking before joining in. | 4. Begins a conversation | Student will initiate conversations with peers across settings. | Yes ☐ | No ☐ | Unsure ☐ |
| Student does not pause to allow listeners an opportunity to react to information during conversations. | 5. Pauses in conversations | In role play, student will pause speaking to allow listeners to speak. | Yes ☐ | No ☐ | Unsure ☐ |

| | | | Yes | No | Unsure |
|---|---|---|---|---|---|
| When student becomes disinterested in a conversation, or prior to the conclusion of a conversation, he/she walks away. | 6. Ends a conversation | In role play, student will conclude conversations. | ☐ | ☐ | ☐ |
| Student frequently interrupts other persons in conversation. | 7. Takes turn in conversation | Student will wait for pauses by speaker before speaking. | ☐ | ☐ | ☐ |
| Student passively observes and stands away from a group during activities *or* jumps in to activities without first being invited/asking permission. | 8. Joins in | Student will ask to join in activities of interest. | ☐ | ☐ | ☐ |
| Student declines offers to engage in games with peers. Student makes up own rules, or refuses to follow rules, when playing games. | 9. Plays a game | Student will accept invitations to play games of interest. Student will ask a peer to play a game. Before beginning a new game, student will verbally report group rules. | ☐ | ☐ | ☐ |
| When needing favor done, student often tells individuals what to do or demands help. | 10. Asks a favor | During role play, student will politely ask for assistance with tasks (i.e., saying please/thank-you). | ☐ | ☐ | ☐ |
| Student ignores requests for assistance from peers. | 11. Offers help to a classmate | During role play, student will recognize peers need for help and offer assistance. | ☐ | ☐ | ☐ |
| Student makes sarcastic remarks regarding accomplishments or positive characteristics of peers. | 12. Gives a compliment | Student will make positive statements about the qualities and accomplishments of others. | ☐ | ☐ | ☐ |
| When given a compliment, the student often belittles themselves or makes negative comments regarding their accomplishments. | 13. Accepts a compliment | In a role play, student will acknowledge and accept compliments. | ☐ | ☐ | ☐ |

| If the Student Makes This Error (does) | Then This Is the Problem: | And This Is the Objective (without criteria) (will) | Does the Student Have the Skills? | | |
|---|---|---|---|---|---|

**Interpersonal**

| If the Student Makes This Error (does) | Then This Is the Problem: | And This Is the Objective (without criteria) (will) | Yes | No | Unsure |
|---|---|---|---|---|---|
| After given assistance, student walks away from situations, often saying nothing in thanks. | 14. Says "thank you" | Student will appropriately (i.e., voice tone, facial expression) thank individuals for assistance. | ☐ | ☐ | ☐ |
| When asked for his opinion on what they want to play, student often reports "I don't know." | 15. uggests an activity | In role play, student will identify activities which they enjoy doing.<br><br>Student will suggest activities to play to peers. | ☐ | ☐ | ☐ |
| When using with objects, student denies access to peers. | 16. Shares | When asked appropriately to share by a peer/adult, student will do so. | ☐ | ☐ | ☐ |
| When student hurts others (with words/ actions), they walk away and say nothing.<br><br>Student does not recognize when they hurt others. | 17. Apologizes | In a role play, student will apologize to others after hurting them (with words or actions).<br><br>In a role play, student will identify when others feeling's have been hurt. | ☐ | ☐ | ☐ |
| Student impolitely interrupts conversations/ activities of others in order to get attention. | 18. Interrupts politely | In role plays, student will wait for pauses in conversations or activities, then say "excuse me" to get attention.<br><br>When watching a video, student will identify impolite interruptions by others. | ☐ | ☐ | ☐ |
| Student often rushes into emotional conversations and speaks before they think. | 19. Gets ready for a difficult conversation | After viewing interactions which failed (messages from speaker to listener not understood) student will identify possible reasons why and rewrite/ plan alternatives. | ☐ | ☐ | ☐ |
| Student responds only to verbal portions of messages. | 20. Deals with contradictory messages | While viewing a video, student will identify contradictions between verbal and nonverbal messages. | ☐ | ☐ | ☐ |
| Student becomes defensive and un- approachable when accused of inappropriate behaviors. | 21. Deals with accusations | In role play, student will deal constructively with accusations. | ☐ | ☐ | ☐ |

| | | | Yes | No | Unsure |
|---|---|---|---|---|---|
| Student ignores or minimizes complaints related to his behavior(s). | 22. Answers a complaint | In role play, student will correct behaviors identified in complaints. | ☐ | ☐ | ☐ |
| Student takes on more responsibilities then they can handle. <br><br>*OR*<br><br> Student engages in any behaviors requested by friends (e.g., fighting stealing, teasing). | 23. Says "no" | In role play, student will refuse unreasonable or unaccomplishable requests of another politely. | ☐ | ☐ | ☐ |
| Student takes items of desire that do not belong to him/her—even after being denied permission. | 24. Deals with wanting something that isn't yours | In role play, student will ask permission to borrow things from others. <br><br> In role play, student will identify reasons for being denied access to other's things. | ☐ | ☐ | ☐ |
| Student refuses to talk about feelings with others and/or bottles feelings up inside. | 25. Recognizes and expresses feelings | In role play conversations, student will describe his/her feelings verbally. | ☐ | ☐ | ☐ |
| In a conflict situation, student employs non-constructive resolution techniques (e.g., walks away from argument, blows up, fist fights, etc.). | 26. Solves arguments | In a role play, student will identify and employ problem solving techniques to constructively solve arguments. | ☐ | ☐ | ☐ |
| Student perceives all actions done to him/her as intentional and treats them accordingly. | 27. Recognizes and deals with intentional and accidental actions | Student will define the terms accidental and intentional. <br><br> In role play or after watching a video, student will identify intentional and accidental actions. | ☐ | ☐ | ☐ |
| Student only concerned about personal well-being and displays behaviors which show disinterest regarding others. | 28. Expresses concern for another | Student will illustrate (acceptable) interest in others. <br><br> Student will express (designated reaction) to others experiencing notable harm or good fortune. | ☐ | ☐ | ☐ |
| Student withholds feelings of affection to peers/adults/family. | 29. Expresses affection | In role play, student will display affectionate behaviors (e.g., smiling, hugging, shaking hands) toward another. | ☐ | ☐ | ☐ |

| If the Student Makes This Error (does) | Then This Is the Problem: | And This Is the Objective (without criteria) (will) | Does the Student Have the Skills? | | |
|---|---|---|---|---|---|
| | | | Yes | No | Unsure |
| | **Interpersonal** | | | | |
| Student views experiences and/or experiences from only his/her perspective. | 30. Has empathy | After watching a video, student will pretend s/he is in the characters position, identify what they were feeling, and the reasons why. | Yes ☐ | No ☐ | Unsure ☐ |
| Student affect remains flat even in times of extreme emotions for others (i.e., happy, sad). | 31. Responds emotionally to another person | In a role play, student will recognize the emotions of another and respond to them in an empathetic way. | Yes ☐ | No ☐ | Unsure ☐ |
| Student attention easily distracted away from key information needed for empathy. | 32. Knows ways to enhance empathy | In role play, student will pay attention to and read emotions from facial expressions, body language, voice tone, and verbal content. | Yes ☐ | No ☐ | Unsure ☐ |
| Student degrades individuals experiencing feelings contradictory to his/her own. | 33. Respects other people's feelings | Student will identify several possible emotions related to the same situation. | Yes ☐ | No ☐ | Unsure ☐ |
| Student believes his/her wants/likes are held by all. | 34. Respects differences in wants and likes | Student will identify differences in wants and likes between himself/herself and those close to them. | Yes ☐ | No ☐ | Unsure ☐ |
| Student engages in behaviors they have not obtained permission for (e.g., leaving the classroom). | 35. Asks permission | Student will appropriately obtain permission for activities requiring it. | Yes ☐ | No ☐ | Unsure ☐ |
| Student tells individuals (i.e. teachers, parents) of his upcoming actions rather then asking. | 36. Asking permission | During role play, student will utilize socially acceptable means (e.g., "may I please") to gain permission for activities. | Yes ☐ | No ☐ | Unsure ☐ |
| Student is surprised when someone is disappointed by his actions. | 37. Recognizes interpersonal expectations | Given situations, the student will correctly label the expectations of other individuals. | Yes ☐ | No ☐ | Unsure ☐ |
| Student does not take steps to maintain relationships. | 38. Maintains interpersonal relationships | Student will use various devices (phone, mail, personal contact) to maintain contact and put effort in working through conflicts that threaten relationships. | Yes ☐ | No ☐ | Unsure ☐ |

| If the Student Makes This Error (does) | Then This Is the Problem: | And This Is the Objective (without criteria) (will) | Does the Student Have the Skills? | | |
|---|---|---|---|---|---|

**Citizenship**

| If the Student Makes This Error (does) | Then This Is the Problem: | And This Is the Objective (without criteria) (will) | Yes | No | Unsure |
|---|---|---|---|---|---|
| Student refuses to compromise or negotiate to resolve conflicts. | 2. Negotiates | In mock conflict situations with others student will identify and offer ways to compromise. | ☐ | ☐ | ☐ |
| Student allows peers to make decisions regarding his/her actions. | 3. Stands up for rights | | ☐ | ☐ | ☐ |
| Student allows peers to pick on his/her friends or listens to gossip about them without stopping it. | 4. Stands up for a friend | . | ☐ | ☐ | ☐ |
| Student "goes along with the crowd" even when he/she is aware of the action's wrongness. | 5. Deals with group pressure | In role play, student will refuse pressures to engage in actions known to be wrong. | ☐ | ☐ | ☐ |
| Student frequently lies when asked questions by peers, teachers or family. | 6. Is honest | In role play, student will accept consequences (+/−) for telling the truth. When asked questions, student will tell the truth. | ☐ | ☐ | ☐ |
| Student believes and behaves as though all people should think/act as he/she does and creates conflict when he/she sees evidence of the contrary. | 7. Takes people's perspectives | In role play, student will identify possible reasons for differing points of views. | ☐ | ☐ | ☐ |
| Student treats peers inconsistently—employing consequences for exact actions on some but not others. | 8. Is fair | Student will identify and employ consistent consequences for actions by others. | ☐ | ☐ | ☐ |
| Student excludes peers from social situations (e.g., games, friendship) or belittles them due to their individual characteristics (e.g., physical). | 9. Respects rights and equality of others | | ☐ | ☐ | ☐ |
| Student refuses to assist with classroom tasks or individuals in need of help. _OR_ Student affect blank and makes negative comments regarding individuals or groups in need. | 10. Is caring and helping | After viewing videos of others in need, student will identify ways in which (s)he can assist them. | ☐ | ☐ | ☐ |

## Problem Solving

| | | | Yes | No | Unsure |
|---|---|---|---|---|---|
| Student generally recognizes problems AS maladaptive behaviors of other.<br><br>Student does not recognize when a problem exists. | 1. Identifies problem | During role play scenarios, the student will identify problems in terms of environmental variables and emotional factors. | ☐ | ☐ | ☐ |
| Student generates one or very few maladaptive solutions for a problem (e.g., hitting). | 2. Generates several solutions | After identifying problems, student will brainstorm a list of possible solutions and their consequences. | ☐ | ☐ | ☐ |
| Student rarely accepts responsibility and blames others for problems. | 3. Decides what caused a problem | In role plays, student will identify the cause and effect relationship in problems. | ☐ | ☐ | ☐ |
| When defining problems and/or in arguments, student blames traits (e.g., physical) of others. | 4. Avoids labels and stereotyping | In role play, student will use objective language during problem solving. | ☐ | ☐ | ☐ |
| Student acts on the first solution they think of. | 5. Chooses solutions | After assessing possible solutions for effectiveness, student will choose one. | ☐ | ☐ | ☐ |
| Student is unaware when his/her solutions to problems are ineffective. | 6. Evaluates solutions for effectiveness | After implementing a solution, student will evaluate it for effectiveness (is the problem solved?) and return to problem solving as necessary. | ☐ | ☐ | ☐ |

## Citizenship

| | | | Yes | No | Unsure |
|---|---|---|---|---|---|
| The student acts without consideration, or modification of actions, for others and society as a whole. | 1. Employs moral reasoning<br>(a) understands morality<br>(b) understands social systems<br>(c) understands conscience<br>(d) understands individualism<br>(e) understands social contracts<br>(f) understands individual rights | Student demonstrates knowledge and use of the following:<br>(a) understands morality<br>(b) understands social systems<br>(c) understands conscience<br>(d) understands individualism<br>(e) understands social contracts<br>(f) understands individual rights | ☐ | ☐ | ☐ |

**Classroom Specific**

| | | | Yes | No | Unsure |
|---|---|---|---|---|---|
| Student is loud and disruptive when entering the classroom. | 1. Enters quietly | Student will enter classroom without disruption. | ☐ | ☐ | ☐ |
| Student places materials/personal effects in places other then specified by the classroom routing. | 2. Puts things away | Student will place materials/personal effects in proper location. | ☐ | ☐ | ☐ |
| Student out of seat when required by teacher or activity. | 3. Sits in seat | Student will remain in seat during times specified by instructor. | ☐ | ☐ | ☐ |
| Student is slow to begin work specified by teachers (e.g., doodles, talks, hums). | 4. Starts work immediately | Student will begin work immediately upon request by teacher. | ☐ | ☐ | ☐ |
| Student talks while others are speaking, makes remarks unrelated to questions that have been asked of them, or engages in other behaviors incongruent to listening. | 5. Listens | During role play conversations, student will employ active listening techniques. | ☐ | ☐ | ☐ |
| Student asks for assistance unrelated to task at hand, or sits idly when confused regarding instructions or information. | 6. Asks for help | Student will request task related assistance when needed. | ☐ | ☐ | ☐ |
| Student refuses to help peers in need and/or makes fun of them for not understanding or knowing information. | 7. Offers help | Student will politely offer assistance to peers having difficulty with classroom tasks. | ☐ | ☐ | ☐ |
| Student enters classroom without necessary materials (e.g., homework, paper, pencil, notebook, books). | 8. Brings materials to class | Student will enter classroom with necessary materials. | ☐ | ☐ | ☐ |
| Student acts contrary to directions given by teachers/adults. | 9. Follows instructions | Student will behave congruent to all instructions given by school adults. | ☐ | ☐ | ☐ |
| Student turns assignments in late or not at all. | 10. Completes assignments on time | Student will turn in completed assignment on time. | ☐ | ☐ | ☐ |

| If the Student Makes This Error (does) | Then This Is the Problem: | And This Is the Objective (without criteria) (will) | Does the Student Have the Skills? | | |
|---|---|---|---|---|---|
| | | | Yes | No | Unsure |
| **Classroom Specific** | | | | | |
| Student makes no comments during classroom discussions and/or makes irrelevant remarks/comments. | 11. Contributes to discussions | During role play, student will make remarks related to discussions. Student will offer relevant contributions to classroom discussions. | Yes ☐ | No ☐ | Unsure ☐ |
| Student talks out, and asks unrelated questions to information being presented or none at all. | 12. Asks questions | Student will raise hand and ask questions related to presentation information. | Yes ☐ | No ☐ | Unsure ☐ |
| Student responds (e.g., talks to peers, watches people) to distractions in and surrounding classroom. | 13. Ignores distractions | Student will remain focused on classroom tasks. | Yes ☐ | No ☐ | Unsure ☐ |
| Student immediately turns in work without checking for errors. OR Student ignores corrective feedback from teachers. | 14. Makes corrections | Student will check for and correct all detected errors on assigned work before turning it in. | Yes ☐ | No ☐ | Unsure ☐ |
| Student accepts failure and seems content just "getting by." | 15. Sets goals | The student will select or produce realistic, yet challenging, goals. | Yes ☐ | No ☐ | Unsure ☐ |
| Student acts before obtaining permission (e.g., using the phone, leaving class). | 16. Asks permission | Student will obtain permission for activities. | Yes ☐ | No ☐ | Unsure ☐ |
| Student engages in off-task behaviors (e.g., talking to peers, leaving seat, doodling) while doing seatwork. | 17. Continues activities (on task) | Student will remain on task throughout school day. | Yes ☐ | No ☐ | Unsure ☐ |
| **Anger/Violence** | | | | | |
| Student denies feelings of anger when physiological indicators are obviously present. | 1. Knows physiological indicators of anger | During role play, student will identify physiological indicators of his anger. | Yes ☐ | No ☐ | Unsure ☐ |
| Student remains in or enters situations that make them angry. OR Student attends to hostile cues in an environment and ignore other social cues. | 2. Recognizes external and internal triggers | During role play, student will identify situations and/or behaviors that contribute to his anger. | Yes ☐ | No ☐ | Unsure ☐ |

| Problem Behavior | Objective | Criterion | Yes | No | Unsure |
|---|---|---|---|---|---|
| Student allows anger to build up. | 3. Uses anger reducers and relaxation<br>(a) uses self-statements in pressure situations<br>(b) uses self-evaluation in pressure situations<br>(c) Anticipates consequences which are:<br>√ short and long term<br>√ most and least probable<br>√ internal and external | Student will use following techniques to reduce anger:<br>(a) Uses self-statements in pressure situations<br>(b) Uses self-evaluation in pressure situations<br>(c) Anticipates consequences which are:<br>√ short and long term<br>√ most and least probable<br>√ internal and external | ☐ | ☐ | ☐ |
| Student cannot explain why he gets angry and/or is surprised when he is. | 4. Knows angry behavior cycle | Student will describe how anger occurs and what may signal its onset. | ☐ | ☐ | ☐ |
| Student taunts others into engaging in behaviors that anger him/her. | 5. Changes own provoking behavior | Student will identify behaviors in his repertoire that anger others. | ☐ | ☐ | ☐ |
| Student blames others for his feelings of anger. | 6. Deals with own anger | During role play, student will accept ownership for his feelings of anger. | ☐ | ☐ | ☐ |
| Student becomes progressively angrier in situations where others are angry. | 7. Deals with another's anger | Student will identify indicators of other's anger. | ☐ | ☐ | ☐ |
| Student confuses and acts on feelings of fear as feeling of anger. | 8. Deals with fear | In role play, student will identify indicators of fear.<br><br>In role play, student will identify the similarities and differences between anger and fear. | ☐ | ☐ | ☐ |
| Student chooses friends and enters environments in which he/she is likely to encounter trouble. | 9. Avoids trouble | In role play, student will identify situations or individuals which precede trouble.<br><br>Student will avoid environments that cause them trouble. | ☐ | ☐ | ☐ |
| Student relies on aggressive problem solving techniques. | 10. Stays out of fights | When faced with conflict, student will utilize non-aggressive problem solving techniques. | ☐ | ☐ | ☐ |

| If the Student Makes This Error (does) | Then This Is the Problem: | And This Is the Objective (without criteria) (will) | Does the Student Have the Skills? | | |
|---|---|---|---|---|---|
| | **Anger/Violence** | | Yes | No | Unsure |
| Student acts before they think about the consequences. | 11. Controls impulses | In role play, student will identify possible consequences before taking action. | ☐ | ☐ | ☐ |
| | | | Yes | No | Unsure |
| Student is often in trouble for fighting. | 12. Employs nonviolent alternative solutions | During role play, student will identify non-violent solutions to possible conflicts and/or problems. | ☐ | ☐ | ☐ |

# Functional Assessment Interview Form

Name of Student _____ Age _____ Date _____

Interviewer _____ Respondent _____

## A. DESCRIBE THE BEHAVIOR(S)

1. What are the behaviors of concern? For each behavior, define the topography (how it is performed), frequency (how often it occurs per day, week, month), duration (how long it last when it occurs), and the intensity (what is the magnitude of the behaviors: low, medium, or high)? Does it cause harm to others or the student?

| Behavior | Topography | Frequency | Duration | Intensity |
|----------|-----------|-----------|----------|-----------|
|          |           |           |          |           |
|          |           |           |          |           |
|          |           |           |          |           |
|          |           |           |          |           |
|          |           |           |          |           |
|          |           |           |          |           |
|          |           |           |          |           |
|          |           |           |          |           |

2. Which of the behaviors above occur together? (e.g., occur at he same time; occur in a predictable "chain"; occur in the same situation).

## B. DEFINE ECOLOGICAL EVENTS THAT MAY AFFECT BEHAVIOR(S)

1. What medications is the student taking (if any) and how do you believe these may affect behavior?

2. What medical complications (if any) does the student have that may his or her behavior (e.g., asthma, allergies, seizures)?

3.     Describe the extent to which you believe activities that occur during the day are *predictable* for the person. To what extent does the student know the activities that will occur (e.g., reading, lunch, recess, group time)?

4.     About how often does the student get to make choices about activities, reinforcers, etc.? In what areas does the student get to make choices (academic activity, play activity, type of task)?

5.     How many other people are in the classroom setting? Do you believe that the density of people or interactions with other individuals affect the target behaviors?

6.     What is the staffing pattern? To what extent do you believe the number of staff, training of staff, quality or social contact with staff, etc. affect the target behavior?

7.     Are the tasks/activities presented during the day boring or unpleasant for the student, or do they lead to results that are preferred or valued?

8.     What outcomes are monitored regularly by you and/or your aide (frequency of behaviors, skills learned, activity patterns)?

**C.   DEFINE EVENTS AND SITUATIONS THAT PREDICT OCCURANCES OF TARGET BEHAVIORS**

1.    **Time of Day:**    When are the behaviors most likely? Least likely?

Most
likely    _____

Least
likely    _____

2.   **Settings:**   Where are the behaviors most likely? Least likely?

Most
likely    _____

Least
likely    _____

3. **Social Control:** With whom are the behaviors most likely? Least likely?

Most
likely _____

Least
likely _____

4. **Activity:** What activity is most likely to produce the behavior? Least likely?

Most
likely _____

Least
likely _____

5. Are there particular situations , events, etc. that are not listed above that "set off" the behaviors that cause concern (particular demands, interruptions, transitions, delays, being ignored, etc.)?

6. What would be the one thing that you could do that would be the most likely to make the undesirable behavior(s) occur?

D. **IDENTIFY THE "FUNCTION" OF THE UNDESIREABLE BEHAVIOR(S). WHAT CONSEQUENCES MAINATIN THE BEHAVIOR(S)?**

1. Use this Exhibit to guide your thinking as you fill out the blank template below.

B-6.3

DOMAINS OF SOCIAL CONTENT

CATEGORIES OF FUNCTIONS:

| | | A. PERSONAL (SELF REGULATION AND CONTROL) | B. INTERPERSONAL (RELATIONS WITH OTHERS) | C. PROBLEM SOLVING | D. CITIZENSHIP | E. CLASSROOM SPECIFIC | F. ANGER/VIOLENCE | G. OTHER |
|---|---|---|---|---|---|---|---|---|
| TYPE 1: EXTERNAL (actions, accomplishments or things) | AVOID "I do not want to…" | Fail to explain my behavior, Give up preferred activities, Act Impulsively, Be shocked or surprised, Be unable to decide | Making confusing statements, Criticize, Talk too much, Physically hurt others, Always be doing what the other person wants | Deal with it now, Organize my materials, Make mistakes, Waste my time or the time of others, Carry out other people's agenda | Experience bias, Be accused of letting others down, Have the quality of education diminished in my local schools, Be dependent on others, Be put in Jail, Fail to help those in need | Fail to learn, do things incorrectly, ignore the teacher or the assignments, receive punishment, be left out. | Be hurt, be attacked, have a friend attacked or hurt, lose things through robbery, hurt others, fight, be abusive and threatening | |
| | OBTAIN "I do want to…" | State why, Reward my self, Make plans, Correctly predict outcomes, List options and resources | Making specific statements, Giving compliments, Listen, Touch appropriately, Suggest alternative activities | Get resolution, Organize my stuff, Catch mistakes before others notice them, Work efficiently, Do what I've decided to do. | Be treated as an individual, Act dependably, Contribute to an adequately supported community structure, Be responsible for my own welfare, Follow rules, Do my part to reduce suffering | Learn, do things correctly, work with the teacher, attend, get rewards and recognition, be a part of the group. | Want to go to school and move about safely, be treated as a friend and someone who can get what he wants through intelligence and honesty | |
| TYPE 2: INTERNAL (feelings, thoughts, emotional status) | AVOID "I do not want to…" | Feel stress, Feel guilt, Be ashamed, Be afraid, Be bored | Be Isolated, Feel rejected, Be manipulated, Be disregard, Feel ridiculed | Worry about getting it done, Feel overwhelmed by the work, be embarrassed because I did the wrong thing, Feel like a bungler, Think I am some else's puppet. | Feel that I am letting my community down, Want to get things through criminal activity, Be deceitful, Think I am lazy, Think I should get things I don't deserve | Feel dumb, confused, feel lost, be bored, be embarrassed, be afraid | Feel afraid, feel like a victim, feel pain, be scared to come to school or move about school or be around some people, regret over what I have done, feel that I can only get things by fighting, feel ashamed, guilty, or embarrassed | |
| | OBTAIN "I do want to…" | Be relaxed, Have pride, Feel satisfied, Be confident, Feel excitement | Feel related to someone, Think I am accepted, Have a sense that there is reciprocity in my life, Feel confirmation, Think I am respected | Have a feeling of closure, Feel on top of things, Feel competent, Be confident that I am an capable, Believe that I'm living the life I choose | Think that I am a responsible member of society, Respect the laws, Be confident that I am honest with others, Feel that I work hard and hold up my part, Feel I am fair | Feel successful, understand, know what to do, be involved and interested, feel secure and confident | Want to feel secure and safe. I also want to know that my teachers, friends, and property are safe. I want to be proud of my actions and confident that others do not simply see me as a threat | |

BLANK FORM FOR YOU TO FILL OUT

| CATEGORIES OF FUNCTIONS: | | A. PERSONAL (SELF REGULATIO N AND CONTROL) | B. INTERPERSO NAL (RELATIONS WITH OTHERS) | C. PROBLE M SOLVING | D. CITIZENS HIP | E. CLASSROO M SPECIFIC | F. ANGER/ VIOLENC E | G. OTHER |
|---|---|---|---|---|---|---|---|---|
| TYPE 1: EXTERNAL (actions, accomplishme nts or things) | AVOID "I do not want to..." | | | | | | | |
| | OBTAIN "I do want to..." | | | | | | | |
| TYPE 2: INTERNAL (feelings, thoughts, emotional status) | AVOID "I do not want to..." | | | | | | | |
| | OBTAIN "I do want to..." | | | | | | | |

2.     Think of each of the behaviors listed in section A and define the function(s) you believe the behavior serves for the student (i.e., what does he/she get and/or avoid by doing the behavior)?

| Behavior | What does he/she get | What does he/she avoid |
|----------|----------------------|------------------------|
|          |                      |                        |

3.  .   Describe the student's most typical response to the following situations:

a.     Are the above behaviors more likely, less likely, or unaffected if you present him or her with a difficult task?

b.     Are the above behaviors more likely, less likely, or unaffected if you interrupt a desired event (e.g., talking with a peer, reading a book, etc.)?

c.     Are the above behavior(s) more likely, less likely, or unaffected if you deliver a "stern" request/command/reprimand?

d.     Are the above behaviors more likely, less likely, or unaffected by changes in routine?

e.     Are the above behaviors more likely, less likely, or unaffected if something the student wants is present, but he/she cannot get it (i.e., a desired object that is visible but out of reach)?

f.     Are the above behaviors more likely, less likely, or unaffected if you are present, but do not interact with (ignore) the student for 15 minutes?

g.     Are the above behaviors more likely, less likely, or unaffected if the student is alone (no one else is present)?

B-6.3

## E. DEFINE THE EFFICIENCY OF THE UNDESIREABLE BEHAVIORS

1.      What amount of physical effort is involved in the behaviors (e.g., prolonged, intense tantrums vs. simple verbal outburst, etc.)?

2.      Does engaging in the behaviors result in "payoff" (getting attention, avoiding work) every time? Almost every time?  Once in  awhile?

3.      How much of a delay is there between the time the student engages in the behavior and receiving the "payoff"?  Is it immediate, a few seconds, longer?

## F. WHAT EVENTS, ACTIONS, AND OBJECTS ARE PERCEIVED AS POSITIVE BY THE STUDENT?

1.      In general, what are things (events/activities/objects/people) that appear to be reinforcing or enjoyable for the student?

## G. WHAT "FUNCTIONAL ALTERNATIVE" BEHAVIORS ARE KNOWN BY THE STUDENT?

1.      What socially appropriate behaviors/skills does the student perform that may be ways of achieving the same *function(s)* as the behaviors of concern?

2.      What things can you do to improve the likelihood that a teaching session will occur smoothly?

3.      What things can you do that would interfere with or disrupt a teaching session?

## H. PROVIDE AHISTORY OF THE UNDESIREABLE BEHAVUIORS AND THE PROGRAMS THAT HAVE BEEN ATTEMPTED

| Behavior | How long has this been a problem? | Programs | Effect |
|---|---|---|---|
| | | | |
| | | | |
| | | | |
| | | | |
| | | | |

B-6.3

_____
_____
_____
_____
_____
_____

The materials in this set of procedures was drawn from the following resources:

Gable, R.A., Quinn, M.M., Rutherford, R.B., Nelson, C.M. and Howell, K.W. (1999). *Addressing student problem behavior: An IEP team's introduction to functional behavior assessment and behavior intervention plans.* American Institute for Research, Center for Effective Collaboration: Washington, D.C.

Gresham, F.M. & Noell, G.H. (1998). *Functional analysis assessment as a cornerstone for non categorical special education.* In D.J. Reschly, W. D. Tilly III & J. P. Grimes, *Functional and noncategorical identification and intervention in special education*, Iowa Department of Education as adapted from O'Neill, Horner, Albin, Sprague, Storey & Newton (1997) *Functional assessment of problem behavior: A practical assessment guide.* (2nd ed.). Pacific Grove: Brooks/Cole.

Kaplan, J. (2000). *Beyond Functional Assessment: A Social Cognitive Approach to the Evaluation of Behavior Problems in Children and Youth.* Austin, TX: Pro-Ed.

O'Neil, R., Horner, R., Sprague, R., Storey, K., & Newton, J. (1997). *Functional assessment of problem behavior: A practical guide* (2nd ed.) Pacific Grove, CA Brooks/Cole

O'Neil, R., Horner, R., Sprague, R., Storey, K., & Newton, J. (1997). *Functional assessment of problem behavior: A practical guide* (2nd ed.) Pacific Grove, CA Brooks/Cole

# CROSS REFERENCE FOR SOCIAL SKILLS, PART 1

| Personal (self-control) | Skill Streaming: Adolescent (page) | Skill Streaming: Elementary (page) | Tough Kid Social Skills (3–6) (page) | Cool Kids (page) | Social Skills for School and Community (page) |
|---|---|---|---|---|---|
| Knows own feelings | 82 | 116 | | | |
| Understands own feelings | 83 | 117 | | | |
| Deals with conflicting feelings | | 121-4, 133 | | | |
| Recognizes changing feelings | | 142 | | | |
| Recognizes another's feelings | | 118 | | | 233 |
| Shows understanding of another's feelings | 84 | 119 | | | |
| Rewards self | 88 | 125 | | | 126 |
| Uses self-control strategies | 93 | 126 | 141 | | |
| Accepts consequences | | 132 | | | 75 |
| Deals with boredom | | 135 | | | |
| Deals with losing | 100 | 139, 140 | | | |
| Deals with being left out | 102 | 141 | 152 | | 214 |
| Deals with embarrassment | 101 | 142 | | | 159 |
| Deals with failure | 105 | 143 | | | 212 |
| Deals with teasing | 95 | 127, 128 | 149 | | |
| Accepts "no" | | 144 | 154 | 183, 194 | 180 |
| Understands reasons for being told "no" | | | | 194 | |
| Eats well | | | | | |
| Exercises | | | | | |
| Manages time | | | | | |
| Relaxes | | 146 | | | |
| Muscle relaxation | | 146 | | | |
| Deep breathing | | 146 | | | |
| Counting backwards | | 146 | | | |
| Positive imagery | | 146 | | | |
| Meditation | | | | | |
| Eliminates distorted thinking | | | | | |
| Identifies feelings triggered by distorted thoughts | | | | | |

| | Skill Streaming: Adolescent | Skill Streaming: Elementary | Tough Kid Social Skills (3–6) | Cool Kids | Social Skills for School and Community |
|---|---|---|---|---|---|
| Identifies distorted thoughts | | | | | |
| Refutes distorted thoughts | | | | | |
| Stops distorted thoughts | | | | | |
| Maintains supportive environment | | | | | |
| Maintains a support group | | | | | |
| | | | | | |
| **Interpersonal** | | | | | |
| Introduces self | 73 | 104 | | 204 | 163 |
| Makes clear statements | | | | 182, 181 | 68 |
| Uses "I" messages | | 121 | | | |
| Begins a conversation | | 105 | 127, 135 | 177, 188, 196 | 78, 167 |
| Pauses in conversation | | 127 | | | 178 |
| Ends a conversation | | 106 | | | 78, 176 |
| Takes turn in conversation | | | 135 | 181, 206 | 70, 178 |
| Joins in | 77 | 107 | 130 | 184, 205 | 170 |
| Plays a game | | 108 | 137 | | 70 |
| Asks a favor | | 109 | | 180, 200 | 81, 132, 183 |
| Offers help to a classmate | | 110 | | 186, 210 | |
| Gives a compliment | | 111 | | 197 | 172, 226 |
| Accepts a compliment | 75 | 112 | | 198 | 155 |
| Says "thank you" | 72 | 93 | | | 65 |
| Suggests an activity | | 113 | | | 84, 134, 223 |
| Shares | 90 | 114 | | | 40 |
| Apologizes | 80 | 115 | | 187, 201 | 174 |
| Interrupts politely | | | | 178, 188, 199 | 33, 38 |
| Gets ready for a difficult conversation | 108 | | 135 | | |
| Deals with contradictory messages | 106 | | | | |
| Deals with accusations | 99 | 133 | | | 209 |
| Makes a complaint | 98 | 137 | | 185, 207 | 228 |
| Answers a complaint | | 138 | | | 230, 243, 251 |
| Says "no" | | 145 | | | 241 |
| Copes with wanting something that isn't his or hers | | 148 | | | |
| Recognizes and expresses feelings | | 116, 117 | 132 | 202 | 123, 128, 130, 216 |

| | Skill Streaming: Adolescent | Skill Streaming: Elementary | Tough Kid Social Skills (3–6) | Cool Kids | Social Skills for School and Community |
|---|---|---|---|---|---|
| Solves arguments | | 131 | 146 | 209 | |
| Recognizes and deals with intentional and accidental actions | | | | | |
| Expresses concern for another | 86 | 120 | | 185, 207 | 130 |
| Expresses affection | | 123 | | | 218 |
| Has empathy | | 118 | | | |
| Responds emotionally to another person | | 119 | | | 86 |
| Knows ways to enhance empathy | | | | | |
| Respects other people's feelings | 84 | | | | |
| Respects differences in wants and likes | | | | 186 | 142 |
| Asks permission | | | | 180, 200 | 33, 81 |
| Recognizes interpersonal expectations | | 124 | | 173, 176, 186 | 255, 257 |
| Maintains interpersonal relationships | | | | 186 | |
| Understands how to listen | | 91 | | 174 | |
| | | | | | |
| Problem Solving | | | | | |
| Identifies problem | | 131 | | | |
| Generates several solutions | | | | | |
| Decides what caused a problem | 111 | 136 | 142 | | |
| Avoids labels and stereotyping | | | | | |
| Chooses solutions | 116 | 131, 149 | | | |
| Evaluates solutions for effectiveness | | 131 | | | |
| | | | | | |
| Citizenship | | | | | |
| Employs moral reasoning | | | | | |
| Understands morality | | | | | |
| Understands social systems | | | | | |
| Understands conscience | | | | | |
| Understands individualism | | | | | |
| Understands social contracts | | | | | |

| | Skill Streaming: Adolescent | Skill Streaming: Elementary | Tough Kid Social Skills (3–6) | Cool Kids | Social Skills for School and Community |
|---|---|---|---|---|---|
| Understands individual rights | | | | | |
| Negotiates | 92 | 134 | | 186 | 249 |
| Stands up for rights | 94 | | | 195 | 201 |
| Stands up for a friend | 103 | | | | 221 |
| Deals with group pressure | 109 | 147 | | 208 | 237 |
| Is honest | | 150 | | | 73, 75 |
| Takes people's perspectives | | | | | |
| Is fair | | 108, 139, 140 | | 186 | 70, 187 |
| Respects rights and equality of others | 91 | 97, 110 | | | 193-5, 235, 255 |
| Is caring and helping | | | | 210 | 140 |
| School-to-work goals | | | | | 47-58, 247, 253 |
| | | | | | |
| Classroom Specific | | | | | |
|   Enters quietly | | | | | 45 |
|   Puts things away | | | | | 43 |
|   Sits in seat | | | | | 29, 31 |
|   Starts work immediately | 110 | 102 | | | |
| Listens | 68 | 91 | | 174, 191 | 136 |
| Asks for help | 76 | 92 | | 180, 200 | 33, 38, 132 |
| Offers help | 91 | 98 | | 186, 203, 210 | 140 |
| Brings materials to class | | 94 | | | |
| Follows instructions | 79 | 79 | | 175, 192 | 29, 75, 93, 107, 109 |
| Completes assignments on time | | 96 | | | 101, 151 |
| Contributes to discussions | 22-3, 25, 27, 31 | 97 | | 181 | 36, 103, 105 |
| Asks questions | 71 | 99 | | 182 | |
| Ignores distractions | | 100 | | | 97 |
| Makes corrections | | 101 | | | |
| Sets goals | 112 | 103 | | | |
| Asks permission | 89 | 127 | | 180, 200 | 33 |
| Continues activities (on task) | | | | | 99 |
| Answers questions | | | | 181 | 36 |
| | | | | | |
| Anger/Violence | | | | | |
| Knows physiological indicators of anger | | | | | |
| Recognizes external and internal triggers | | 116, 121, 122 | | | |
| Uses anger reducers and relaxation | | 121, 122 | | | |

| | Skill Streaming: Adolescent | Skill Streaming: Elementary | Tough Kid Social Skills (3–6) | Cool Kids | Social Skills for School and Community |
|---|---|---|---|---|---|
| Uses self-statements in pressure situations | | 142 | | | |
| Uses self-evaluation in pressure situations | | 132 | | | |
| Anticipates consequences | | 132 | | | |
| Short and long term | | | | | |
| Most and least probable | | | | | |
| Internal and external | | | | | |
| Knows angry behavior cycle | | 120, 122 | | | |
| Changes own provoking behavior | | 121 | | | |
| Deals with own anger | | 122 | | | |
| Deals with another's anger | 85 | 129 | | | 239 |
| Deals with fear | 87 | 130 | | | |
| Avoids trouble | 96 | | | | |
| Stays out of fights | | | | | |
| Controls impulses | | | | | |
| Employs nonviolent alternative solutions | | | | | 128 |

## CROSS REFERENCE FOR SOCIAL SKILLS, PART 2

| | Second Step Violence Prevention K | Second Step Violence Prevention 1-3 | Second Step Violence Prevention 4-5 | Second Step Violence Prevention 6-8 | Beyond Functional Assessment |
|---|---|---|---|---|---|
| Personal (self-control) | (unit.lesson) | (unit.lesson) | (unit.lesson) | (unit.lesson) | (unit) |
| Knows own feelings | 1.2 | 1.5, 1.7, 1.8, 1.13 | | 2.1 | |
| Understands own feelings | | 1.5 | 2.2 | | |
| Deals with conflicting feelings | 1.3 | 1.14 | | 2.1 | |
| Recognizes changing feelings | 1.5 | 1.5, 1.8, 1.13 | 1.3, 1.7, 1.10 | 2.1 | |
| Recognizes another's feelings | 1.2, 1.3, 1.4 | 1.2, 1.3, 1.4, 1.8, 1.13 | 1.2, 1.10 | | |

| | Second Step Violence Prevention K | Second Step Violence Prevention 1-3 | Second Step Violence Prevention 4-5 | Second Step Violence Prevention 6-8 | Beyond Functional Assessment |
|---|---|---|---|---|---|
| Shows understanding of another's feelings | 1.6 | 1.4, 1.6, 1.10, 1.13, 1.17 | 1.4, 1.11, 1.16, 3.9 | 2.2 | |
| Rewards self | | | | | |
| Uses self-control strategies | | | | | 1-10 |
| Accepts consequences | | 3.11 | 3.12 | | 5, 6, (1-10) |
| Deals with boredom | | | | | |
| Deals with losing | | | | | |
| Deals with being left out | | 3.10 | 3.8 | | |
| Deals with embarrassment | | | | | |
| Deals with failure | | 3.13 | | | |
| Deals with teasing | 3.4 | 3.7 | 3.6 | 4.4 | 8 |
| Accepts "no" | | | | | |
| Understands reasons for being told "no" | 3.6 | 3.11 | 3.12 | | |
| Eats well | | | | | |
| Exercises | | | | | |
| Manages time | | | | | |
| Relaxes | | | | 3.2 | 8-10 |
| Muscle relaxation | | | | | 8-10 |
| Deep breathing | 3.1 | 3.3, 3.8, 3.12 | 3.3 | 3.2, 4.1 | 8-10 |
| Counting backwards | 3.1 | 3.3, 3.8, 3.12 | 3.3 | 3.2, 4.1 | |
| Positive imagery | 3.1 | 3.3, 3.8, 3.12 | 3.3 | 3.2, 4.1 | 8-10 |
| Meditation | | | | | |
| Eliminates distorted thinking | | | | | |
| Identifies feelings triggered by distorted thoughts | | | | | |
| Identifies distorted thoughts | | | 2.9 | | |
| Refutes distorted thoughts | | | | | |
| Stops distorted thoughts | | | | | |
| Maintains supportive environment | | | | | |
| Maintains a support group | | | | | |
| Interpersonal | | | | | |
| Introduces self | | | | | |
| Makes clear statements | | | | | |

| | Second Step Violence Prevention K | Second Step Violence Prevention 1-3 | Second Step Violence Prevention 4-5 | Second Step Violence Prevention 6-8 | Beyond Functional Assessment |
|---|---|---|---|---|---|
| Uses "I" messages | 1.10 | 1.7, 1.8 | 1.9, 1.10 | 2.4 | |
| Begins a conversation | | 2.16 | 2.8 | | |
| Pauses in conversation | 2.10 | | | | |
| Ends a conversation | | 2.16 | 2.8 | | |
| Takes turn in conversation | | | | | |
| Joins in | | 2.4, 2.11 | | | |
| Plays a game | | 2.12 | | | |
| Asks a favor | | | | | 6 |
| Offers help to a classmate | | | | | |
| Gives a compliment | | | 2.7 | | 9 |
| Accepts a compliment | | | 2.7 | | 9 |
| Says "thank you" | | | | | |
| Suggest an activity | | | | | |
| Shares | 2.6, 2.8 | 2.8 | | | |
| Apologizes | | 2.14 | 2.9 | | |
| Interrupts politely | 2.10 | 2.7 | | | |
| Gets ready for a difficult conversation | | | | | 8 |
| Deals with contradictory messages | | | | | |
| Deals with accusations | | 3.14 | 3.11 | | |
| Makes a complaint | | 3.15 | 3.14 | 4.1 | 9 |
| Answers a complaint | | | 3.6, 3.14 | 4.1 | |
| Says "no" | | | | | 8 |
| Copes with wanting something that isn't his or hers | | 2.8 | | | |
| Recognizes and expresses feelings | | 1.7 | 1.2, 1.3, 1.10 | | 5-10 |
| Solves arguments | | | | | |
| Recognizes and deals with intentional and accidental actions | 1.8 | 1.11, 1.13 | 1.12 | | 5, 8 |
| Expresses concern for another | | 1.16 | 1.15 | | |
| Expresses affection | | | | | |
| Has empathy | | 1.8, 1.10 | 1.8, 1.10, 1.16 | 2.2, 2.3 | |
| Responds emotionally to another person | | | | | |
| Knows ways to enhance empathy | | | | 2.3 | |
| Respects other people's feelings | | | 1.5, 1.10 | 2.2 | |
| Respects differences in wants and likes | 1.7 | 1.9, 1.13 | 1.6 | | |

234

| | Second Step Violence Prevention K | Second Step Violence Prevention 1-3 | Second Step Violence Prevention 4-5 | Second Step Violence Prevention 6-8 | Beyond Functional Assessment |
|---|---|---|---|---|---|
| Asks permission | 2.7, 2.10 | 2.13 | | | |
| Recognizes interpersonal expectations | | | 2.1, 2.6 | | 1-10 |
| Maintains interpersonal relationships | | | | | |
| Understands how to listen | | 1.15 | 2.14 | 2.4 | |
| **Problem Solving** | | | | | |
| Identifies problem | 2.1, 2.2 | 2.1, 2.2, 2.9, 2.14 | 2.3 | 3.3 | 5, 8 |
| Generates several solutions | 2.3 | 2.3, 2.9, 2.14 | 2.4 | 3.4 | 5, 8 |
| Decides what caused a problem | 2.1 | | 2.9 | | 5, 8 |
| Avoids labels and stereotyping | | | | | |
| Chooses solutions | | 1.12, 1.13, 2.5, 2.6, 2.8, 2.9, 2.14, 2.18, 2.19 | 1.13, 2.4, 2.5, 2.11, 3.10 | 3.4 | 5, 8 |
| Evaluates solutions for effectiveness | 2.5 | 2.3, 2.5, 2.9, 2.14 | 2.4, 2.5, 2.11 | 3.4, 3.5 | 5, 8 |
| **Citizenship** | | | | | |
| Employs moral reasoning | | | | | |
| Understands morality | | | | | |
| Understands social systems | | | | | |
| Understands conscience | | | | | |
| Understands individualism | | | | | |
| Understands social contracts | | | | | |
| Understands individual rights | | | | | |
| Negotiates | | | | | |
| Stands up for rights | | | | | |
| Stands up for a friend | | | | | |
| Deals with group pressure | | 2.17 | 2.13 | 4.2 | |
| Is honest | | | 2.15 | | |
| Takes people's perspectives | | | 1.8, 1.10, 1.16 | 2.2 | |
| Is fair | 1.9 | 1.12, 1.13 | 1.13 | | |
| Respects rights and equality of others | 1.9 | 1.12, 1.17 | 1.7, 1.13, 1.16 | 2.3 | 5 |

B-6-4

| | Second Step Violence Prevention K | Second Step Violence Prevention 1-3 | Second Step Violence Prevention 4-5 | Second Step Violence Prevention 6-8 | Beyond Functional Assessment |
|---|---|---|---|---|---|
| Is caring and helping | 1.12 | | 1.15 | | |
| School to work goals | | | | | |
| | | | | | |
| Classroom Specific | | | | | |
| Enters quietly | | | | | |
| Puts things away | | | | | |
| Sits in seat | | | | | |
| Starts work immediately | | | | | |
| Listens | 1.11 | 1.15 | 1.14 | | |
| Ask for help | | 2.10 | | | 4-6 |
| Offers help | | | | | |
| Follows instructions | | | | | 1-10 |
| Completes assignments on time | | | | | 1 |
| Contributes to discussions | | 1.1 | 1.1 | | |
| Ask questions | | | | | |
| Ignores distractions | 2.9 | 2.6 | | | 1 |
| Makes corrections | | | | | |
| Sets goals | | | 2.16 | | |
| Asks permission | 2.10 | | | | 6 |
| Continues activities (on task) | | | | | |
| | | | | | |
| Anger/Violence | | | | | |
| Knows physiological indicators of anger | 3.1 | 3.1, 3.8, 3.12 | 3.1, 3.10 | 3.1 | 5-10 |
| Recognizes external and internal triggers | | 3.2, 3.8, 3.12 | 3.2 | 3.1 | 5-10 |
| Uses anger reducers and relaxation | | 3.3, 3.6, 3.7, 3.8, 3.11, 3.12 | 3.3, 3.10 | 3.2, 4.1 | 5-10 |
| Uses self-statements in pressure situations | | 3.4, 3.8, 3.12 | 3.4 | 3.2 | 5-10 |
| Uses self-evaluation in pressure situations | | 3.5, 3.8, 3.12 | 3.5 | 3.2 | 5-10 |
| Anticipates consequences | | 2.18, 2.19, 3.6 | 2.2, 3.1, 3.13 | 3.1 | |
| Short and long term | | | | | |
| Most and least probable | | | | | |
| Internal and external | | | | | |
| Knows angry behavior cycle | | | | 3.1 | |
| Changes own provoking behavior | | | | | |

| | Second Step Violence Prevention K | Second Step Violence Prevention 1-3 | Second Step Violence Prevention 4-5 | Second Step Violence Prevention 6-8 | Beyond Functional Assessment |
|---|---|---|---|---|---|
| Deals with own anger | | | | | 5-10 |
| Deals with another's anger | | | | 3.2 | 5-10 |
| Deals with fear | | | 2.9 | | 2-4 |
| Avoids trouble | | | 2.13 | | |
| Stays out of fights | 3.5 | 3.6, 3.8, 3.12 | 3.13 | 4.5 | 8-10 |
| Controls impulses | | 2.18, 2.19 | | | 2, 4, 7, 10 |
| Employs nonviolent alternative solutions | | 3.6, 3.8, 3.12 | 3.13 | 4.5 | 6-8 |

Committee for Children (1992). Second step: A violence prevention curriculum (Series: preschool/kindergarten, grades 1–3, grades 4&5, grades 6–8). Seattle, WA.

Fister, Conrad, Kemp (1998). Cool Kids. Sopris West.

Goldstein, McGinnis, Skilstreaming the Adolescent, revised edition. Research Press, 1997.

Kaplan, J. S. (2000) Beyond Functional Assessment: A Social Cognitive Approach to the Evaluation of Behavior Problems in Children and Youth. Pro-Ed, Austin, TX.

McGinnis, Goldstein (1997). Skillstreaming the Elementary School Child, revised edition. Research Press.

Sargent (1998). Social Skills for School and Community Systematic Instruction for Children and Youth with Cognitive Delays. Council for Exceptional Children (MR/DD).

Sheridan, S. M. (1995). Tough Kid Social Skills, Sopris West, Longmont, CO.

# Domains of Social Content.

Domains of Social Content

| Categories of Functions: | | A. Personal (Self Regulation and Control) | B. Interpersonal (Relations with Others) | C. Problem Solving | D. Citizenship Specific | E. Classroom | F. Anger/ Violence | G. Other |
|---|---|---|---|---|---|---|---|---|
| Type 1: External (actions, accomplishments, or things) | Avoid "I do not want to . . ." | Give up preferred activities. Act impulsively. Be shocked or surprised. Be unable to decide. | Fail to explain my behavior. Make confusing statements. Criticize. Talk too much. Physically hurt others. Always be doing what the other person wants. | Deal with it now. Make mistakes. Waste my time or the time of others. Carry out other people's agenda. | Experience bias. Be accused of letting others down. Have the quality of education diminished in my local schools. Be dependent on others. Be put in jail. Fail to help those in need. | Fail to learn, do things incorrectly. Ignore the teacher or the assignments. Receive punishment. Be left out. | Be hurt. Be bullied. Be attacked. Have a friend attacked or hurt, lose things through robbery, hurt others. Fight. Be abusive and threatening. | |
| | Obtain "I do want to . . ." | State why. Reward myself. Make plans. Correctly predict outcomes. List options and resources. | Make specific statements. Give compliments. Listen. Touch appropriately. Suggest alternative activities. | Get resolution. Organize my stuff. Catch mistakes before others notice them. Work efficiently. Do what I've decided to do. | Be treated as an individual. Act dependably. Contribute to an adequately supported community structure. Be responsible for my own welfare. Follow rules. Do my part to reduce suffering. | Learn. Do things correctly. Work with the teacher. Attend. Get rewards and recognition. Be a part of the group. | Go to school and move about safely. Be treated as a friend and someone who can get what he wants through intelligence and honesty. | |
| Type 2: Internal (feelings, thoughts, emotional status) | Avoid "I do not want to . . ." | Feel stress. Feel guilt. Be ashamed. Be afraid. Be bored. | Be isolated. Feel rejected. Be manipulated. Be disregarded. Feel ridiculed. | Worry about getting it done. Feel overwhelmed by the work, be embarrassed because I did the wrong thing. Feel like a bungler. Think I am someone else's puppet. | Feel that I am letting my community down. Want to get things through criminal activity. Be deceitful. Think I am lazy. Think I should get things I don't deserve. | Feel dumb, confused. Feel lost. Be bored. Be embarrassed. Be afraid. | Feel afraid. Feel like a victim. Feel pain. Think of ways to hurt others. Regret over what I have done. Feel that I can only get things by fighting. Feel ashamed, guilty, or embarrassed. | |
| | Obtain "I do want to . . ." | Be relaxed. Have pride. Feel satisfied. Be confident. Feel excitement. | Feel related to someone. Think I am accepted. Have a sense that there is reciprocity in my life. Feel confirmation. Think I am respected. | Have a feeling of closure. Feel on top of things. Feel competent. Be confident that I am capable. Believe that I'm living the life I choose. | Think that I am a responsible member of society. Respect the laws. Be confident that I am honest with others. Feel that I work hard and hold up my part. Feel I am fair. | Feel successful. Understand. Know what to do. Be involved and interested. Feel secure and confident. | Feel secure and safe. I also want to know that my teachers, friends, and property are safe. I want to be proud of my actions and confident that others do not simply see me as a threat. | |

Source: Howell, K. W., Zucker, S. H. & Morehead, M. K. (2000b). Multilevel Academic Skills Inventory. Bellingham, WA: Applied Research and Development Center. To order contact the Student Co-op Bookstore, Western Washington University. FAX (360) 650-2888. Phone (360) 650-3656.

# Common Prerequisite Sheet.

Directions:

1. Only use this status sheet after:
✓ the maladaptive behavior(s) has been specified
✓ the function of behavior has been specified
✓ the target behavior(s) has been specified

2. The sheet should be filled out through collaboration with people who know the student.

3. Each question should be answered.

Type 1 (Do Behaviors)

| If a student does not engage in the target behavior, ask yourself if . . . | Status: Yes-No-Unsure Odd Items | Even Items |
|---|---|---|
| 1. . . . the student can discriminate the target and maladaptive behaviors from each other and from other behaviors. | _____ | |
| 2. . . . target and maladaptive behaviors are clearly and consistently labeled and reviewed. | | _____ |
| 3. . . . the student can monitor his own behavior well enough to know he is engaging in the target or maladaptive behavior. | _____ | |
| 4. . . . the student is encouraged to reflect on his behavior and is praised for self-corrections and/or early recognition of problems. | | _____ |
| 5. . . . the student can monitor the environment well enough to recognize events that should prompt the target behavior or inhibit the maladaptive behavior. | _____ | |
| 6. . . . cause and effect relationships between events in the environment and the student's behavior are clearly explained and reviewed. | | _____ |
| 7. . . . the student knows what behavior is expected of him. | _____ | |
| 8. . . . expectations are clearly explained and/or demonstrated to the student (they are also frequently reviewed). | | _____ |
| 9. . . . the student has the skills/knowledge to engage in the target behavior | _____ | |
| 10. . . . the student is taught how to engage in the target behavior. | | _____ |
| 11. . . . the student knows the consequences of engaging in the target behavior. | _____ | |
| 12. . . . the student is taught the consequences of engaging in the target behavior. | | _____ |
| 13. . . . the student knows the consequences of engaging in the maladaptive behavior. | _____ | |
| 14. . . . the student is taught the consequences of engaging in the maladaptive behavior. | | _____ |
| 15. . . . the student understands that his behaviors cause certain consequences. | _____ | |
| 16. . . . the reasons for the reactions of others to the student's behavior are explained. | | _____ |
| 17. . . . there are no physical factors that work against the target behavior and/or promote the maladaptive behavior (such as allergies or seizures). | _____ | |

|  | Status: Yes-No-Unsure | |
|---|---|---|
|  | Odd Items | Even Items |

18.  . . . there are environmental factors which promote the target
behavior and/or work against the maladaptive behavior.
For example:
3 examples of the target behaviors are commonly found in the
student's environment.
3 appropriate instruction occurs in the student's classroom.
3 appropriate management techniques are used in the
classroom.    _____

19.  . . . the student generates solutions to problems that include the
target behavior.    _____

20.  . . . the student is taught to solve problems.    _____

21.  . . . the student knows that a target behavior may become
maladaptive and that maladaptive behaviors may become
targets, depending on the situation/context in which the student
is functioning.    _____

22.  . . . the situational cues promoting various behaviors are identified
and adequately taught to the student, along with skills for
analyzing new situations.    _____

## Type 2 (Select Behaviors)

If a student does not engage in the target behavior, ask yourself if . . .

23.  . . . the student considers the consequences of engaging in the
target behavior to be rewarding.    _____

24.  . . . the advantages of the target behavior are taught to the student.    _____

25.  . . . the student considers the consequences of engaging in the
maladaptive behavior to be aversive.    _____

26.  . . . the disadvantages of the maladaptive behavior are taught to the
student.    _____

27.  . . . the student values the target behavior more than the
maladaptive behavior.    _____

28.  . . . the student is taught to consider how the target and maladaptive
behaviors fit within the student's belief system.    _____

29.  . . . the student holds beliefs which are compatible with the target
behavior and incompatible with the maladaptive behavior.    _____

30.  . . . the student is taught to develop beliefs through the active
application of hypothesis formation, hypothesis testing, and
reflection. This instruction must include public thinking by an
exemplar and stress the need for beliefs to be "valid."    _____

31.  . . . the student maintains an adaptive explanatory style when
attributing the causes of events.    _____

32.  . . . the student is taught to avoid permanent and persuasive
attributions to external causes and/or internal abilities.    _____

33.  . . . the student avoids errors in thinking when developing and
employing belief systems.    _____

34.  . . . the student is taught to avoid errors in cognition, irrational
thoughts, and a helpless cognitive set.    _____

# Example Assessments.

| Prerequisites | Specific-Level Probes |
|---|---|
| **Type 1 (Do Behaviors)** | |

1. . . . the student can discriminate the target and maladaptive behaviors from each other and from other behaviors.

Give the student a list of behaviors, a series of pictures, or role-playing examples and ask him to indicate the target and maladaptive behavior.

3. . . . the student can monitor his own behavior well enough to know when he is engaging in the target or maladaptive behavior.

Ask the student to record his own behavior or to think back and state whether or not he engaged in two specific behaviors.

5. . . . the student can monitor the environment well enough to recognize events that should prompt the target behavior or inhibit the maladaptive behavior. playing) and ask him to match scenes to behaviors.

Ask the student how he can tell what to do or give the student statements of the behavior and various scenes (through pictures, descriptions, or role-

7. . . . the student knows what behavior is expected. "What should you be doing?" If the student is unable to produce the desired response, give some choices and ask him to identify which one is correct. Say, "Should you be in your seat, or should you be out of your seat?" Use cue sorts.

Ask him. Say "What do I want you to do?" or

9. . . . the student has the skills/knowledge to engage in the target behavior successfully. the behavior first if it is fairly complex.

Conduct an assessment using criterion-referenced measures to check necessary skills. Task analyze

11. . . . the student knows the consequences of engaging in the target behavior. some choices and ask him to identify which one is correct. Say, "Do you get to go to recess?" or "Do you get to read?"

Ask him. Say, "What happens to you when you . . . ?" If he is unable to produce the desired response, give

13. . . . the student knows the consequences of engaging in the maladaptive behavior. some choices and ask him to identify which one is correct. Say, "Do you miss recess?" or "Do you have to stay after school?"

Ask him. Say, "What happens to you when you?" If he is unable to produce the desired response, give

15. . . . the student understands that his behaviors cause certain consequences. to beliefs and preferences of others, or if he simply knows what the reactions will be.

Ask the student to explain the reactions of others to his behaviors. Note if he attributes these reactions

17. . . . there are no physical factors which militate against the target behavior and/or promote the maladaptive behavior (such as allergies or seizures). behavior.

Look for any evidence of personal or environmental factors that might trigger the maladaptive behavior or prevent the student from engaging in the target

19. . . . the student generates solutions to problems that include the target behavior. they do to get what they want?" Use a forced-choice questioning format, such as "Which would you rather have [the problem solved] or [the resource required to solve it]?

Supply the student with various restatements of the problem, involving other people. Ask, "What could

21. . . . the student knows that a target behavior may become maladaptive and that maladaptive behaviors may become targets, depending on the situation/context in which the student is functioning.

Supply a picture or role-play of a situation and several behavioral options. Ask the student to select the best, or worst, behavior. Note if the student adjusts his answers according to the situation.

| **Type 2 (Select Behaviors)** | |

23. . . . the student considers the consequences of engaging in the target behavior to be rewarding. and ask him to sort them according to value (which he likes the most to the least). Use the ABC technique to determine thoughts about receiving various rewards.

Give him a list of rewards including ones you have used in the past and are presently using with him

25. . . . the student considers the consequences of engaging in the maladaptive behavior to be aversive. (which he finds the most aversive to the least). Use the ABC technique to determine thoughts about receiving various punishers.

Give him a list of punishers, including ones you have used in the past and are presently using with him, and ask him to sort them according to value

B-6-7

27. . . . the student values the target behavior more than the maladaptive behavior. importance to him. If he cannot complete this; type of exercise, ask a series of restricted alternative questions such as, "Which would you rather do, work by yourself or with a group?"

Give him a list of behaviors (including the target behavior) and have him sort them according to their

29. . . . the student holds beliefs which are compatible with the target behavior and incompatible with the maladaptive behavior.

Use the control investment technique or other forms of structured interview.

31. . . . the student maintains an adaptive explanatory style when attributing the causes of events.

Refer to Appendix A.13.

33. . . . the student avoids errors in thinking when developing and employing belief systems.

Refer to Appendix A.13.

Howell, K. W., Zucker, S. R & Morehead, M. K. (2000b). Multilevel Academic Skills Inventory. Bellingham, WA: Applied Research and Development Center.

To order contact the Student Co-op Bookstore, Western Washington University. FAX (360) 650-2888. Phone (360) 650-3656.

# Content of Task-Related Knowledge

Part A: Class Support
The Student Has the Skill and Knowledge
Needed to Learn in this Setting:
Descriptors:
    Instructional presentation
    Classroom environment
    Teaching expectations
    Cognitive emphasis
    Motivational strategies
    Relevant practice
    Academic engaged time
    Informal feedback
    Adaptive instruction
    Progress evaluation
    Instructional Planning
    Checks for student understanding

Part B: Prior Knowledge

The Student Has Required Prior Knowledge:
Descriptors:
    Has taken prerequisite classes
    Received acceptable grades in prerequisite
    classes
    Understands text and presentations
    Knows topical vocabulary
    Is familiar with related topics

Part C: Study and Test-Taking Skills

Study and Test-taking Skills Are Adequate:
Before Class:
Descriptors:
    Arrives on time
    Enters in a pleasant manner
    Brings materials to class
    Gets ready for learning
During Class:
Descriptors:
    Follows classroom rules
    Listens carefully
    Works during class
    Asks for assistance
    Moves quickly to new
    activity
After Class:
Descriptors:
    Takes materials home
    Completes homework
    Brings homework back

Part D: Self-Monitoring and Evaluation

The Student Monitors and Evaluates Work:
Descriptors:
    Self-monitors
    Recognizes errors
    Judges quality of work given criteria
    Judges quality of work on own

Part E: Problem Solving

The Student's Problem Solving/Self-
Monitoring
Is Adequate:
Descriptors:
    Defines problems
    Identifies goals
    Identifies obstacles
    Recognizes types of problems
    Anticipates problems
The Student Recognizes Types of Problems:
Descriptors:
    Identifies open system
    Identifies closed system
The Student Recognizes Solution:
Descriptors:
    Generates options
    Considers resources
    Anticipates outcomes
    Selects solutions
The Student Plans:
Descriptors:
    Thinks before acting
    Explains what will happen
    Has immediate goals
    Allocates time
The Student Works:
Descriptors:
    Follows plan
    Follows schedule

Part F: Academic Motivation

The Student Holds and Expresses These
Beliefs:
Descriptors:
    My goals are important, my learning
    Depends on what I do
    I'm a success as long as I improve
    My goals are interesting
    If I make a mistake I need to work hard to
fix it


Organization:
Descriptors:
    Organization of materials (e.g., use of
    Notebook or folders)
    Organization of time (e.g., use of calendar,
    Scheduling work)
    Organization of content on paper (e.g.,
    heading, margins)
Gaining Information:
Descriptors:
    Reading expository material
    Reading narrative material
    Gaining information from verbal
    presentations (lectures, demonstrations)
Demonstrating Knowledge or Skills:
Descriptors:
    Completing daily assignments

Answering written questions
Writing narrative and expository products
Preparing for and taking tests
I am an important member of my class
and my school

Part G: Basic Learning Skills

The Student Uses Selective Attention:
Descriptors:
Focuses on relevant cues
Ignores irrelevant cues
Uses effective techniques to focus and
maintain attention

The Student Uses Recall/Memory:
Descriptors:
Recalls information
Uses effective techniques to store and
recall
material

The Student Uses Motivation:
Descriptors:
Perseveres in the face of difficulty
Perceives value of task
Maintains an adaptive explanatory style
(i.e.,
Is not "learned helplessness")
Indicates feelings of control
Uses effective techniques to maintain
motivation

**Summary Form for Student Knowledge**

Student Name_____
Topic_____
Date_____
Evaluator Name_____

Directions:

1. List key ideas.
2. Mark conditions; test, essay, interview.
3. Mark the student's status using this key:
   C = answers correct
   CP = answers correct with prompts
   EP = error made with prompts
   E = error

| Key Idea(s) | Facts | Concepts | Principles/Rules | Note incorrectly Used Terms Here |
|---|---|---|---|---|
| 1. | | | | |
| 2. | | | | |
| 3. | | | | |
| 4. | | | | |
| 5. | | | | |
| 6. | | | | |
| 7. | | | | |
| 8. | | | | |
| 9. | | | | |
| 10. | | | | |

# Checklist for Study/Test Taking and Problem Solving/Self-Monitoring.

Directions:

1. Start on the right and move left if skill is not passed.
2. Designate skills as passed (P) or no-pass (NP).
3. Judge each heading by summarizing the status of the majority of descriptors under that heading.

| | Know | | Apply | |
|---|---|---|---|---|
| | Recognize | Explain | With prompts | Spontaneously |

### Study and Test Taking

| | Recognize | Explain | With prompts | Spontaneously |
|---|---|---|---|---|
| **Before Class:**<br>Arrives on time<br>Enters in a pleasant manner<br>Brings materials to class<br>Gets ready for learning | ____ | ____ | ____ | ____ |
| **During Class:**<br>Follows classroom rules<br>Listens carefully<br>Works during class<br>Asks for assistance<br>Moves quickly to new activity | ____ | ____ | ____ | ____ |
| **After Class:**<br>Takes materials home<br>Completes homework<br>Brings homework back | ____ | ____ | ____ | ____ |
| **Organization:**<br>Organization of materials<br>(use of notebook or folders)<br>Organization of time<br>(use of calendar, scheduling work)<br>Organization of content on paper (heading, margins) | ____ | ____ | ____ | ____ |
| **Gaining Information:**<br>Reading expository material<br>Reading narrative material<br>Gaining information from verbal presentations (lectures, demonstrations) | ____ | ____ | ____ | ____ |
| **Demonstrating Knowledge or Skills:**<br>Completing daily assignments<br>Answering written questions<br>Writing narrative and expository products<br>Preparing for and taking tests | ____ | ____ | ____ | ____ |

| | Know | | Apply | |
|---|---|---|---|---|
| | Recognize | Explain | With prompts | Spontaneously |

### Problem Solving

| | Recognize | Explain | With prompts | Spontaneously |
|---|---|---|---|---|
| **Recognizes Problem:**<br>Defines problems<br>Identifies goals<br>Identifies obstacles<br>Recognizes types of problems<br>Anticipates problems | ____ | ____ | ____ | ____ |

B-7-3

Identify Problem Type: ___  ___  ___  ___
  Open system
  Closed system
  Identify or develop solutions

Select Solutions: ___  ___  ___  ___
  Generates options
  Considers resources
  Anticipates outcomes
  Selects solutions

Plans: ___  ___  ___  ___
  Thinks before acting
  Explains what will happen
  Has immediate goals
  Allocates time

Works: ___  ___  ___  ___
  Follows plan
  Follows schedule

# MOTIVATION TEST

This box is the Key. It would be a good idea to cover it before giving the test.

|  | 1 | 2 | 3 | 4 | 5 | 6 |
|---|---|---|---|---|---|---|
|  | Goal | Internal | Success | Interest | Persevere | Partnership |
| YES | 1, 13 | 8, 20 | 3, 15 | 10, 22 | 5, 17 | 12, 24 |
| NO | 7, 19 | 2, 14 | 9, 21 | 4, 16 | 11, 23 | 6, 18 |

Directions: Answer "yes" or "no" to the following questions. Take your time---but your answer can only be "yes" or "no":

1)  I work best when I know what I am trying to learn.
2)  If I fail it is most likely because the task is too hard.
3)  I don't need to get the best score in class, I just need to do better than I have before.
4)  I don't find most school work to be interesting.
5)  If I make mistakes it means I should think about changing the way I am studying.
6)  During class my teacher sometimes compares our work.
7)  I only study what the teacher wants me to know.
8)  If I fail it is my job to fix the problem.
9)  I like to pick simple things to do so I now I'll get a good grade.
10) I find most school work interesting.
11) If I'm doing well I don't need to study as much.
12) The teacher knows my goals and helps me reach them.
13) It is hard for me to learn when I don't know exactly what I'm suppose to by the end of the lesson.
14) I often get high grades because I am very smart.
15) I like to pick hard things to do because I feel good when I learn something challenging.
16) If I could pick stuff to learn it wouldn't be what we have to study.
17) When I am having trouble learning something it means I must work harder.
18) Sometimes it seems like my teacher is more interested in my finishing the work than in my learning.
19) Knowing that I must reach a certain target makes the lesson scary and/or unpleasant.
20) My teacher doesn't give me grades, I earn them.
21) It doesn't matter if I get a higher score then last time, all that matters is that I get a good score.
22) The things I am learning in class are the things I would like to be learning anyhow.
23) If I make mistakes I should stop working because I've run into something I can't do.
24) In our school there are as many rewards for improvement in classes as there are for attendance and sports.

B-7.5

# Task Related Interview

Directions: Use these questions to talk about classes in which student is having trouble.

⇒ 1.1 When you do school work in [name subject of class] do you like to know exactly what is expected of you, or would you rather the expectations were open or vague?

**Follow-up**

1.2 Why?

1.3 Does your [name subject of class] teacher usually supply vague expectations or clear expectations?

⇒ 2.1 Who is mainly responsible for you meeting goals in [name subject of class], you or your teacher?

**Follow-up**

2.2 Why?

2.3 What does your [name subject of class] teacher say to let you know if he or she is mainly responsible for your learning or if you are responsible?

⇒ 3.1 Do you feel most successful in [name subject of class] when you think you've learned a lot or when you get a high grade?

**Follow-up**

3.2 Why?

3.3 What does your [name subject of class] teacher do to let you know if he or she thinks high grades or learning is most important?

⇒ 4.1 If something seems uninteresting to you do you study it anyhow, try to get interested in it, or avoid studying it?

⇒ 5.1 In [name subject of class] when you run into something that seems hard to do, do you usually stop working or try working harder?

**Follow-up**

5.2 Why?

5.3 When you run into something that seems hard what does your [name subject of class] teacher do?

⇒ 6.1 Do you feel like you are a part of this school and that you belong here?

**Follow-up**

6.2 Why?

6.3 What does your [name subject of class] teacher do that might help make you feel you don't belong, or that you do belong?

# Content Vocabulary Tests
## For Task-related Knowledge

These tests cover vocabulary from four domains. For every domain there are three tests at each of these levels: primary (grades 1 & 2), intermediate (grades 3-5), and advanced (grades 6-8). The primary tests are given individually and require the student to say the answer. The other tests are multiple-choice and the student marks the answers. The words on the tests were drawn from an analysis of textbooks. Words were selected if they appeared in several sources.

Performance criteria for these tests will have to be established locally, although a big difference in a student's score in one domain as opposed to the others may also be of interest.

All of the tests are supplied in the next few pages. The questions for the oral tests are presented first followed by the eight written tests, and then the answer key for the written tests. The correct answers for the oral tests are supplied with the questions.

Allow at least five minutes for each of the multiple choice tests.

Here are the written test numbers and what they sample:

|  | Primary | Intermediate | Advanced |
|---|---|---|---|
| Math/Science | oral | 1 | 2 |
| Social studies | oral | 3 | 4 |
| Language/Arts | oral | 5 | 6 |
| Everyday living | oral | 7 | 8 |

Howell, K.W., Zucker, S.H. & Morehead, M.K. (2000). Multilevel Academic Skills Inventory. Bellingham, WA: Applied Research And Development Center. To order contact the Student Co-op Bookstore, Western Washington University. FAX (360)650-2888. Phone (360)650-3656

# Primary Level (grades 1, 2)
## Content Vocabulary

*Acceptable Responses*

1. galaxy – **star system**
   **Milky Way**
   **group of stars**
2. pulse – **heartbeat**
   **regular beat**
   **throb**
3. vibrating – **shaking**
   **moving back and forth**
   **unsteady motion**
4. cycle – **repeating**
   **time period**
   **regularly occurring**
5. electricity – **electric current**
   **power**
   **runs lamps, appliances**
6. root – **part of a plant**
   **under the ground**
   **feeds the plant**
7. plus – **addition sign**
   **add**
   **symbol used in arithmetic**
8. equal – **having the same value**
   **the same amount**
   **symbol used in arithmetic**
9. height – **how tall**
   **vertical side of a figure**
   **length of the vertical side**
10. factor – **part of a product**
    **reduce**
    **part of a multiplication problem**

### Math/Science
### Primary
*Acceptable Responses*

11. minus – **subtraction sign**
    **subtract**
    **comparison of two variables**
12. quotient – **answer in division problem**
    **how many times**
    **answer to ratio**
13. angle – **slant**
    **corner**
    **distance between diverging lines**
14. average – **mean**
    **add up and divide**
    **total score divided by number**
    **of scores**
15. diameter – **width of a circle**
    **length across a circle**
    **line which bisects a circle**
16. graph – **chart**
    **figure**
    **symbol used in arithmetic**
17. melt – **change to liquid**
    **dissolve**
    **turn into water**
18. gravity – **having weight**
    **pull of the earth**
    **center of gravity**
19. liquid – **water**
    **fluid**
    **pours freely**
20. heat – **warmth**
    **hot**
    **high temperature**

---

### Social Studies
### Primary

*Acceptable Responses*

1. west – **direction**
   **where the sun sets**
   **reference point**
2. lake – **body of water**
   **inland water**
   **pond**
3. travel – **take a trip**
   **go someplace**
   **journey**
4. east – **direction**
   **where the sun rises**
   **reference point**
5. mayor – **elected official**
   **head of the city**
   **chief of the city**

*Acceptable Responses*

6. explorer – **discoverer**
   **travels to faraway places**
   **seeks information**
7. woodland – **forest**
   **timberland**
   **covered with trees**
8. trade – **exchange**
   **swap**
   **business**
9. transportation – **carrying goods**
   **moving goods**
   **system of movement**
10. climate – **weather**
    **weather conditions over time**
    **region of the earth**

## Content Vocabulary Tests Instructions

11. goods – **things bought**
    **things sold**
    **equipment, cloth, stuff**
12. citizen – **member of society**
    **lives in the town**
    **member of state**
13. factory – **place where things are made**
    **manufacturing facility**
    **building where things**
        **are made**
14. frontier – **wild country**
    **border**
    **unknown area**
15. disaster – **sudden bad event**
    **destruction**
    **terrible event**

16. foreign – **another country**
    **not from here**
    **outside the country**
17. atlas – **map book**
    **charts**
    **maps**
18. communication – **message**
        **sending and receiving**
            **messages**
        **exchange of information**
19. harbor – **where ships load**
    **protected body of water**
    **deep water close to shore**
20. capital – **location of government**
    **main city**
    **important place**

---

**Language/Music**
**Primary**

1. props – **objects used in a play**
   **scenery**
   **objects**
2. parentheses – **curved lines**
        **used to separate words**
        **contain an explanatory**
            **phrase**
3. conversation – **talk**
        **discussion**
        **exchange of ideas**
4. vocabulary – **words you know**
        **words you use**
        **list of word meanings**
5. character – **person**
        **someone in a story**
        **strange person**
6. paragraph – **unit of writing**
        **contains one idea**
        **begins on a new line**
7. sentence – **a written statement**
        **says one thing**
        **related group of words**

8. dictionary – **book of words**
        **explains words**
        **reference**
9. plural – **more than one**
        **many**
        **grammar form**
10. synonyms – **same meaning**
        **two words mean the same**
        **sometimes mean the same**

11. poems – **verse**
        **story that rhymes**
        **story in verse**
12. rhymes – **sounds alike**
        **same endings**
        **same sounds at the end**
13. riddle – **puzzle**
        **problem**
        **question**
14. solo – **one voice**
        **singing alone**
        **playing alone**
15. chords – **musical notes**
        **tone**
        **blended sounds**
16. melody – **tune**
        **arrangement of sounds**
        **nice music**
17. stage – **platform**
        **where the actors are**
        **theatre**
18. actor – **man in a play**
        **plays a character**
        **plays a part**
19. author – **writes books**
        **writer**
        **writes stories**
20. audience – **those watching**
        **those listening**
        **spectators**

Content Vocabulary Tests Instructions

## Everyday Living
### Primary

*Acceptable Responses*

1. boy – **young man**
   **male child**
   **school-age male**

2. woman – **lady**
   **adult female**
   **older girl**

3. come – **get closer**
   **get over here**
   **walk over**

4. sit – **take a seat**
   **take a chair**
   **stay still**

5. water – **a liquid**
   **drink it**
   **lake, river**

6. year – **12 months**
   **January to December**
   **from one birthday to the next**

7. say – **tell**
   **speak**
   **talk**

8. follow – **go along**
   **go behind**
   **obey directions**

9. price – **cost**
   **value**
   **how much**

10. stop – **cease motion**
    **prevent**
    **quit**

11. children – **kids**
    **boys and girls**
    **young boys and girls**

12. walk – **go by foot**
    **path for walking**
    **sidewalk**

13. boss – **person in charge**
    **chief**
    **order around**

14. save – **keep money**
    **don't waste**
    **keep for later**

15. tool – **utensil**
    **for working with**
    **hammer, screwdriver**

16. name – **what you're called**
    **what something is called**
    **description**

17. date of birth – **when you were born**
    **birthday**
    **day and year of birth**

18. age – **how old you are**
    **time of life**
    **get older**

19. left – **direction**
    **opposite of right**
    **(indicates hand or points)**

20. emergency – **need help**
    **immediate action**
    **immediate need**

1. membrane
   a) unit of the body
   b) layer of tissue
   c) long bones

2. solar cell
   a) three-dimensional mass
   b) produced during sunspot activity
   c) converts sunlight to electricity

3. nonconductor
   a) does not allow transmission of current
   b) goes against society
   c) made out of hard metal

4. hibernate
   a) period of dormancy
   b) go into seclusion
   c) foolishness

5. ecosystem
   a) lawmaking group
   b) monetary policies
   c) environmental interrelationships

6. spore
   a) boxing practice
   b) germ cell
   c) poisonous

7. reproduction
   a) process giving rise to offspring
   b) lengthy mining process
   c) to start over again

8. reptile
   a) type of floor covering
   b) to give information
   c) scaly, creeping animal

9. counterclockwise
   a) right around the clock
   b) left around the clock
   c) regular dweller

10. fossil fuel
    a) coal, oil, natural gas
    b) petrified remains
    c) oat, corn, barley

11. microorganism
    a) a microscope
    b) a microbe
    c) a type of paper

12. ore
    a) manually propel a boat
    b) narrow minded
    c) metal bearing mineral

13. circuit
    a) electrical path
    b) travelling show
    c) point of crossing

14. tangent
    a) a power hammer
    b) a juicy citrus fruit
    c) trigonometric function

15. negative number
    a) an odd number
    b) less than zero
    c) no place value

16. circumference
    a) percent of inside area
    b) committee meeting
    c) perimeter of a circle

17. cylinder
    a) roller shaped object
    b) equal sided triangle
    c) a reference book

18. decimal
    a) a fraction
    b) loudness of sound
    c) type of dessert

19. common factor
    a) representing the same issue
    b) divides evenly into two numbers
    c) same size rectangles

20. mean
    a) highest score
    b) average score
    c) combination of parts

*Content Vocab* 1, *(math/sc. int.)*

1. abyss
   a) infected cyst
   b) bottomless pit
   c) road equipment

2. axis
   a) being able to reach something
   b) to keep changing one's mind
   c) straight line about which things revolve

3. condense
   a) to make more compact
   b) change from solid to liquid
   c) a general agreement

4. epicenter
   a) part of a continuing story
   b) earth's surface above the center of an earthquake
   c) inside concentric circle of a geometric form

5. diatom
   a) unicellular algae
   b) four-sided figure
   c) combination of proton and electron

6. saturation
   a) holding up to ridicule
   b) make a strong promise
   c) maximum concentration

7. solstice
   a) point of greatest distance from sun
   b) point of closest distance from sun
   c) electromagnetic switch

8. species
   a) one of a kind
   b) biological classification below genus
   c) a scale of values

9. blood pressure
   a) pressure exerted by the blood
   b) pressure at which the veins burst
   c) hemoglobin count

10. convex
    a) curved in
    b) curved out
    c) violent shaking

11. pasteurization
    a) soft, pale colors
    b) branching out from the center
    c) partial sterilization by heat

12. reflex
    a) related to the subject of the sentence
    b) type of blood vessel
    c) an inborn act

13. algorithm
    a) step-by-step procedure
    b) letters representing numbers
    c) musical composition

14. arc
    a) a scenic representation
    b) line from center of circle to perimeter
    c) curved line between two points

15. ellipse
    a) partial blocking of the sun
    b) a glowing fragment
    c) oval shape

16. equilateral
    a) having all angles equal
    b) having all sides equal
    c) many sided figure

17. exponent
    a) symbol indicating power of a number
    b) an integral part
    c) a structural form

18. median
    a) average score
    b) fortune teller
    c) middle score

19. pi
    a) 6.28
    b) 3.14
    c) 1/2 of 3.14

20. rational number
    a) number used only in equations
    b) divisible a finite number of times
    c) computer related

Content Vocab 2  (math/sc. adv.)

255

1. settler  a) a type of dog
          b) a pioneer
          c) a highway

2. altitude  a) height above sea level
          b) grassy farmland
          c) magnitude of an angle

3. liberty  a) freedom
          b) growing up
          c) office building

4. colony  a) sail-making factory
          b) disorder of the digestive system
          c) new settlement ruled by another country

5. assembly line  a) waiting in line for a meeting
          b) each worker does one part over and over
          c) imaginary line of demarcation

6. income  a) amount of money received
          b) a softball game
          c) immigrating to the U.S.

7. amendment  a) the healing of broken bones
          b) ratified change in the Constitution
          c) a long dark alleyway

8. scab  a) a strike breaker
          b) a bank branch
          c) a kind of spider

9. boycott  a) a group of strangers
          b) a harbor-marking device
          c) refusal to buy a product

10. veto  a) refuse to approve
          b) one who fought in the war
          c) a type of outer garment

11. civil  a) war between nations
          b) to strain out impurities
          c) relating to citizens

12. textile  a) a ceramic floor covering
          b) a woven cloth
          c) a chemical compound

13. executive branch  a) part of the government
          b) longest limb on the tree
          c) a portion of the upper atmosphere

14. glacier  a) a very smooth surface
          b) the flexible part of a shoe
          c) a large moving body of ice

15. fiscal year  a) 12-month period used for accounting
          b) a year signifying sunspots
          c) relating to the Roman calendar

16. jury  a) very thick forest or jungle
          b) gold rings and bracelets
          c) group of people appointed to give a verdict.

17. poverty  a) being poor
          b) a holiday drink
          c) a large area of land

18. ballot  a) a secret vote
          b) a poem set to music
          c) certain radio frequencies

19. lobbying  a) waiting downstairs in a hotel
          b) planting a tree
          c) influencing lawmakers

20. strait  a) a line that does not curve
          b) a narrow waterway
          c) special way of folding paper

1. archaeologist
   a) someone who designs buildings
   b) someone who studies old things
   c) an evil person

2. nationalism
   a) patriotic feeling
   b) chemical reaction
   c) all the citizens

3. monarchy
   a) structure in water
   b) multicolored butterfly
   c) country ruled by a king

4. immigrant
   a) one who comes to a country to live
   b) a small gland in the brain
   c) about to take place

5. bipartisan
   a) involving members of two parties
   b) wings above and below the fuselage
   c) without legal force

6. isolationist
   a) not rightly named
   b) having two equal sides
   c) believer in noninterference

7. caucuses
   a) prickly desert plant
   b) closed meetings to decide on policy
   c) hot red pepper

8. primary
   a) voting for election candidates
   b) mounted on horseback
   c) undercoat of paint

9. martial law
   a) a city law officer
   b) serious cattle disease
   c) military government

10. due process
    a) rotational axis
    b) calling in a loan
    c) adherence to proper procedure

11. featherbedding
    a) a quilt stuffed with down
    b) requiring more jobs than necessary
    c) adjacent to the forehead

12. constituents
    a) residents in an electoral district
    b) parts something is made of
    c) an area near the North Pole

13. annexation
    a) being next to
    b) incorporate within government domain
    c) reserved for the clergy

14. commonwealth
    a) a state or union of nations
    b) national treasury
    c) water-cooled pipe

15. summit meeting
    a) top of the mountain
    b) conference of high level officials
    c) divide into triangles

16. impeachment
    a) charge a public official with misconduct
    b) a skin infection found in children
    c) grove of fruit trees

17. ordinance
    a) weapons
    b) a law
    c) a bay window

18. revenue
    a) income
    b) worthless
    c) variety act

19. AFL-CIO
    a) football conference
    b) NATO
    c) labor organization

20. ratification
    a) random
    b) approval
    c) exterminate

Content Vocab 4  (soc. stu. adv.)

257

1. biography    a) harvesting machine
                b) written history of a person's life
                c) study of living tissue

2. pronunciation    a) manner of saying words
                    b) part of speech referring to persons
                    c) a dangerous twig

3. byline    a) farewell
             b) piece of cloth
             c) line indicating author's name

4. dialogue    a) conversation between two or more persons
               b) clock face
               c) religious belief

5. primary colors    a) navy uniforms
                     b) yellow, blue, red
                     c) mostly red colored

6. fantasy    a) outer space
              b) a safety platform
              c) an imaginary happening

7. science fiction    a) tale based on unproven extensions of current knowledge
                      b) the acquisition of knowledge through stories
                      c) a deep shovel for digging in soft soil

8. characterization    a) a special feature
                       b) portrayal of a role
                       c) preserved foods

9. flashback    a) return to earlier occurrence
                b) unit of weight
                c) waterproofing around chimney

10. abstract    a) absent-minded
                b) in poor condition
                c) difficult to understand

11. novel    a) fictional book
             b) short story
             c) combining of atoms

12. card catalog    a) collection of greeting cards
                    b) list of books arranged systematically
                    c) loud, ringing sound

13. entertainment    a) a steep grade
                     b) adventurous
                     c) a show

14. return address    a) address of sender
                      b) reply address
                      c) controls electricity

15. essay    a) to analyze ore
             b) short piece of writing
             c) tuba-like instrument

16. adjective    a) modifier of a noun
                 b) mixing up
                 c) having a common border

17. present tense    a) making a gift
                     b) expressive of present time
                     c) big reputation

18. harmony    a) employed in industry
               b) severe injury
               c) melody arrangement

19. improvisation    a) not decent
                     b) a kind of rhythm
                     c) unrehearsed act

20. volume    a) surface area
              b) loudness
              c) paraffin

1. plot   a) to fall flat
          b) plan of a story
          c) agreeable person

2. unabridged   a) complete
               b) strange
               c) road washed out

3. abbreviation   a) not present
                  b) stream of charged particles
                  c) shortened form of a word

4. subordinate clause   a) dependent on another clause
                        b) a legal document
                        c) dependent child

5. interrogative   a) shellfish
                   b) question
                   c) disrupt continuity

6. narration   a) less than normal width
               b) a safety platform
               c) telling a story

7. index card   a) found in card catalogue
                b) left side of a ship
                c) contains contents of book

8. outline   a) contours
             b) plan
             c) treachery

9. script   a) text of a play
            b) paper money
            c) a piece of wood

10. analogy   a) skilled in analysis
              b) belief in yourself
              c) correspondence

11. edit   a) give desired result
           b) prepare for publication
           c) command

12. drama   a) story depicting serious events
            b) unit of measurement
            c) the space between things

13. thesis   a) plural of this
             b) introductory statement
             c) main point in an essay

14. metaphor   a) part of a poem
               b) figure of speech
               c) radioactive chemical

15. chronological   a) according to the order of time
                    b) high-quality sound
                    c) instrument that tells time

16. ballad   a) a voting slip
             b) a story song
             c) a clumsy fellow

17. ballet   a) dance performance to convey story
             b) working only for money
             c) a travelling minstrel

18. overture   a) an exaggeration
               b) a type of check
               c) orchestral introduction

19. hue   a) a gardening implement
          b) gradation of color
          c) Greek letter

20. stage right   a) use an opportunity
                  b) to set up correctly
                  c) position in the acting area

260

1. hazardous  a) cloudy
                 b) dangerous
                 c) untrue

2. credit  a) paying later
            b) business slump
            c) a small fish

3. employee  a) hires people
               b) imaginary
               c) paid worker

4. maiden name  a) nickname
                  b) name before marriage
                  c) military title

5. appointment  a) a set time and day
                  b) a sharp edge
                  c) work done at home

6. full-time  a) no time clock
              b) very thin
              c) work all day

7. investment  a) outlay of money for profit
               b) type of special clothing
               c) interchange

8. personal property  a) where you live
                      b) large tract of land
                      c) one's possessions

9. market value  a) consumer interest in a product
                  b) price agreeable to buyer and seller
                  c) closeness to shopping area

10. interest  a) fee for using money
             b) something unusual
             c) insurance

11. net proceeds  a) amount taken in
                 b) conduct estimate
                 c) amount left after expenses

12. admission price  a) discount price
                   b) ticket cost
                   c) confession

13. schedule  a) timetable
              b) appointment
             c) division

14. fare  a) unbiased
          b) ticket cost
          c) a long way

15. holiday  a) day off from work
            b) sick day
            c) temporary

16. bank  a) handkerchief
         b) save or borrow money
         c) school building

17. savings account  a) safe-deposit box
                 b) curved edge
                c) money in the bank

18. postal service  a) process the mail
               b) bookkeeping office
              c) answering service

19. utility companies  a) street paving
                   b) phone, electric, water, gas
                 c) landscaping

20. probation  a) on-the-job trial period
             b) professional athlete
             c) pre-retirement period

1. FICA
   a) state retirement tax
   b) social security tax
   c) proceeds

2. exemption
   a) taxable at a higher rate
   b) argument over money
   c) portion not taxable

3. double time
   a) twice the hourly wage
   b) work twice as many hours
   c) two time clocks

4. commission
   a) hourly salary
   b) large agency
   c) percent of sales

5. collateral
   a) security for a loan
   b) investment
   c) applies only to bonds

6. depreciation
   a) nasty remarks
   b) decrease in value over time
   c) increase in taxes

7. estimate
   a) estate tax due
   b) statement of approximate cost
   c) hard to bear

8. dependents
   a) trustworthy
   b) all sources of income
   c) those needing another's support

9. employment history
   a) record of previous jobs
   b) where you would like to work
   c) government job

10. take-home pay
    a) pay that does not go in the bank
    b) total pay including vacation pay
    c) amount of pay left after all deductions

11. withholding
    a) deduction of taxes from pay
    b) keeping information secret
    c) profitable investment

12. qualifications
    a) skills related to a job
    b) what you like to do
    c) market value

13. punch in
    a) note departure time
    b) fight at work
    c) note arrival time

14. overtime
    a) working the night shift
    b) more than eight hours in one day
    c) getting to work late

15. finance charge
    a) fee for paperwork
    b) applies only to credit cards
    c) interest on purchase

16. safe-deposit box
    a) for night deposits
    b) rented compartment in vault
    c) box for overdue library books

17. express mail
    a) foreign mail delivery
    b) next day delivery
    c) shipped by freight

18. answering service
    a) service that answers personal letters
    b) information directory
    c) service that answers client's telephones

19. prime rate
    a) interest banks charge other banks
    b) long-term home mortgage interest
    c) interest banks pay to individuals

20. promissory note
    a) written loan application
    b) written agreement to pay money
    c) consolidation of bad debts

261

*Content Vocab 8 (evydy. liv. adv.)*

# ANSWER KEY

## Math/Science

| | Advanced (Obj. 12i) | | Intermediate (Obj. 11i) |
|---|---|---|---|
| 1. | b | 1. | b |
| 2. | c | 2. | c |
| 3. | a | 3. | a |
| 4. | b | 4. | a |
| 5. | a | 5. | c |
| 6. | c | 6. | b |
| 7. | a | 7. | a |
| 8. | b | 8. | c |
| 9. | a | 9. | b |
| 10. | b | 10. | a |
| 11. | c | 11. | b |
| 12. | c | 12. | c |
| 13. | a | 13. | a |
| 14. | c | 14. | c |
| 15. | c | 15. | b |
| 16. | b | 16. | c |
| 17. | a | 17. | a |
| 18. | c | 18. | a |
| 19. | b | 19. | b |
| 20. | b | 20. | b |

## Social Studies

| | Advanced (Obj. 9i) | | Intermediate (Obj. 8i) |
|---|---|---|---|
| 1. | b | 1. | b |
| 2. | a | 2. | a |
| 3. | c | 3. | a |
| 4. | a | 4. | c |
| 5. | a | 5. | b |
| 6. | c | 6. | a |
| 7. | b | 7. | b |
| 8. | a | 8. | a |
| 9. | c | 9. | c |
| 10. | c | 10. | a |
| 11. | b | 11. | c |
| 12. | a | 12. | b |
| 13. | b | 13. | a |
| 14. | a | 14. | c |
| 15. | b | 15. | a |
| 16. | a | 16. | c |
| 17. | b | 17. | a |
| 18. | a | 18. | a |
| 19. | c | 19. | c |
| 20. | b | 20. | b |

## Language/Music

| | Advanced (Obj. 6i) | | Intermediate (Obj. 5i) |
|---|---|---|---|
| 1. | b | 1. | b |
| 2. | a | 2. | a |
| 3. | c | 3. | c |
| 4. | a | 4. | a |
| 5. | b | 5. | b |
| 6. | c | 6. | c |
| 7. | a | 7. | a |
| 8. | b | 8. | b |
| 9. | a | 9. | a |
| 10. | c | 10. | c |
| 11. | b | 11. | a |
| 12. | a | 12. | b |
| 13. | c | 13. | c |
| 14. | b | 14. | a |
| 15. | a | 15. | b |
| 16. | b | 16. | a |
| 17. | a | 17. | b |
| 18. | c | 18. | c |
| 19. | b | 19. | c |
| 20. | c | 20. | b |

## Everyday Living

| | Advanced (Obj. 3i) | | Intermediate (Obj. 2i) |
|---|---|---|---|
| 1. | b | 1. | b |
| 2. | c | 2. | a |
| 3. | a | 3. | c |
| 4. | c | 4. | b |
| 5. | a | 5. | a |
| 6. | b | 6. | c |
| 7. | b | 7. | a |
| 8. | c | 8. | c |
| 9. | a | 9. | b |
| 10. | c | 10. | a |
| 11. | a | 11. | c |
| 12. | a | 12. | b |
| 13. | c | 13. | a |
| 14. | b | 14. | b |
| 15. | c | 15. | a |
| 16. | b | 16. | b |
| 17. | b | 17. | c |
| 18. | c | 18. | a |
| 19. | a | 19. | b |
| 20. | b | 20. | a |

# Study Questions

**TEACHER THOUGHT PROCESS**
*Conceptualization of curriculum*

1. In order to understand the authors' suggestions for making decisions about curriculum, it is important to know how they think about curriculum. Which of the following best represents the textbook's definition of curriculum?

Published materials adopted by a school district.

Learning outcomes expected to result from instruction.

A set of organized activities that keep students actively engaged during the     school day.

*Inside and Outside decisions*

2. Educational decisions serve two functions. Consider each of the following and identify whether it is a outside decision or a inside decision. The first item is completed as an example.

a.  _I_    Sally's teacher has decided to teach her the periodic table of elements.

b. _____Brad has been assigned to work with the Chapter 1 remedial reading teacher.

c. _____Juan will learn to use a specific learning strategy to improve his reading comprehension.

d. _____Willard's teacher suggests that he use a number line to help solve arithmetic problems.

e. _____Kathleen will work with a cooperative learning group as a strategy to help her learn to write a report.

f. _____Susan scored low on her achievement test, so she will work with the lowest reading group.

*Effective decision making procedures require good judgement.*

3. Which of the following provides the best analogy for the role of teachers' decision making?

Teachers are like orchestra leaders. They need to get the group playing the same note, in tempo, all together.

Teachers are like detectives trying to solve a case. They gather information, form a possible explanation, and then test the accuracy of their assumptions by gathering more evidence.

Teachers are like pilots. They file a flight plan and take off facing weather, wind velocity, and the chatter of their passengers as they wing their way across a three-dimensional landscape. Sigh. (Occasionally, they crash.)

Teachers are like artists. They may be spontaneously inspired by theme, attitude, or other characteristics of the moment. Their medium is the classroom.

C.1

**THINKING ABOUT LEARNING AND STUDENTS**

4. The ease or difficulty a student has in learning is influenced by the interaction between  a) the nature of the task the student is asked to complete, b) the characteristics of the student, and c) the quality of the instruction. Many of the characteristics of the student will be **unalterable** variables.  Task and instruction characteristics are more easily changed.  For each of the following, label the item **T** for task variable, **S** for student variable, or **I** for instructional variable.  After labeling, state whether it is an **unalterable** or an **alterable** variable within the context of a teacher's role.

|  | Alterable | Unalterable |
|---|---|---|
| a)  _S_   Chemically dependent parents. |  | X |
| b)  ____  Assignments given directly from a textbook that is two grade levels above the student's reading level. |  |  |
| c)  ____  The teacher uses a "hands off" approach to reading instruction. |  |  |
| d)  ____  The student is a tough looking 6-foot 5-inch 13-year-old. |  |  |
| e)  ____  The teacher maintains a 50% engagement rate with students during group lessons. |  |  |

5. The waitress came rushing over to the table and said, "I've got something to show you."  She began, "Johnnie's mother had three children."  She laid a penny on the table and said, "She named the first one Penny."  Next, she laid a nickel on the table and said, "She named the second one Nicole."  Then she laid a dime on the table and asked,  "What did she name the third one?"
What was that third child's name, and which of the big three (attention, memory or motivation) is important in solving this question?

6. Which of the following students is the most motivated?
a)  Willie believes that his "personal best" time at the swim meet was the result of poor competitors and that he will never be able to replicate it.
b)  Waylen gave a poor performance at the talent show, but he refuses to be embarrassed about it.  He simply won't play the accordion again.
c)  Dolly isn't such a great musician either, but she intends to add back-up  rhythm to her vocal and try it again at the junior class Karoke night  next week.
d)  Garth has difficulty following the coach's rules about attending extra study  sessions if any grade drops below a "C."  However, instead of singing he wants to play ball. So he pays his twin brother to attend study hall for him.

*THINKING ABOUT CURRICULUM*

7.  Should curriculum for remedial students differ from that of their typical peers?  Justify your response.

8. If a student has trouble learning, a teacher should use a task analysis and/or concept analysis to identify what the student does and does not know. Try your hand at each of the three by responding to the following scenarios:

**TASK ANALYSIS** List at least three skills that the student would have to perform in order to add 2 and 2/3 to 12/9.

**CONCEPT ANALYSIS** Identify at least three concepts that a student must understand in order to complete the problem described in the task analysis section above.

9. Quality goals and objectives must be measurable, useful, and calibrated in units that are both small enough to show variation in the behavior when change occurs and large enough to maintain an achievable pace through the breadth of the curriculum.
Only one of the following has all three qualities. Which one is it?

a) Franklin will improve his appreciation of numerical systems used around the world throughout history. He will demonstrate his appreciation orally and in writing.
b) Emilio will master the content of the audio library's series on inventors. Mastery will be judged as 85% or better on tests that are given on the material.
c) Agnes will get better at reading prose and poems in reading materials both in school and out of school.
d) Leah will improve writing skills so that all of ten randomly selected written assignments will contain complete sentences with correct punctuation.

10. Which of the following statements about criterion levels is _false_?

a) Proficiency level standards are arbitrary, but _some_ statement about them must be made so the objective can be measured.
b) Some standards are established by sampling other students who have already mastered the skill.
c) Criteria for accuracy, fluency, and automaticity for any given skill should be considered and specified.
d) Although criterion standards may be individualized for a student, teachers should be careful not to routinely ask less of students with remedial or special needs lest their performance remain substandard.

11. Here's the objective:
Sven will orally read words in context from literature based chapter books at the fourth-grade level at 125 words per minute with no more than 3 errors per minute.

⇒ Modify the objective for individualization purposes by changing the criteria.

⇒ Modify the original objective by changing the content.

⇒ Modify the original objective by changing the behavior.

⇒ Modify the original objective by changing the conditions.

⇒ Modify the original objective by recalibrating the objective (the size of the curricular "slice").

*THINKING ABOUT INSTRUCTION*

12. Since the primary defining characteristic of students in need of remedial or special education is their failure to keep pace with their general-education peers while moving through the curriculum, the authors of this text advocate a "hands on" approach to instruction. "Hands on" means direct, teacher driven instruction. Consider the following items and categorize them as hands on Yes or student centered No .

____    a. Ms. Perkins asks the group to speak in unison, listing in sequence the three steps necessary to solve the problem.  As they respond, she listens to be sure they know the right steps in the correct sequence.

____    b. The history teacher assigns chapter five and the first ten questions of the summary section. Students are expected to copy each question and then write its answer using information from the textbook.

____    c. Mr. Murray is a good lecturer.  He always starts with an entertaining story and then develops three or four major points, supporting each with related information.  As he lectures, he moves around the classroom to make sure students are taking notes in an organized manner.  At the end of his lecture, he always summarizes the important content and usually gives a brief preview of the content that will be covered next.

____    d. As students finish writing the in-class essay assignment, Ms. Bower checks each one to be sure that each student has used paragraphs that begin with a topic sentence and include at least three supporting sentences.  When she finds instances where that format was not followed, she asks the student to list the characteristics of a paragraph.  She then pairs that student with a peer partner who has finished the assignment so that they can work together to reconstruct one of the troublesome paragraphs.

____    e. Mr. Leckvold is very clear about his expectations for class assignments.  They must be neat, they must be finished within the allotted class period, and they must be placed in the tray labeled "Assignments." Once the assignment has been turned in, Mr. Leckvold gives credit for its completion by placing a check mark by students' names in the grade book.  If any student fails to turn in two or more assignments in the grading period, his or her grade will be decreased by one full grade.

13. The text states, "One of the biggest threats to good instruction is the belief that the core of teaching is assignment giving."  Here is your opportunity to change a threat to a promise.  Change each of the following assignments into a teacher action that will have a higher probability of influencing student learning.  Hint: consider using explanation, demonstration, guided practice, timely correction, task specific feedback, or other teacher action supported by the effective teaching literature.  The first example is completed for you.

⇒  Today's lesson has been on mammals.  As a group we listed the critical and noncritical attributes of a mammal.

The assignment:
    Now use  your textbook to help as you answer the first eight questions at the end of chapter five titled, Facts About Mammals.

Revised:
    Now, work with your partner as you sort this list of 20 animals into  mammal and nonmammal categories. Be prepared to explain why you categorized each as you have. (This teacher has presented an activity designed to provide practice for students as they demonstrate their level of comprehension about the defining characteristics of mammals.)

⇒  Yesterday, I showed you the chemical abbreviations used for elements on the periodic table.  Today, you'll have a chance to review that information.

The assignment:

C.1

This worksheet lists all of the elements. You are to fill in the chemical abbreviation for each and turn in the worksheet when you are finished.

Revised:

⇒ So that is how you should use the punctuation marks of commas, colons, and semi-colons.

The assignment:

Write an essay at least three pages long, and pay attention to how you punctuate it.

Revised:

14. Sometimes students need to learn strategies to either apply what they already know or to learn new information. When teachers want to teach strategies, they should use good instructional techniques to do so. Which of the following best represents the critical attributes for strategy instruction?
a) Define the strategy. List its critical and non-critical attributes. Give examples and non-examples, then present test items to see if the student understands.
b) The teacher orally talks through the process, demonstrating use of the strategy. The student uses the process, also orally talking through each step. Experiences are arranged to provide practice, and the student self-monitors application.
c) The teacher describes when the strategy should be used, assigns work that might require its use, then reinforces the student when he or she does choose to use it.
d) The strategy is broken down into its component parts, each part is written on a flashcard and the student memorizes the sequence by drill and practice.

15. Sometimes...let's be honest, MANY times... a student will demonstrate mastery of a task in an instructional setting, but fail to generalize that skill to other settings where its use would be appropriate. Which of the following is not a reasonable explanation of why that occurs?

a) The skill was not learned to a fluent level.
b) The student is uncertain about how to do the larger task of which the previously learned skill is only part.
c) The student, because she is learning disabled, lacks the capacity to generalize.
d) The student fails to recognize the situational cue that should prompt use of the skill.

16. Somewhere out there is a teacher who does not follow the guidelines suggested by TIES or this textbook. The following description might be from a lesson in that teacher's classroom. Underline the teacher behaviors that violate the guidelines described in this text, and suggest an alternate behavior.
a) Teacher X expected her students to know how to act like good
b) students since seventh graders have already had six years of practice
c) at being students, but sometimes their behavior really got out of hand.
d) Today's lesson had to begin with a stern reprimand and a reminder that
e) seventh-grade students should be more sophisticated than fourth-grade
f) students. The lesson started a little late, but once everyone settled down,
g) Ms. X presented a lesson on levers as simple machines. She hadn't had
h) time to organize the equipment for the lesson, so she assigned pairs of
i) students to select one person to go get the fulcrums and levers from two
j) locations in the back of class. When everyone returned to their desk, she
k) asked students to tell her what they already knew about levers.
l) Responses indicated that there was great diversity in what students
m) already knew, so she reassigned peer partners so that the high performers
n) were with high performers and low performers with low performers.
o) Ms. X then began the lesson. She talked about how levers could be used
p) to move heavy objects and showed pictures of workers removing stumps,
q) moving rocks, and using crowbars. Students appeared to be listening to
r) some of her lecture while they set up playful uses of the levers and

C.1

s)   fulcrums at their desks.  Ms. X had to interrupt her lesson once or twice
t)   to intervene in an object-flipping contest that developed between Larry
u)   and Bridget who had learned that the levers could be used as a primitive
v)   catapult for pieces of eraser, paper clips, and other small objects.
w)   Time seemed to slip away very quickly because of all the interruptions,
x)   but at the end of the period, Ms. X asked if there were any questions
y)   about levers; no one seemed to have any.  Ms. X inferred that the
z)   students would have attended better without the levers at their desks,
aa)  and planned for a continuation of the lesson for the next day that would
bb)  be based on written essay responses rather than "hands on" lever
cc)  experimentation.


**EVALUATION**

17. What is a status sheet and what purpose does it serve?

18. Let's play a game.  The guide-master (that's Dr. Fox) will describe a series of teacher actions, and the guide-reader (guess who that is) will name the thought process.  Remember the thought process categories are: Facts, Concepts, and Strategies.

a)   The teacher has reviewed relevant prior knowledge and demonstrated how an example of the core idea discussed in the lesson can be changed to a non-example.  He has asked several students to explain how they know an answer given by another student is correct, and he periodically challenges correct answers by asking students to support a response.  After the teacher is finished with the group lesson, students are assigned an activity that requires them to sort items into categories and to change some non-examples into examples by changing the necessary attributes.
Thought process: _____

b)   The teacher has demonstrated a procedure for arriving at a solution to a problem.  She hasn't emphasized the answer, only the way to obtain the answer.  Students are asked to supply rules, steps, and procedures and during seat work, they are required to identify the missing steps when given an incomplete series of directions.  They are also asked to practice identifying situations where the procedure will and will not work.
Thought process: _____

c)   During this lesson, students are encouraged to make rapid responses to simple, direct questions.  The instructor uses drill and practice that is distributed across the day in several short sessions rather than one long lesson.  Students receive frequent feedback on accuracy and rate, and items that are missed are repeated several times.
Thought process: _____

d)   Ms. Jackson's lesson encouraged students to focus on the process, not the completion of the task.  She didn't care if students finished every problem, only if they knew how they solved the problem.  Students were asked to explain what went wrong when they made a mistake, and to practice generating and evaluating alternative solutions.
Thought process: _____

19. Now let's try the same thing for behavior outcomes.  Given a description of student performance, identify whether the student is operating at an accuracy, mastery, or automatic level.

C.1

a) The student requires extensive explanation and demonstration of the lesson. The teacher monitors all responses and makes sure the student does not practice errors. The student engages in guided practice, but not in independent practice.

Behavioral outcome level: _____

b) The teacher emphasizes answers, not the process, and praises fluent work. The student engages in drill and practice and completes independent practice activities with a success rate of 90% to 100%.

Behavioral outcome level: _____

c) The lesson emphasizes how existing skills can be generalized to other tasks and environments. The student is asked to modify the skill to meet new demands in "real world" examples. The student meets or exceeds the criterion expected in the basic core skill.

Behavioral outcome level: _____

20. The text listed a number of "do's" and "don't's" to remember while developing assumed causes. Some of each have been scrambled in random order below. Sort the good advice from common evaluation errors by indicating **Do** or **Don't** by each and then stating a rationale for your judgment.

a) Be comprehensive. Don't assume that the first thing a student can't do is the only, or most important, thing he needs to be taught.

**DO**                    **DON'T**          (Circle one)

**Rationale:**

b) Assume that if a student skips an item, he doesn't know it. If he had <u>known</u> it, he wouldn't have skipped it.

**DO**                    **DON'T**

**Rationale:**

c) Stick to alterable variables that can be influenced by instruction. Don't focus on variables such as I.Q. score, family status, low birth weight, or other variables not likely to be changed through classroom interaction.

**DO**                    **DON'T**

**Rationale:**

d) Understand that for a student to pass content class objectives (like literature, science, social studies), she must read the textbook, and must therefore be taught to read first.

**DO**                    **DON'T**

**Rationale:**

e) Select instructional goals that match a teaching style that you like. Go with your personal teaching strengths.

**DO**                    **DON'T**

**Rationale:**

f) Test <u>all</u> the elements of a task, including content behavior, conditions, and criteria.

**DO**                    **DON'T**

**Rationale:**

21. Identify at least two limitations of curriculum-based measurement.

1)

2)

**ANSWER KEY**

1. The authors define curriculum as a set of learning outcomes resulting from instruction. _B_ is the correct choice. Both choices _A_ and _C_ are common misconceptions that result in teachers designing lessons around material that is available rather than around a student's instructional needs. The authors believe that when a teacher defines learning outcomes and teaches to them, learning has a greater probability of being more relevant and efficient.

2. Outside decisions are concerned sending messages to someone outside of the instructional interaction. For example: assignment to a particular category of students; grade retention; or, school accountability. Inside decisions focus on what to teach and how it will be taught.

   a. Inside.  The decision concerned what to teach.

   b. Outside.  This example focused on assignment to a specific service.

   c. Inside.  Juan's teacher has identified a teaching strategy that will  determine the instructional process.

   d. Inside.  Willard is being taught how to solve problems.

   e. Inside.  The cooperative learning group is being used as an instructional  process to teach a specific skill.

   f.  Outside. Lisbeth is being placed in a group, but no indication was given  of what she will be taught or how she will be taught.

3.  Although it's true that some teaching functions may resemble the orchestra leader, the pilot or the artist, the role that is the best analogy for effective decision making is that of the detective.  Teachers gather assessment information related to the interaction between  task-student-instruction, form an idea of the nature of the problem and its potential solutions, and then test the student's response changes in the task or instruction.

4.

a)  _Student variable_.  Since it is usually not within the role of the teacher to treat chemical dependence or change family dynamics, this is an **unalterable** variable.

b)   _Task variable_.  The student's ability to successfully complete the assigned task is limited by the reading level of the text.  The nature of the task is **alterable**.  The teacher could change the assignment to either reading a less difficult text with similar content or by providing audio tapes with the content.

c)  _Instructional variable_.  Since the teacher has chosen the type of instruction used, this is an **alterable** variable.  The teacher could choose to use a direct instruction approach if student success rate indicated it was necessary.

d)  _Student variable_.  His size and other physical characteristics are just as **unalterable** as is his parent's choice of occupation.  Hey, don't judge a book by its cover.  This kid is known to read poetry by flashlight under his covers late at night.

e)  _Instructional variable_.  This is an **alterable** pattern that the teacher could change by structuring lessons that would focus students by increasing active participation.

5. The third child's name is Johnnie...as in, "Johnnie's mother had three children". Since all of the problem solving information was presented in just a few short sentences, only short term memory played a part in finding the answer. Most adults who care enough to voluntarily work their way through a study guide have the motivation necessary to expend the 1/1000th of a calorie necessary to continue. The remaining possibility is attention, and that is, in fact, the variable involved in this cheap trick. If you did not focus on the introductory information, "Johnnie's mother had three children", it is probable that you returned to the beginning of the story to read it again to learn if you had missed critical information. The second time through, you probably had ATTENTION on your side, and solved the riddle. We sincerely hope so. Some of our friends who still haven't figured this one out are still mad at us.

6.     Willie attributes his success to external forces and is not likely to persist at a task when he doesn't believe his efforts matter. We cannot identify him as motivated given the information we have about him.

    Waylen is not motivated. He is giving up the accordion forever!

    Dolly is motivated. She did not perform well, but she is sticking to the task and will try again. She is behaving in a way that suggests she believe what she does will make a difference.

    Garth has found an easy way out. He has not demonstrated that he is motivated.
Students who believe that success is related to things they can control, view difficulty as a cue to work harder.

7.     No. Curriculum for remedial and special education students in general education settings should not be different from their typical peers. What students need to learn remains constant. Instructional strategies, calibration of tasks, or learning pace may vary, but the goals and objectives are the same.

8.     The following are potential correct answers. There may be others.

### TASK ANALYSIS

Addition would be a necessary skill.
Finding a common denominator would be required.
Reduction of improper fractions would be necessary.

### CONCEPT ANALYSIS

The concepts of "more" and "less"
The concepts of whole numbers and fractions
The concepts of proper/improper fractions

9.     _D_ is the only example that is measurable, useful and calibrated in "reasonable" units.

10.     _A_ is false. Proficiency level standards are <u>not</u> arbitrary. They should be set at a level comparable to the standards used for general education peers. Remember, it is not a student's capacity that is the major identifying feature of students with remedial or special education needs. It is the poor use of attention, memory and motivation that distinguishes them from peers who succeed in the curriculum. Attention, memory and motivation can all be taught.

11.     You may have made any of hundreds of possible changes to individualize Sven's objective. We have identified <u>what part</u> of the objective should have been changed under each condition.

a.     Criteria should have changed:
       125 words per minute with no more than 3 errors

b.     Content changes should have focused on:
       words in context

c.     Behavior changes should have altered:
       orally read words

d.     Conditions should have changed:
       from literature based chapter books

e.     Calibration of the objective:
       fourth grade level

**Instruction**

12.     a.     <u>Yes</u>  Ms. Perkins is engaging students in an overt behavior that allows her to monitor their level of mastery of a strategy. The teacher action represented in this example is <u>asking questions</u>.

       b.     <u>No</u>  The history teacher has not chosen a teacher action in this example. Students are expected to independently read the chapter and answer the questions at the end. There is no teacher interaction here.

       c.     <u>Yes</u>  Mr. Murray is relying on two types of student responses to keep them engaged in this example. He is hoping for covert attention to his lecture and the chances of that are increased by his expectation that his students will overtly take notes. This is an example of the teacher action of <u>delivery of information</u>.

       d.     <u>Yes</u>  Ms. Bower is <u>responding to student efforts</u> by checking their paragraphs and asking them to self correct after overtly reviewing the strategy used to develop a complete paragraph.

       e.     <u>No</u>  This teacher has carefully defined how to complete assignments, but has not chosen any action that would require active interaction focused on learning the curriculum objectives. His students may complete assignments, but that is not the same as LEARNING.

13.     Your answers are correct if they engaged students in activities that required thoughtful responses directly related to the lesson content. Teacher directed instruction that targets curriculum objectives requiring active participation of the students is powerful. It is more powerful than dittos, workbooks,

coloring, puzzles, non academic discussions, or feeding Squeezy - the class gerbil. Teacher directed instruction is what enables learning to occur and what gives us the professional label: "teac*her*".

14.     _B_. The strategy is demonstrated, practiced orally, applied and the student monitors its use.

15.     We hope you answered _C_ . We danced that capacity myth out again just to see if you remembered that you shouldn't trust old stories. All of the other options are reasonable explanations why a student may fail to generalize.

16.     By now, you should understand that there are many choices that a teacher could make to effectively organize the teaching learning environment. The "key" presents only some suggestions that would improve the lesson as presented by Ms. X.. Our hope is that you identified errors in teacher actions and replace them with appropriate suggestions. Here are some better ideas:

Line 1:  Teacher X maintained a small number of important rules and communicated them through discussion of rules and routines.

Line 5-7:  Today's lesson began with a review of information presented in a previous related lesson and a statement of how this lesson contributes to the unit goal. The lesson started on time.

Line 9-10:  Students knew the established routine for obtaining equipment used in science lessons and collected the materials Ms. X had organized before class and placed in the equipment pick-up area.

Line 10-13:  The steps involved in completing the lesson were identified through a task analysis and the student's instructional skill levels were considered when Ms. X assigned tasks.

Line 13-14:  Peer partners were assigned at the onset of the lesson based on similar instructional needs, not on labels reflecting assumed abilities.

Line 15-18:  Ms. X required frequent guided practice responses from students and she monitored their responses so she could adjust instruction by providing more examples or alternate explanations. Students were actively engaged as they responded to teacher directed questions throughout the lesson.

Line 18-19:  The practice activities were directly related to the instructional goal.

Line 19-22:  Disruptions were infrequent because Ms. X maintained lesson momentum with high rates of student engagement by asking frequent, relevant questions and providing clear guided practice activities using the fulcrums and levers.

Line 24-25:  Students were asked to show, demonstrate, explain, and display their responses overtly.

Line 25-29:  All of the activities students were asked to complete were closely related to the objective of the lesson.

C.1

17. A status sheet is simply a list of the things a student should know about (prior knowledge) to work with competence on a task. Another way to view one is that it contains a list of skills which, if missing, will become "assumed causes" for failure. They are good things to have around because they help you narrow the scope of your evaluation and save you time. With a good status sheet you won't need to do much in the way of task-analysis.

18.    The thought processes go like this:
a = concept
b = strategy
c = fact
d = strategy

19. Accurate behavior, Fluent behavior and Automatic behavior

20.    a.    **Do**    Rationale: Students seldom have only one missing prerequisite and it isn't safe to assume the first thing they can't do is the only thing they can't do.

b.    **Don't**    Rationale: The absence of behavior is not the same as observable behavior. Cue the student to complete that, or similar, items in order to obtain observable behavior.

c.    **Do**    Variables that are not easily changed through school experiences may be interesting but not cost effective to measure for teaching purposes.

d.    **Don't**    What a student needs to know is determined by the curriculum, not by the way the curriculum is taught. The <u>content</u> can be taught through means other than reading.

e.    **Don't**    Personal preference for teaching actions should not determine teacher choice. Student need should determine teacher action.

f.    **Do**    Since tasks contain behavior, conditions and criteria, all elements should be tested or observed.

21. Limitations of CBM include:

1.Most CBM measures have focused on basic skills and there are not many examples of complex concept or strategic knowledge bases that have been measured with CBM.

2.Most CBM has been used at the elementary level, and although it has been used to make <u>teaching</u> decisions at the secondary level, information about making <u>eligibility</u> decisions is not as available.

274

**Templates for studying the evaluation process for each chapter**

1. For each chapter you study copy the blank template.
2. Fill in the questions asked during the CBE process in that chapter (you may need to add rows).
3. Look up the answers in the text and write them in the grid (you may want to include the page numbers where you found the answers).
4. Repeat the process but fill in the grid from memory.

BLANK TEMPLATE

| LIST QUESTIONS FROM CHAPTER FLOW-CHART DOWN LEFT. | A: WHAT WOULD CAUSE YOU TO ASK THIS QUESTION? | B: HOW WOULD YOU ANSWER THIS QUESTION? | C: WHAT THINGS, DEPENDING ON THE ANSWERS, SHOULD YOU DO NEXT? |
|---|---|---|---|
| | | | |
| | | | |
| | | | |
| | | | |
| | | | |
| | | | |
| | | | |
| | | | |

CHAPTER 8: READING COMPREHENSION

| QUESTIONS FROM CHAPTER FLOW-CHART. | A: WHAT WOULD CAUSE YOU TO ASK THIS QUESTION? | B: HOW WOULD YOU ANSWER THIS QUESTION? | C: WHAT THINGS, DEPENDING ON THE ANSWERS, SHOULD YOU DO NEXT? |
|---|---|---|---|
| 1) Does the student seem at risk of a comprehension problem? | Referral. When screened student continues reading when he makes errors that violate the meaning of the text. | I would have student read a passage at expected level and ask basic comprehension questions. | If "YES", then begin by assessing student's oral reading rate in a text at the expected level. Also give either a cloze or maze test. |
| 2) Is comprehension OK? | Student guesses when asked comprehension questions on a passage he is able to orally decode. | I would assess oral reading rate, give cloze or maze test and establish PLOP. | If "YES", then record present level of performance and discontinue. If "NO", then I would use S-B-D formula to summarize discrepancy, set a goal, and use status sheet to develop assumed causes for comprehension problem. |
| 3) What problems have you found? | There may be several areas that are contributing to overall inadequate reading comprehension performance. | I would use a status sheet (collaboratively if applicable) and mark pass, no-pass, or unsure. If enabling skills are the primary area of deficiency, I would consult other chapters on enabling skills. If a category in the area of reading comprehension is marked a clear no-pass, then give respective SLP, and go to applicable teaching recommendations as indicated. | If "NO" problems are found, then assume student has the skill and record as PLOP. Monitor for maintenance and generalization. If problems are found, then use specific level procedures, record PLOP, select objectives to address discrepancy, and teach missing skills. |
| 4) Is more information needed? | If you have marked any areas as "unsure" when using the status sheet you need more information. | I would review problems already found, re-check the status sheet to make adjustments if necessary, and select and indicated teaching recommendations. | If "NO", then list objectives and teaching procedures. If "YES", then use specific level procedures to arrive at teaching recommendations. |

| 5) Are there teaching recommendations you should follow? | Inadequate reaction to reading may be further complicated by lack of enabling skills. | Review results of SLP's that you have given. If more information is needed re-assess/modify or modify. | If "NO", then double check to make sure this is a problem. If there is start over or try another process.<br>If "YES", then follow the recommendations, monitor progress and make how to teach decisions as necessary. |

## CHAPTER 9: DECODING
## TEMPLATE FOR STUDYING THE CBE PROCESS

| QUESTIONS FROM CHAPTER FLOW-CHART | A:<br>WHAT WOULD CAUSE YOU TO ASK THIS QUESTION? | B:<br>HOW WOULD YOU ANSWER THIS QUESTION? | C:<br>WHAT THINGS, DEPENDING ON THE ANSWERS, SHOULD YOU DO NEXT? |
|---|---|---|---|
| 1) Is the student's reading acceptable? | Referral.<br>Suspected reading problem. | Screening with a timed oral reading measure. (Survey level /GOM ) | If oral reading is OK discontinue.<br>If oral reading is not OK summarize the discrepancy and ask:<br>Is the student in 1$^{st}$ grade or below?<br>Did the student decode some words? |
| 2) Is the student in 1$^{st}$ grade or below? | When reading at the expected level the student's oral reading was inadequate. | Review of student records.<br>Current knowledge of student. | If "YES", then I would check early reading skills.<br>If "NO" then I would ask if the student decoded some words. |
| 3) Did the student decode some words? | The student's oral reading was inadequate and he is above 1$^{st}$ grade level. | I would review the results of the survey level (oral reading) sample. | If the student did not decode some words, then I would check his early reading skills.<br>If the student did read some words, then I would ask "Is reading accurate but slow?" |

| 4) Is the student missing some early reading skills? | The student is currently in, or below, the first grade. The student, regardless of grade level, did not decode words. | I would assess early reading skills (concepts of print and sound). | If the student is missing early skills, then I would teach them. If the student is not missing early skills, then I would ask "Is reading at the expected level accurate but slow?" |
|---|---|---|---|
| 5) Is reading accurate but slow? | When reading at the expected level the student's oral reading is not acceptable However, he did read some words, and there are no problems with missing early reading skills. | By reviewing the summary of the oral reading sample collected at the expected level. | If the answer is "YES", then I would try a re-reading test. If the answer is "NO", then I would need to obtain an error sample. |
| 6) Does reading rate increase significantly with re-reading? | The student's reading is inadequate because, while it is accurate, it is slow. | By using the re-reading SLP. | If the student's rate increased by 40%, then I would teach the student by emphasizing fluency. If the student's rate did not increase, then I would obtain an error sample. |
| 7) Are important errors self-corrected? | The student's reading is inaccurate and/or slow at the expected level (no increase in rate with rereading). | By obtaining a sample of errors from material on which the students is 80-85% accurate. This may mean sampling above or below the expected level. I would also note if errors violating meaning are self-corrected. | If errors are self corrected, then I would teach by emphasizing accuracy and active reading. If the errors are not self corrected then I would ask "At what level must the kid read before you elicit important errors?" |
| 8) At what level did the kid read before you elicited important errors? | When reading at the expected level the student does not increase rate when re-reading or accuracy is low. Also, when important errors are made he does not self correct them. | Review the information collected while trying to obtain a sample of errors from material on which the student is 80-85% accurate to find the level. | If the errors could only be collected by pushing the student above his expected level, then I would teach using Active Reading instruction. If the errors were obtained from passages below the expected level I would try the assisted monitoring SLP. |

| 9) Did accuracy improve with assistance? | The student makes reading errors at levels below that expected. These errors are not self-corrected. | Sit with the student while he reads and signal the student as soon as meaningful errors take place. Then note to see if the student immediately corrects most of the errors (50-70%). | If errors were corrected, then I would teach by emphasizing self-monitoring. If the errors were not corrected, then I would try to categorize and analyze them. |
|---|---|---|---|
| 10) Are there patterns to the errors? | The student makes reading errors at levels below that expected. He does not correct them when given monitoring assistance. | Try to categorize errors. | If errors violate meaning, then I would continue with reading but check for language problems. If the errors fall into patterns, then I'd teach to correct those error patterns. If the errors seem phonetic, then I'd evaluate phonics and teach any missing skills. If there are no clear patterns, then use Active Reading Instruction. |

## CHAPTER 10: LANGUAGE
## TEMPLATE FOR STUDYING THE CBE PROCESS

| QUESTIONS FROM CHAPTER FLOW-CHART | A: WHAT WOULD CAUSE YOU TO ASK THIS QUESTION? | B: HOW WOULD YOU ANSWER THIS QUESTION? | C: WHAT THINGS, DEPENDING ON THE ANSWERS, SHOULD YOU DO NEXT? |
|---|---|---|---|
| 1) Do certain areas seem weak? | Referral or screening. | Determine language history, collect a language sample | If "NO", then discontinue. If "YES", then survey pragmatics, survey syntax, and/or survey semantics. |
| 2) Is language acceptable? | Student's oral expression violates rules of pragmatics, syntax and/or semantics. | Collect a language sample to get a baseline and tally errors on checklist of language content and follow assessment recommendation. | If "YES", student is competent in all three areas, then cease evaluation. If "NO", then use S-B-D formula to derive discrepancy for each area of concern and convert to instructional goals. |
| 3) Are errors in | Student's oral | After tallying baseline | If "YES", then I would |

| semantics? | expression violates rules of semantics, or in other words, the kid uses a word in a way that it shouldn't be used. | language sample, I would follow assessment recommendation. | probe vocabulary.<br>If "NO"      I would ask:<br>"Are there errors in pragmatics or syntax?" |
|---|---|---|---|
| 4) Are errors in pragmatics? | For example, student does not shift from speaker to listener. | After tallying baseline language sample, I would follow assessment recommendation. | If "YES", then I would use pragmatics and communication status sheet.<br>If "NO" , then I would ask:<br>"Are there errors in syntax?" |
| 5) Are errors in syntax? | Student's oral expression violates rules of syntax. | After tallying baseline language sample, I would follow assessment recommendation | If "YES", then I would use syntax status sheet.<br>If "NO", then I would ask:<br>"Is the class/school environment supportive of language learning?" |
| 6) Is the class/school environment supportive of language learning? | Are there discrepancies in the way students with communication problems are addressed in the educational setting. | I would observe the student in the school setting. | If "YES", then ask:<br>"Is vocabulary OK?"<br>If "NO", then follow teaching recommendation to modify setting. |
| 7) Is the student's vocabulary OK? | Student uses words in ways that violate their meaning. | I would follow procedure for probing vocabulary and morphology. | If "NO", teach semantics.<br>If "YES", then ask:<br>"Are pragmatics OK?" |
| 8) Are pragmatics OK? | The student engages only in one-way communication. | I would follow procedure for analysis of pragmatics content, in collaboration with others if possible, and then record pass/no-pass/unsure, and summarize results. | If "NO", check performance in communication with Analysis of Communication assessment plan and teach pragmatics.<br>If "YES", then ask:<br>"Are there syntactical errors?" |
| 9) Are there Syntactical Errors? | While speaking the student is unaware of noun/verb agreement. | Have student try to imitate modeled sentence structures as well as expanding responses to see if he has the skill to expand responses. | If "YES", teach syntax.<br>If "NO", then calculate MLU (mean length of utterance) and use S-B-D formula to summarize any discrepancy. |

| 10) Is MLU OK? (Is Sentence Complexity Adequate?) | The form of the student's oral expression remain unchanged regardless of setting or communication purposes. | I would calculate MLU by using other students as the exemplar(s) and summarizing the discrepancy with the S-B-D formula. | If "YES", and there were problems identified in other areas of language, then discontinue or return to survey level assessment. If "NO", then build fluency by using teaching recommendations for expansion. |
| --- | --- | --- | --- |
| 11) Is the setting OK? | Are opportunities to learn language being presented to this student in any setting. | Observe student in the school setting. | If "YES", then review results of assessments of semantics, pragmatics and syntax. If "NO", then modify setting to increase opportunities for communication. |

CHAPTER 11: WRITTEN EXPRESSION
TEMPLATE FOR STUDYING THE CBE PROCESS

| QUESTIONS FROM CHAPTER FLOW-CHART. | A: WHAT WOULD CAUSE YOU TO ASK THIS QUESTION? | B: HOW WOULD YOU ANSWER THIS QUESTION? | C: WHAT THINGS, DEPENDING ON THE ANSWERS, SHOULD YOU DO NEXT? |
| --- | --- | --- | --- |
| 1) Is written communication acceptable? | Referral. Screening. | Collect and score a writing sample. | If "YES", then discontinue. If "NO", then ask: "Is there evidence of a problem in expression and/or mechanics?" |
| 2) Evidence of problem in expression? | When prompted to write the student exhibits difficulty completing the task on materials at expected level. | I would collect a writing sample and score on the Tindal/Hasbrouk analytical scales for dimensions of writing using five-point anchors of quality. | If "YES" for expression, then establish the discrepancy using S-B-D formula. Set a goal. Then interview/observe the student writing, and do the word sequence test. If "NO", then ask: "Is the writing product OK?" |

| | | | |
|---|---|---|---|
| 3) Is writing product OK? | The student follows the writing process adequately but the product is of low quality. | Collect a writing sample and score it. | If "NO", then follow teaching recommendation emphasizing fluency. If "YES", follow teaching recommendation on balanced expression, and then ask: "Is the writing process OK?" |
| 4) Does the student use the writing process effectively? | When prompted to write the student's sample is of low quality and steps of the writing process were absent. | Observe collection of writing sample and rate on status sheet. | If "YES", then follow teaching recommendation on balanced expression. If "NO", then follow teaching recommendation on the writing process. |
| 5) Are word sequences correct? | When prompted to write the student's sample contains disjointed and fragmented information. | Review results of word sequence test or apply word sequence analysis to writing sample collected in survey-level testing. | If "YES", follow teaching recommendation on balanced expression. If "NO", then ask: "Is there a mechanics problem?" |
| 6) Is there a spelling, handwriting, or convention problem? | Student's sample contains errors in spelling, handwriting, and/or conventions. | Collect sample and score it for spelling, handwriting, and conventions. | If "YES", establish discrepancy using S-B-D formula, conduct interview/observation of student, and collect writing samples under different conditions. If "NO", then ask: "Is sentence complexity OK?" |
| 7) Are sentences adequately complex (syntax)? | Student's writing sample contains sentences with one primary sentence structure. | Collect writing sample or analyze sentence structure of survey-level assessment. | If "YES", then check semantics (A.5). If "NO", then increase syntactic complexity with TR 4. |
| 8) Are sentences adequately complex (semantics)? | Student's writing sample is syntactically adequate but still not expressive. | Check vocabulary to determine if the proportion of lengthy and unique words is adequate. | If "YES", then use a balanced approach to written expression (TR1). If "NO", then go to chapter 10 for advice on teaching vocabulary. |
| 9) Is there a handwriting problem? | The student's sample is not always legible. | Collect sample and/or review other samples and analyze handwriting. | If "YES", use Action 7. If "NO", then ask: "Is there a spelling problem?" |

| 10) Is there a spelling problem? | Writing sample contains spelling errors. | Collect sample and/or review other samples and analyze spelling. | If "YES", use Action 8. If "NO", then ask: "Is there a punctuation and/or capitalization problem?" |
|---|---|---|---|
| 11) Are there convention problems? | Writing sample contains problems with conventions. | Collect and score a sample that has at least 50 errors and identify errors. | If "YES", then use Action 9. If "NO", then use Mechanics Teaching Recommendation 5. |
| 12) Are there patterns to the errors? | When analyzed patterns in errors emerge. | Collect and score a sample that has at least 50 errors and identify error patterns. | If "NO, then follow teaching recommendation on balanced expression. If "YES", then ask: "Do errors increase with fatigue or context?" |
| 13) Do errors increase with fatigue or context? | Errors increase as writing sample gets longer, or when the student is writing about a certain topic. | If "YES" or "NO", go to teaching recommendations on mechanics fluency. | Use TR 7 and place your emphasis on fluency building and automaticity. Practice on the topics that seem associated with fatigue. |

CHAPTER 12: MATH
TEMPLATE FOR STUDYING THE CBE PROCESS

| QUESTIONS FROM CHAPTER FLOW-CHART | A: WHAT WOULD CAUSE YOU TO ASK THIS QUESTION? | B: HOW WOULD YOU ANSWER THIS QUESTION? | C: WHAT THINGS, DEPENDING ON THE ANSWERS, SHOULD YOU DO NEXT? |
|---|---|---|---|
| 1) Is the student accurate and fluent? | Referral. Suspected problems in math computation and/or math comprehension. | I would administer timed fact test for each area. | If "YES", discontinue. If "NO", then I would calculate the discrepancy on each fact test given. I would then use that information to state long-term goals. |
| 2) Is the student accurate but slow? | Perhaps the student is slow at adding *and* writing, or is simply slow at writing. | I would administer a timed writing digits or copying digits test. | If "YES", I would teach fact fluency. If "NO", I would teach fact accuracy. |
| 3) Are oral responses at rate? | Perhaps the student correctly responds when assessed orally. | Administer a timed basic facts test having the student say the answers rather than write them. | If "YES", I would ask: "Is writing adequate?" If "NO", then I would teach fact accuracy. |

| 4) Is writing adequate? | While the student's accuracy and fluency are adequate when tested orally, they are inadequate on written tests. | I would re-administer basic facts test(s) without an emphasis on fluency. | If "YES", then I would teach fact fluency. If "NO", then I would set an intermediate aim based on approximated level of writing skill. |
|---|---|---|---|
| 5) Did the student become more accurate? | The original errors were really rate induced. | I would compare previous score (timed) with new score (not timed). | If "YES", I would teach fluency. If "NO", then I would ask: "Is accuracy extremely low?" |
| 6) Is accuracy extremely low? | When student was tested at expected level he scored at below 50% accuracy. | I would teach missing basic tools and/or conceptual prior knowledge. | If "YES", I would look to see if the student is missing basic tools and concepts to perform tasks. If "NO", I would teach fact accuracy. |
| 7) Can the student correctly work operation items at the expected level? | There is an error pattern presented when tested on operational items. | I would review results and list correct items as indicators of PLOP. Missed items would be listed on student's teaching plan. | If "YES, then I would discontinue. If "NO", then I would use S-B-D formula to determine discrepancy. |
| 8) Were some operation items correct? | If there is no pattern in the small sample a larger one might reveal it. | I would get a larger sample by administering the survey-operation tests. | If "YES", then I would look to see which operations needed to be taught. If "NO", I would check basic tools and concepts. |
| 9) Does the student have tools/concepts? | When interviewed student answered questions about tools/concepts incorrectly. | I would use basic concept status sheet to mark items which the student does/doesn't know. | If "YES", then I would determine which operations need to be taught. If "NO" then I would teach basic tools and concepts. |
| 10) Are operational skills adequate? | If student has basic tools and concepts and misses items on operational items assessment. | I would use error-analysis materials to determine what operational skills the student is missing. | If "YES", then I would discontinue or check skills at next higher curriculum level. If "NO", then I would check for missing prior knowledge and look for error patterns. |

| 11) Which type of prior knowledge seems to account for the errors? | The student struggles with any of the following: selecting operations, setting up equations, estimating answers, following algorithms, discriminating relevant/irrelevant information. | I would review results of survey-operation tests and conduct an interview to determine missing skills. I would select or construct new assessment on problem solving skills if necessary. | If missing sub-skills or making factual errors, I would teach computation. If missing conceptual prior knowledge, I would assess use of strategies and teach missing skills. |
|---|---|---|---|
| 12) Does student know how to solve problems? | Student gets computation problems correct in isolation but misses items when problems are embedded and must be set up. | I would review sample and analyze computational process errors along with interviewing the student. If computational errors were already noted I would re-test student but let him use a calculator for accuracy. | If "YES", then I would teach computation. If "NO", then I would teach problem solving strategies. |
| 13) Is student working at expected level? | Student is falling behind in the curriculum. | I would list the standard and behavior, determine the discrepancy and use increase needed to remove the discrepancy to formulate my goal. | If "YES", then I would discontinue or test at the next higher curriculum level. If "NO", then I would use S-B-D formula to set goal. I would ask: " Are there computation, problem solving, and/or content errors indicated?" |
| 14) Are there computational errors? | The student understands the operation, vocabulary and problem solving process, but doesn't correctly compute problems. | I would review results of survey-facts rate and if acceptable then review results of survey-operations test. | If "YES", then I would survey fact accuracy and fluency. If "NO", then I would ask: "Are there problem solving errors?" |
| 15) Are there problem solving errors? | The student is accurate with computation, understands vocabulary, but struggles with attacking problems. | I would review results of survey-operations test and conduct interview to determine missing skills. | If "YES", then I would teach problem solving strategies. If "NO", then I would ask: "Are there content errors?" |

| 16) Are there content errors? | The student attacks problems and computation is accurate but is based on incorrect understanding of content terminology. | I would review results of applications content test summary and interview student. | If "YES", I would construct a test to sample the student's knowledge of vocabulary, tools, and content for the material of concern and teach missing skills. If "NO", then I would ask: "Is the student's application performance within expectations?" |
| --- | --- | --- | --- |
| 17) Does the student know content, tools and vocabulary? | Student misses items directly relating to specific content, tools or vocabulary. | I would assess student to determine missing application skills and use results to design instruction. | If "YES", then teach student to apply what he knows through application strategies. If "NO", then teach the missing content knowledge, tools and vocabulary. |

## CHAPTER 13: SOCIAL SKILLS
## TEMPLATE FOR STUDYING THE CBE PROCESS

| QUESTIONS FROM CHAPTER FLOW-CHART | A: WHAT WOULD CAUSE YOU TO ASK THIS QUESTION? | B: HOW WOULD YOU ANSWER THIS QUESTION? | C: WHAT THINGS, DEPENDING ON THE ANSWERS, SHOULD YOU DO NEXT? |
| --- | --- | --- | --- |
| 1) Does the student have maladaptive behavior ? | The student exhibits maladaptive behavior and/or is referred for disruptive classroom behavior. | Simple observation by myself or other qualified staff members of the student. Summarize on a Status Sheet. | If "NO" then discontinue. If "YES", then I would ask: "Is the behavior dangerous?" |
| 2) Is the behavior dangerous? | The student exhibits behavior that places the student or others at risk of injury. | Check to see if those that contact the student feel threatened. Also check to see if anyone around this student feels that he is likely to injure himself. | In either "YES" /"NO" I would still complete Parts A & B of the functional evaluation interview. However, if the answer is "YES", then I develop an interim plan to insure safety. Next I'd complete a specific level status sheet in order to clearly define the maladaptive behavior. |

| | | | |
|---|---|---|---|
| 3) Does the description of the maladaptive behavior pass the stranger test? | If the student is referred by someone else and it is unclear what specific, observable maladaptive behavior is occurring. | If another person has referred the student then I would help them to state the maladaptive behavior as an objective, or as the target behavior. | If the behavior doesn't pass stranger test, then I would revisit specific level status sheet to pinpoint problem. If the answer is "YES" would observe student and look to see if the maladaptive behavior can be observed. |
| 4) Does the description of the maladaptive behavior pass the so-what test? | Does the behavior significantly interfere with his learning or that of his peers? | I would review class management guidelines to address behavior in large group context. | If "NO" then I would practice ignoring it or return to question 1. If "YES" then I would use the S-B-D formula and begin addressing behavior. |
| 5) Is the behavior tied to poor class management? | There are other students struggling with the class management techniques currently employed. | I would look at the options & indicators for class management. I would determine the form/function of the behavior of the individual student. | If "YES" or probably, then I would improve class management. If "NO" or unsure, I would find forms and functional evaluation parts C & D of functional evaluation interview and write target pinpoints that meet the function of the behavior. |
| 6) Does the description of the target behavior pass the stranger test? | Other professionals read this goal and can easily recognize and count occurrences of the replacement behavior. | Have another professional come into room and try to count occurrences of the replacement behavior. | If "NO", then I would review form and function evaluation interview and rewrite pinpoints to pass the stranger test. If "YES", then I would ask: "Do they pass the so-what test?" |
| 7) Does the description of the target behavior pass the so-what test? | The pinpoint has passed the stranger test but must also be proactive, addressing the student's needs, and a true replacement for the maladaptive behavior. | Review parts C&D of the functional evaluation interview and make determination of both accuracy and significance of the form of the behavior. | If "NO", then I would forget it and ask: "Does the student have maladaptive behavior?" If "YES", then I would use the survey-level status sheet collaboratively to narrow down the area(s) of concern. |

| | | | |
|---|---|---|---|
| 8) Could you categorize the problem into one or more of the social-skill subdivisions? | One or more areas may have been marked. | I would review the survey-level status sheet to narrow down areas of concern. | If "YES", then I would go to the corresponding specific-level sheet of expanded skills. If "NO" then I would review survey-level status sheet and include others in my rating of this student's behavior. |
| 9) Can you find goals and/or objectives? | Survey level status sheet has at least one category marked as "YES" and "The student makes this error." has been marked on the specific-level status sheet. | I would review survey-level status sheet and refer to specific-level status sheets to locate objectives. | If "YES", then I would use common prerequisite status sheet. If "NO", then return to Part A & B of the functional evaluation interview. |
| 10) Did you find subskills and/or objectives | The kid's got problems and I've to used the common prerequisite sheet. | Review results of survey-level status sheet, common prerequisite sheet, and specific-level procedures. | If "YES", I'd consider if the problem may be associated with task-related, academic, or language skills. If "NO", then return to Part A & B of the functional evaluation interview. If necessary, conduct additional specific-level probes for additional information. |
| 11) Is the problem related to task related skills? | Task-related skills are contributing to the student's maladaptive behavior. | Go to chapter 14 and begin following flowchart for task-related skills. | If "YES" or maybe, then go to chapter 14 and follow procedures for assessing and teaching task-related skills. If "NO", then ask: "Is there an academic problem resulting in the display of the maladaptive behavior?" |
| 12) Is the problem related to academics? | Missing prior knowledge in the area of academics is contributing to the student's maladaptive behavior. | Do a screening in the areas of concern and go to appropriate chapters and follow flowchart. | If "YES" or "MAYBE", then screen in the areas involved and go to appropriate chapter. If "NO", then ask: " Is there a problem with language?" |

| | | | |
|---|---|---|---|
| 13) Is the problem related to language? | Missing language skills are contributing to the student's maladaptive behavior. | Do a language screening and go to chapter 10 and follow flowchart. | If "YES" or "MAYBE", include a language screening in the evaluation and go to chapter 10.<br>If "NO", then ask: "Are there missing type 1 skills?" |
| 14) Missing type 1 skills? | I have objectives but don't know what prior knowledge I need to teach. | Look for missing type 1 skills by reviewing prerequisite status sheets and specific-level probes. | If "YES", I'd focus on type 1 skills.<br>If "NO", then I would ask about missing type 2 skills? |
| 15) Missing type 2 skills? | I have objectives but don't know what prior knowledge I need to teach. | I look for missing type 2 skills (student's beliefs, feelings, perceptions and/or expectations) that might contribute to the maladaptive behavior. | If "YES", then I'd focus on the type 2 skills I found.<br>If "NO", then ask: "Are there missing enabling skills?" |
| 16) Missing enabling skills? | I have objectives but don't know what prior knowledge I need to teach. | I would review all information, including details from other content areas (language, academic skills, task-related skills) | If "YES", then I'd focus on the skills I found.<br>If "NO", then I'd have to return to Action 2. |

## CHAPTER 14: TASK-RELATED
## TEMPLATE FOR STUDYING THE CBE PROCESS

| QUESTIONS FROM CHAPTER FLOW-CHART. | A:<br>WHAT WOULD CAUSE YOU TO ASK THIS QUESTION? | B:<br>HOW WOULD YOU ANSWER THIS QUESTION? | C:<br>WHAT THINGS, DEPENDING ON THE ANSWERS, SHOULD YOU DO NEXT? |
|---|---|---|---|
| 1) Is student failing to learn from classroom instruction? | Referral or screen for inadequate progress. | Frequent monitoring of student progress in the curriculum. | If "NO", then discontinue.<br>If "YES", then carefully define the topic and the indicators of failure. |
| 2) Does the problem pass the stranger test? | Is the problem formulated such that any professional would be able to identify the problem you are working to correct. | After working to pinpoint the specific problem areas I would have other professionals that work with the student be my strangers. | If "NO", go back to defining the topic and the indicators of failure.<br>If "YES", ask: "Do my definitions pass the so-what test?" |
| 3) Do definitions pass the "so-what" test? | The problem, while disruptive, is not significant enough to pass the so-what test. | If the problem is significant I would summarize the discrepancy | If "NO", then forget about it.<br>If "YES", then summarize the discrepancy as a score in summary 1. |

| | | | |
|---|---|---|---|
| 4) Can you specify problem areas? | The student's progress may be affected by missing skills in one or more areas. | I would fill out status sheet on content of task-related knowledge. | If "NO", then review the TR status sheet and look again at the so-what test. If "YES", then narrow the focus down to specific areas and follow flow chart. |
| 5) Should the environment be changed? | Materials that the student is assigned is above their present level of performance. | I would conduct a series of short observations of the student in the setting where he struggles and summarize results according to the TIES descriptors of effective classes. | If "NO", work with teacher and student to determine if student has access to the curriculum, if materials and activities are OK, and if instructional alignment is sufficient. |
| 6) Are there problems with topical knowledge? | Student's progress in the curriculum is impeded because he is missing key concepts and vocabulary. | I would assess student's topic-specific vocabulary and prior knowledge by designing an assessment and teach missing vocabulary. | If "YES", teach topical knowledge. If "NO", then try to specify one of the other areas as the primary problem. |
| 7) Adequate study skills? | When interviewed on how the student studies at home, the student says he never studies. | I would review status sheet on content of task-related skills and apply checklist for study/test taking skills and problem solving/self-monitoring in the areas the student struggles. | If "NO", then teach study skills and test taking strategies. I also would teach basic learning skills. If "YES", then ask: "Is the student's self-monitoring and problem solving OK?" |
| 8) Adequate self-monitoring and problem solving? | Student struggles to judge the quality of his own work (self-monitoring). Student struggles in approach to problems. | I would observe student and interview. I would complete status sheet on study skills and test taking strategies. | If "YES", then assess academic motivation and interview. If "NO", then teach self monitoring and problem solving strategies as applicable. |
| 9) Is academic motivation OK? | Student is uninterested in material he is being asked to learn. | I would give student motivation test and conduct interview. | If "YES", then ask: "Can other problem areas be specified?" If "NO", then ask: "Are basic learning skills adequate?" |
| 10) Are basic learning skills adequate? | The student forgets, is unorganized, gives up too soon and/or does not appear to pause for thought before, during, or after completing a task. | I would review the evaluation to try to find the level of assistance the student requires on the task of interest and then select most relevant instructional activities from areas of attention, memory and motivation. | If "YES", then something must have been missed and its time to collect more information or review flowchart. If "NO", then I would employ the sequence of assistance while teaching basic learning skills. |

# <u>NOTES</u>

# NOTES

# NOTES

# NOTES

# <u>NOTES</u>

# NOTES